THE WORLDS OF
DOROTHY
L. SAYERS

First published in Great Britain in 2025 by
Pen & Sword History
An imprint of
Pen & Sword Books Ltd
Yorkshire - Philadelphia

ISBN 978 1 03611 130 4

Typeset in INDIA by IMPEC eSolutions
Printed and bound in England by CPI (UK) Ltd.

The Publisher's authorised representative in the EU for product safety is
Authorised Rep Compliance Ltd., Ground Floor, 71 Lower Baggot Street,
Dublin D02 P593, Ireland.
www.arccompliance.com

For a complete list of Pen & Sword titles please contact

PEN & SWORD BOOKS LIMITED
47 Church Street, Barnsley, South Yorkshire, S70 2AS, England
E-mail: enquiries@pen-and-sword.co.uk
Website: www.pen-and-sword.co.uk

or

PEN AND SWORD BOOKS
1950 Lawrence Rd, Havertown, PA 19083, USA
E-mail: uspen-and-sword@casematepublishers.com
Website: www.penandswordbooks.com

MIX
Paper | Supporting
responsible forestry
FSC
www.fsc.org
FSC® C013604

THE WORLDS OF
DOROTHY
L. SAYERS

THE LIFE AND WORKS OF THE
CRIME WRITER AND POET

STEPHEN WADE

PEN & SWORD HISTORY

AN IMPRINT OF PEN & SWORD BOOKS LTD.
YORKSHIRE – PHILADELPHIA

Contents

Introduction

It isn't enough merely to warm both hands at the fire of life ... the art of living lies in warming one's whole body...

- Ethel Mannin

A Note to the Reader

Every writer has to face the question: for whom am I writing this book? Sometimes the audience is a clear concept; but often, there is a realisation that there are multiple readers imagined as a book takes shape. That has been the case with this enquiry into such a strikingly individual life. Basically, my first notion was to provide an introduction, rather similar to Janet Hitchman's book, *Such a Strange Lady* (1975), which is openly defined as an introduction. Then there is the issue of what may be provided for those specialists and fans of Dorothy. The bare biographical facts are so easy to access that a repetition of that seemed pointless from the inception. It had to be a different read.

My answer is that I was thinking of: (a) a reader new to the overall work, from the detective fiction to the Dante scholarship and translation, and (b) readers who probably know and enjoy the Peter Wimsey experience but know little of the other aspects of the oeuvre. In addition, there was the question of what to do about the poetry? Dorothy was a poet and versifier from the beginning. Barbara Reynolds's magisterial biography covers virtually all aspects of the work, but the poetry itself presents very specialised knowledge.

I reflected on exactly what concepts, such as scansion, assonance or end-stopped rhymes, would mean to the average reader today. I decided that some brief explanations were needed, and a short glossary as an appendix. After all, the vocabulary of Old French literature required a knowledge of metrics and verse forms in order to have the impact the poets desired. Dorothy's own notes on this are helpful, but a quick reference seemed necessary.

Dorothy was a writer who followed a current enthusiasm, whether that was bell-changing for *The Nine Tailors* or laws of inheritance for *Unnatural Death*. I have always been that kind of writer, and so I understand that such aims may not align with contemporary commercial notions of readership. But her abilities as a storyteller were so magnificent that she could transmute quite arcane enthusiasm into compelling novels. The reader who makes it to the end of *The Documents in the Case* will find that he or she is transfixed with the anticipation of the results of a laboratory test.

In my plans there was always a wish to offer something that might address the reasons why Dorothy's work has been in print for so long, what her influence has been on readers and writers, and exactly what her overall impact has been, in disciplines both within and beyond literary study.

Finally, I also wanted to write a book in which I was a presence, albeit rather shadowy. This is a popular work, with the primary intention of drawing new readers to the cause of Dorothy L. Sayers, in addition to entertaining readers who know her work well. My principal contribution here comes from my backstory as a social historian; my work in topics such as medicine, forensics and police history have provided some of the foundation for this element of social context. Writing as an enthusiast for popular biography, I wanted to include anecdotes, experiences and instances from my own writing life.

Overview

I open the enquiry into the force of nature that was Dorothy Leigh Sayers with some words from Ethel Mannin, almost as productive and energetic as Sayers in her writing life. It seems to me that the image Mannin presents is applicable to the woman who not only gave us the literary marvel of Lord Peter Wimsey, but also made a mark in the world in the spheres of poetry, translation, theology, drama and criminology. Her writing career began at a time when several women were also making their presence felt in the world of letters. One could mention F. Tennyson Jesse, who wrote fiction and criminological studies, or even perhaps Agatha Christie, whose forensic knowledge was immense and impressive, but one has to concede that it was Sayers who stood out from the crowd as having excelled in so many other fields of writing and scholarship after completing her last work of crime fiction.

She has been much misunderstood and her work distorted; even her name is rarely pronounced as she wanted it to be. She wrote in a letter that it should be spoken to rhyme with 'stairs'. More important, she has arguably been limited in terms of her media presence and image by the immense success of the Wimsey novels. Many people will know these through television adaptations, and often place Wimsey alongside Bertie Wooster, not fully perceiving that under the bluff and humour there is a powerful investigative mind at work, as weighty and learned as that of Holmes or Poirot. As with so many hugely successful writers and artists, maybe her achievement has not been fully appraised because of the wide base and variety of her interests and projects.

My aims in this new look at Sayers stem from the fact that I came to her work late: having always written and read both fiction and non-fiction, I was so busy in my research and writing that I left some classic works and writers to one side until time allowed me to embark on questions of achievement and stature. Sayers was one of these writers, along with one of her favourite authors, Wilkie Collins, and other literary giants such as Thomas Mann and Goethe. I was not disappointed. Beginning with Wimsey and then plunging into the mass of biographical writing, I soon understood that here was a very special creative personality, and one who made very large claims for the significance of creativity itself. I also soon saw that her genius was in setting free a wayward imagination that brushed aside any number of accepted modes and voices in narrative. Here was the real thing, I reflected, after reading *Strong Poison*.

Here was an astounding crime novel: one with a bold reach into so many cultures in modernity. Here also was a protagonist with a challenge as formidable as any trope in storytelling that might hinge on a quest. I was aware that, simultaneously, the writer was inviting me to share in that quest; she was also inviting me to accept that here, in the immediate lifestyle and culture of her investigator, was a gaggle of intriguing characters, with the usual undercurrents dealing with greater and deeper themes.

Who is this writer? One asks this on first impact. How on earth could such a mix of voices and minds work as a set of concurrent interests? Other Wimsey novels spread the interest yet further, with such techniques as extended monologues of demotic English, dotty eccentrics meandering across subjects with the fascination we see in the best of Alan Bennett. But the more one reads, the more it all comes together. Then, after the explanations of biographical interest, notably in the work of Barbara Reynolds, the whole crazy, concocted whimsy of Wimsey coalesces, and a unique achievement emerges.

Equally fascinating is the catalogue of other Sayers's personae within her art and work. This is where this book begins; I wanted to share questions as well as enthusiasms, and open up a wider interest than another chronological narrative would offer. I decided to advance by theme and topic, to look through a prism at the person who was

Dorothy L. Sayers the friend, the mother, the lover, the speaker, the scholar and the poet, as well as the writer who created the Denvers and Climpson, Harriet and D.I. Parker.

Aspiring to present the 'real' Dorothy L. Sayers may suggest a certain arrogance, but one has to read that word with an undertone of what a cultural historian might discern, one who works hard to be objective when fundamentally, that historian is an advocate for the subject. Why might one enter into literary biography at all? For me, it is to gather new readers for a writer who continues to impress, and whose fiction goes on appealing to readers of crime stories, in spite of the demands sometimes made, such as the linguistic bravado of all the foreign phrases and literary references. In spite also of the metafictional forays piercing the fabric of the suspension of disbelief that any story demands of us, as in this from *Unnatural Death*, in reply to a question about poisons from Parker:

> Oh by one of those native poisons which slay in a split second and defy the skill of the analyst. They are familiar to the meanest writer of mystery stories. I'm not going to let a trifle like that stand in my way.

So much has been written about Sayers, and so many fans exist, that an objective view might be difficult to achieve. But where large claims have been made, great efforts have to be made to add to what is already established or perhaps debated, though always with the delight of celebrating a rare creative soul in this instance.

When one tries to assess exactly what criteria we use in order to apply some judgement to fiction, the notion of playfulness, the pleasure taken in the text, comes to mind. This is something in literary theory which always relates to the quality of reader and writer sharing the story; the term 'carnival' has been used linked to this: the notion that, with the willing suspension of disbelief, the reader invests in the creation of the fictional world and characters. The evidence of the success of this is in the mediation of the fiction across the various commercial and aesthetic arms of the representation of a book. Hence, we have letters from the public addressed to Sherlock Holmes at 221B Baker Street. Equally, Lord Peter Wimsey, so startlingly 'alive' is in that status. Such has been the success of Sayers's outstanding creation.

One of the many secrets of her craft in fiction was the tendency to create a knotty problem stemming from human transgression, and that situation has to generate a labyrinth of journeys, both real and mental, for Wimsey, Parker, Climpson and anyone else concerned; even more than this, however, is the universal theme running through the mystery. Arguably, it is the embellishment of this material, largely through secondary characters and Wimsey's own multilateral wit, playfulness and need to indulge in a performance that really makes the Sayers difference. In a classic biographical essay on Dr Samuel Johnson, Bertrand H. Bronson chose the title 'Johnson Agonistes' (Johnson in opposition or in a struggle) and Sayers similarly gives to Wimsey the need to make a conversation the linguistic equivalent of a game of tennis, or a dramatic dialogue in which a need to entertain dominates proceedings.

In one respect, the Sayers oeuvre falls simply into two: the crime novelist, followed by the theologian and serious academic translator; but if we spin the material a little, it is not hard to discern a fluent progression of her creative energies and interests, all unified, from the first poems through to the intense immersion in Dante studies. She thought Dante to be the greatest storyteller, and had her own crusade on his behalf, to demonstrate that. What emerges as a spin-off from this is her own impressive adaptability as a weaver of tales, whether the form be prose or poetry.

Sayers's achievement has been evaluated in so many ways, but I tend to adopt the verdict of Barbara Reynolds, relating to the concept of Wimsey, when trying to comment on such a varied and staggering literary career. 'His creator was to say that Lord Peter became more real to her than many living persons. This is partly because she wove the threads of her own experience, thoughts and feelings into the fabric of his character.' In my own experience of planning and writing novels, I concur that the skills required to fashion a successful work of fiction are deeply worked into that illusive 'fabric' of 'character'. The trick is to make the resulting fictional creation utterly convincing, and Sayers did this in spite of the Wimsey genius being a sparkling fusion of earthbound good sense and sheer, wild fancy.

If one had to choose something in the oeuvre which would illustrate Sayers's almost unique quality and skill, arguably, a couple of chapters of *Unnatural Death* (1927) would be perfect. In chapters 17 and 18 the solicitor, Mr Trigg is involved in a mix of legal explanation and a cooperative exploration of his memory, all in the cause of the reader understanding the potentially murderous implications related to a new Property Act. Sayers wants the reader to follow the complicated routes to the link between a murder and the motives inherent in the impact of the legislation. All this emerges from a paragraph in which we are prepared for some brain-work: when Mr Towkington asks, 'You show a remarkable disposition of crime, don't you. Eh?' This then follows:

'Well, if I did go in for it, I'd take reasonable precautions,' retorted Wimsey. 'Swonderful, of course, the tomfool things murderers **do** do. But I have the highest opinions of Miss Whittaker's brains. I bet she covered her tracks pretty well.'

The reader has to follow extensive legal talk and explanation in the following chapters. Everything in the context leads to the subterfuge committed on the victim, and we stay with the legal explorations because such things as 'mercy killings' and murder by opium have so often been central in murder cases. In fact, not long after the publication of this novel, the notorious Dr Bodkin Adams was practising, and in the role of the GP who helped the sick from this world – though he was never charged with murder and was acquitted at his trial. Sayers had chosen a most outstandingly current theme for the novel.

One of the arguments against reading Sayers's work is that she gives no quarter to her readers, and her work carries a burden of quotation and literary reference that only the best scholars would understand and appreciate. This is far from the truth. In fact, enthusiasts for the Wimsey character often argue that there is a special pleasure in the place of the reference of this kind in the books. Surely, the use of epigrams, in the right hands, may be an integral element in the narrative.

In the last analysis, the influential effects of a great writer prove the achievement, and this is the case with Sayers. Elizabeth George, given the enviable task of introducing the Wimsey novels for the New English Library edition, has a familiar comment on this feature of the work: 'The passions felt by characters created eighty years ago are as real today as they were then. The motives behind people's behaviour are no more complex now than they were in 1923 when Lord Peter Wimsey took his first public bow.'

One could add to this that the power of creating an empathic understanding through fictional means is the special quality of successful fiction, and beneath the mind games and apparent triviality of much that Wimsey says and does there is the true essence of a fine mind, created by an equally fine mind who maintains Wimsey's personality and keeps the reader involved, sharing in the enterprise of the story.

It has to be added that, along with every other advocate for and admirer of, Sayers's work, one would enjoy the thought that perhaps one day her writing beyond the crime fiction would be more widely known and admired. There are many strands in the case for presenting Sayers's special contributions to crime fiction, but one stands out: she demonstrated for other writers the possibility of using and enjoying the author's own range of knowledge and interest. Not only does her crime fiction have the entire repertoire of her interests, from crosswords to forensics, rare books to languages, it also has an arguably unique appropriation of the minutiae of her life and acquaintances, all knitted into the fabric of her narratives. When one considers the appeal of crime whodunits, which is largely the pleasure of the reader being in a dangerous world which is assuredly safe, and which presents reflections of the puzzle of life itself, then Sayers shows her understanding of how a fictional microcosm works.

When the theory of crime fiction is discussed, it is often said that this is literature that always ensures a bourgeois illusion of rationality. That is, the 'baddie' is punished and the virtues of the integrated community survive. The detective is the heroic figure who protects that community. As Raymond Chandler famously said, putting words into the mouth of his detective, Philip Marlowe, 'Down these mean streets a man must go.' The key word is 'must'. Lord Peter must work tirelessly for the truth, and in his case he walks through a bizarre world, as well as a challenging one. Not only does he almost die in the bog of Peter's Pot (in *Clouds of Witness*) but he is constantly in danger, in his world of fast travel, unseen enemies and foolhardy behaviour in the face of the unknown. He is, in many ways, the opposite of the traditional hero. In the short story *The Abominable History of the Man With Copper Fingers*, Sayers describes the Egotists' Club, and she notes that 'Nobody is ineligible per se, except strong, silent men.'

The whodunit's immense popularity may largely be explained by the notion of a story as teleological; that is, the reader is always looking to the end, and building the shape of a tale in their own mind; if we add to this the reader's desire to share in the construction of a plot, and to exercise the grey matter as if a puzzle is being presented, then everything else is adornment. But that is only in the smallest, least ambitious fiction. It is quite possible to write in the whodunit genre with only the tiniest character building and contextual material. But this is not for Sayers. Generally, in a Wimsey novel, running parallel to the course of the murder itself there are strands of knowledge, contemporary reference and themes of a more profound nature.

Yet matters run deeper still. There is also Sayers's love of metafictional playfulness. That is to say, she exploits the nature of fiction itself by applying the double ruse of having characters refer to crime fiction, as if the illusion of the 'realism' of her novels is soundly supported by the narrative's comments on make-believe tales. This happens, for instance, in *Clouds of Witness*, when Wimsey is tracing the movements of a potential killer outside Riddlesdale Hall: 'I have always maintained that those obliging criminals who strew their tracks with little articles of personal adornment ... were an invention of detective fiction.' The metafiction often gives Sayers an ideal opportunity for humour, and of course, the reader, sharing in the pretence, enjoys another layer of interest in this technique.

Not only did Sayers utilise every facet of her life experience in the fiction: she also tended to use abstruse knowledge as well as her deep learning. Her degree in French, together with her experience of living and working in France (notably with Eric Whelpton at L'École des Roches) is often used to great effect. In the short story, 'The Entertaining Episode of the Article in Question', she uses French as part of a dabble into basic forensic linguistics by Lord Peter when he develops a clue on the would-be thief Jacques San-culotte, by spotting the criminal's error in the misuse of the adjectives beau/belle.

The author's voice and the character's dialogue in the detective fiction tend to be seamlessly integrated, and the foundation is a mix of deep learning and extravagant whimsicality. The effect Sayers works for is difficult, but her great resource is that she clearly had an extremely retentive memory, a true involvement in her scholarship, and a love of 'playing the part' which had been in her from her childhood, when she loved dressing up and mimicking the heroes of the tales of adventure she adored. There is always a flavour of the romantic adventure in her stories, a presence of the Scarlet Pimpernel or of a Musketeer. She enjoyed building an entire episode or story around academically based subjects, as in a 1939 anthology in which a Wimsey story, 'The Dragon's Head,' is entirely concerned with the theft of an ancient volume, convincingly titled Münster's *Cosmographia Universalis*.

All this explains why true readers and lovers of Sayers's fiction are intensely involved. They tend to re-read, share their enthusiasm and see Wimsey from every angle. Yes, he is similar to the great Sherlock; he has a personal Who's Who reference work and he revels in forensic knowledge; he is eccentric, full of obscure learning, and above all, he is good company in spite of the occasional crassness and the inability to speak and behave as a context dictates.

In short, for reasons both popular and academic, Sayers created a fictional creation who will stand alongside the Pickwicks, the Father Browns and the Holmeses as long as books are in existence.

There is far more to Dorothy L. Sayers than detective fiction of course. However, by 1936 there is no doubt about the status she had achieved in English letters. One national paper asked at that time, 'Who stands highest among the writers of modern thrillers?' The writer answered his own question: 'Edgar Wallace, Sydney Horler, Dorothy L. Sayers, "Sapper," J.S. Fletcher, Valentine Williams, "Seamark".' They had all been featured in *The Book of a Thousand Thrills*. Dorothy L. Sayers was up there with the elite, barely thirteen years after the first Wimsey book. She was undoubtedly well known in that genre, but there was also the Sayers of religious drama, of poetry, and so much more.

My own particular delight, among all the expressions and achievements of this remarkable writer, is in her poetic heart. Her very first book was a poetry collection, published by her employer at the time, Basil Blackwell, and its title promised much more: *Op.1*. Moreover, the poetry in her repertoire was expressed everywhere. In the fiction, it is never so functional as to be scene-setting or plain visual description. One could think of the close of Chapter 15 of *Clouds of Witness*, when she gives us this: 'A scurry of swift black clouds with ragged edges was driving bleakly westwards as they streamed out into Parliament Square, and the seagulls screeched and wheeled inwards from the river.' This could be presented in lines, as a free verse elegy, but of course the word 'clouds' is probably not accidental. The clouds in the intricate story have obfuscated and now they may even enlighten. Who knows? That is the deeper mystery, far beyond the confines of a novel.

In the end, we read Dorothy L. Sayers to remind us that so much of our highbrow literary attitudes are illusory; in the end, if a story is sound and compelling, the vehicle for its delivery will be enjoyed. Her achievement backs up an enduring appeal from many crime writers (notably Ian Rankin) to give crime fiction a status on a par with the narratives defined as highbrow as opposed to 'popular'. As far back as the 1930s, journals such as the seriously high-cultural *London Mercury* were separating 'detective fiction' from the blanket term 'fiction' in their listings, and even now, a similar dichotomy is seen in publications whose book review space often includes a brief mention of the crime fiction titles, in contrast to fuller reports on *literary* works. The Sayers approach invites the reader to enjoy the intellectual demands in her fiction, contrary to the criticism that her Wimsey stories demand too much. A perfect example of this is a long letter written in French, in *Clouds of Witness*. A translation follows in the book, but the reader doesn't know this at the beginning. Consequently, one copes or skims. Most readers probably brush up their school French and understand some of the letter, but others may despair and feel frustrated.

Personally, I admire the storyteller who delivers the words just as they emerge from the imagination, and I think Sayers respected that concept so much that she wanted her readers to join in the challenge of assembling a satisfactory narrative.

My biographical work will not aim to challenge any accepted view of Dorothy. Full chronological works have been supplied by, among others, Barbara Reynolds, Janet Hitchman and David Coomes. Neither will my word 'the real' Sayers claim any startling discoveries. What I offer is more in the order of the woman who was dedicated to the 'itch to write,' but who drank from life's cup to the full. I was attracted to her tireless need to create and to struggle to express her own truth. I would like something ordinary but heroic to emerge from my version of the Sayers story.

I feel that I need to add to this a short explanation regarding my approach. I have included a small amount of material linked to my own life as a writer and poet; obviously, as I explain in the text, the status and popularity of some genres and literary conventions have changed radically in the century since Dorothy L. Sayers embarked on her writing career. As I am a social and a literary historian, I felt it necessary to use autobiographical sources and references at times to help to clarify such things as the factual bases of some categories of writing. My aim from the start has been to avoid a dry scholarly analysis, as much as I wished to avoid yet another chronological presentation of facts and events. I have freely used sources from across the historical spectrum, from local history to specialist sources, and I have even allowed some forays into areas of explanation (notably in the chapter on marriage and children) in which anecdotal material fuses with academic research.

I know that the readership for such texts as *The Song of Roland* or Dante's *La Divina Commedia* require massive supportive material if a full knowledge of the translation abilities of DLS are to be understood, so consequently I have used a process of selection. As invariably happens in a biographical project, research uncovers a mass of vaguely related material and a few topics which tend to be very close to the life itself. I have enjoyed mixing both.

Aside from the fact that her work in fiction was always going to be a product defined somewhere between the detective story she knew and loved, with roots in diverse places, from the Scarlet Pimpernel to Sexton Blake, the literary quality is always there. Howard Jacobson, in his memoir, expresses the issue with 'literary' for popular fiction: 'Literary is a word writers run from. Literary Editor describes a job you hope you will never have to take. Literary Novelist is an insult. Literary fiction is atrocious marketing. Writers are meant to have read a lot but not to let the reading show.' Dorothy lets the reading show, with aplomb, entertainment and of course, relevance. This issue will appear again later in the book, as it is crucially important in understanding and enjoying Dorothy's particular variety of fiction, with its multiple generic roots and its special, unique mix of the startling and the documentary. This produces the kind of novel that we feel, as readers of crime fiction, may have had the actions of characters meticulously planned, but nevertheless there are shocks which transfer from text to reader in a way that suggests something is a surprise to everyone involved.

There are crime novelists who plan in great detail, using grids to note chapter events and character development. They know what will happen and to whom in chapter ten, and everything happening in that chapter will align with links and details in other chapters. With a Sayers novel, the feeling is always that the story has been made following the lead of the people. From being a child and dressing up, to act or tell stories, Dorothy had to embellish a tale; in a play or a dialogue written for fun, that will always entertain, but care has to be taken when it comes to the adornment of the action in a genre novel. She mastered that skill, and her sales and success prove the case.

Note: In the text, I use DLS for every use of Dorothy's name, to make the presentation more succinct.

Chapter 1

Formative Years 1893–1920

Happy bells of eighteen-ninety,
bursting from your freestone tower!
recalling laurel, shrubs and privet,
red geraniums in flower...

– John Betjeman

DLS was born in Oxford, at 1 Brewer Street, on 13 June 1893, the daughter of the Rev. Henry Sayers. The date of her birth immediately tempts the historian to note that she was 21 years old when the First World War began, and 26 when one of the most important Acts in the history of women's lives was passed: the 1919 Sex Disqualification (Removal) Act. She had been a student at Oxford just before and during the war, and her degree was awarded in 1920, as that university decided to issue degrees to women students. All this means that in her early adulthood, DLS had lived through a momentous period in the story of our islands. In her formative years she had experienced a society in a world war, ravaged by a pandemic of influenza (the years 1918-19) and a revolution in women's rights.

The 1918 Act on women's suffrage had given the vote to some women, and ten years later, women voted alongside men on an equal footing. But there had been a succession of further revolutionary effects of all this, principally regarding the professions and the world of education. The crucially important words from 1919 are: 'A person shall not be disqualified by sex or marriage from the exercise of any public function, or from being appointed to or holding any civil or judicial office or post or from entering or assuming or carrying on any civil profession or vocation.' Now, women could even sit in the House of Lords.

Of course, this was not as sweepingly revisionist as the wording above implies. There were still reservations and qualifications. We might ask what statute was ever an action with simple and comprehensive consequences? However, this meant that there was a profound impact on the lives of DLS and her circle of friends. Britain was behind the USA in the status of women in the legal profession; in the board of directors for the Women's Bar Association of Illinois, for instance, we have Edith Gabel, who was admitted to that bar in 1917. Margaret Hall, in Britain, noted in 1901 that 'It must be acknowledged that the prejudice which existed against women entering other professions or businesses has been gradually removed of recent years.' Not long after the 1919 Act readers of the daily papers were being told about women on juries or serving as magistrates. On Christmas Eve 1919, Helena Normanton was the first woman admitted to the Inns of Court. Today, a stroll around those Inns and some glances at the staff lists shows a high proportion of women barristers.

As has been widely reported and described, there had also been a revolution in the general world of work, largely because of the war; women had served as nurses in the theatre of war, and also as drivers and in all kinds of secondary roles. At home they had worked in the munitions factories. There were still some limitations for women seeking a civil service career, mainly the marriage bar; neither could women serve in the armed forces or in ecclesiastic positions.

One might deduce from this that there were still social problems and unrest in this sphere of life, and such groups as the Women's Freedom League (WFL) created in 1907, which was militant in its aims and actions, shows this. The ethos was direct action and passive resistance, and in the Grille Incident of 1908 three WFL women unfurled a banner in the House of Commons and chained themselves to a grille in the ladies' gallery. There are plenty of other incidents which could be invoked to show the extreme dissent around the land, in spite of the new attitudes and the changes in the law, including a bomb that exploded a summer house that was being built for Lloyd George in 1913.

However, in the world and immediate culture of DLS, which was largely in education, one of the most resounding events was that from 1920, women at Oxford could be awarded their degrees. In the last decades of the nineteenth century, at Oxford, higher education for women had progressed, with women's colleges being founded. Somerville, DLS's college, was opened in 1879. Matters always moved slowly though. In fact, there was no full professorship awarded to a woman until that of Agnes Headlam-Morley in 1948. But as far as DLS was concerned, the important turning-point was in October 1920, a while after finishing her studies. She wrote home: 'Of course, I am going to Oxford on the 13th for my degree Christine Blackwell is putting me up.' Barbara Reynolds, in her biography of DLS, explains the situation: 'a ceremony was held in the Sheldonian at which the first batch of qualified women … were formally invested with a B.A. and immediately afterwards with an M.A.' DLS could now wear the gown and cap.

Oxford had been well behind other institutions. At Aberystwyth in Wales, for instance, Mary Louis Williams had been the first woman graduate, awarded her degree (from London) in 1888. The first woman student at that college, studying there in the years 1884–88, was Mrs Louisa Pattrick, and she recalled some of the restraints of student life:

We women now proclaimed our intention to be present [at dinners] and consternation reigned. There were hurried meetings of the powers to discuss it and finally we were allowed to appear on consideration of our being duly chaperoned. One august lady said 'It would be the death of her.'

The college might have been advanced in respect of women students, but there were difficulties. At least in Oxford there were women's colleges; they were in advance of the age in many respects, and DLS benefited immensely, as will be described in a later chapter.

Naturally, the old brigade complained. In a letter to *The Times* in March 1922, Dr Charles Pring simply could not cope with the new breed of student; he wrote on women medical students, and his stance was indicative of how some of the establishment saw DLS's generation:

> No matter how choice the demeanour and character of the feminine neophyte, after a few months of the students' common room she becomes coarse, immodest and vulgar ... It is because of these things that those of us who have daughters view the prospect of their possible association with the advancing sisterhood with misgiving and dismay.

Still, between her first spell at university and her return to receive the degree, her life had been one typical of a middle-class woman of her time working to carve out some kind of career. We know from the autobiographies of women writers such as Ethel Mannin and Storm Jameson that women aspiring to be professional writers generally had to strive for a foot in the door wherever they could find one. Unless an individual had established contacts or circles of friends, the years now marked and celebrated as the period of the birth of Modernism and Bloomsbury values was one in which the majority of people from the working class found it hard to be noticed, and their work considered. Fortunately, there was a new world of news media: commerce, advertising, and in particular, the popular press. This was the era when the hunger for reading matter among the new commuter groups was being met by cheap paperback editions of fiction, and – in particular – by short stories in newspapers and magazines.

Ethel Mannin and Storm Jameson found some kind of progress in work with popular magazines or even literary, 'niche readership' publications. In the career of DLS the equivalent experience was more a mixture of finding time to think, to be with friends, and with teaching. Between leaving Oxford for the first time, as the war began, and the early 1920s, she dipped her foot in the great river of teaching, the place for writers that offered some time to write - in the vacation of course. Before that, there had been school: in the Godolphin School in Salisbury mainly, following on from tutoring at home, where her education had begun very early, and included Latin (with her father) and music lessons.

Godolphin School was to be very important for DLS. Her imagination in childhood was nurtured by tales of romance and adventure, by authors such as Dumas and Baroness Orczy. Her letters show the depth of influence in this reading, but by her time at the Godolphin, where she was already on track for Oxford and Somerville, some important traits of character were showing boldly through.

At the Godolphin, where she was to pass the exam for her Gilchrist scholarship to Somerville College, she met two particular women who would impress her, and indeed become very dear to her: Miss White, her teacher, and Fraulein Fehmer, who taught her piano. The Godolphin was founded in 1784, and extended in 1904. DLS would have relished the school motto, as she was always deeply involved in language; it was in Cornish – 'Franc haleal eto ge' – and translated as 'Frank and loyal art thou'.

Her activities are stunningly impressive; from her arrival at the school in January, 1909, until leaving to start her degree studies, DLS was so busy that she must hardly have had time to sleep. She was involved in music, playing her violin where and when she was needed; she acted in plays and used the texts of her own dramas written earlier; she also studied French and German, and when a French theatre company arrived in Salisbury to perform classic French drama, she chatted in fluent French to a Monsieur Roubaud. On top of all this, she was taking piano lessons with Fraulein Fehmer, whom she liked very much, together with Miss White, for whom, as Barbara Reynolds described in her biography, DLS had a 'pash'. In fact, as is often the case with adolescents, stirrings of affection and passion arise and cause emotional crises. Barbara Reynolds uses the German word *Schwärmerei* to explain this, and there is plenty of evidence to show that several girls felt emotionally drawn to Miss White. Much is explained when we learn that the teacher, on being asked to provide an autograph by another girl, referred the pupil to some lines of Wordsworth, from *Laodamia*:

Be taught, o faithful consort, to control
Rebellious passion; for the Gods approve
The depth, and not the tumult, of the soul;
A fervent, not ungovernable, love.
Thy transports moderate, and meekly mourn,
When I depart, for brief is my sojourn.

One of the most interesting aspects of her time at the Godolphin was a work of fiction she wrote, entitled *Cat O'Mary*. Barbara Reynolds notes that this work shows a very different girl from the one in her letters home; there is much unhappiness and internal conflict. But the simple answer to this is that DLS was trying her apprentice hand at narrative, and generating fictional selves. As the poet Charles Causley once said, all literature is autobiographical in some way. He meant that writers will find a way to make strands of material from their inner feelings, or form fantasy from interpretations of the reality they create.

The fact that DLS adored drama, dressing up and being in a role is also essential information in the attempt to identify the roots of her later work; after all, Lord Peter Wimsey, Parker, Miss Climpson and the rest, all perform, as they are projected in their speech, and one only has to reflect on the sheer delight DLS had in letting working-class characters have their head and produce their monologues to see how the writer in Sayers was profoundly embedded in the spoken word. At school, though, in spite of various illnesses, she had protean energy. Barbara Reynolds notes that DLS had confidence to manage 'several activities at the same time'.

There she was, with her plays and studies, expressing her passions for writers, famous actors, adults who had obvious charisma; her boundless energy had to create some kind of difficulties at some point. She contracted measles in 1911, and her suffering was most severe. She was so ill that Reynolds writes that she was 'delirious and close to death' when a specialist was called. Yet finally, a doctor brought her back to health; she spent some time at a nursing home in Salisbury and obviously her family were worried about her. In the hot summer of 1911 she was not well; one symptom was alopecia, and she wore a wig for some time; she must have used the time to read and think, and her letters reveal someone intellectually more mature than her years might suggest. She was reading Chesterton, for instance, and deciding on her views of Christianity and faith.

In relation to her Christian life, her confirmation came along, and she notes that she went for classes on the subject with a local canon called Myers. She was confirmed in Salisbury Cathedral. Barbara Reynolds neatly sums up the attitude of DLS to her faith; she perceived two kinds of Christianity: 'the sentimental, which made her feel uncomfortable, and the Christianity she glimpsed in the lovely language of the Scriptures and in the great churches.'

In spite of the illness and the constant hard work which focused her academic projects productively, DLS did so well in exams that in 1911 she discovered she had come first in all England in the Cambridge Higher Local Examination. What really drives home the depth and significance of her scholarly interests – the drive that made her into the translator of *The Song of Roland* and of Dante – is important in understanding DLS, and the best explanation is in her juvenilia, where she writes of her fictional self settling to her study: 'When Katherine sat down to prepare a passage from Moliere she experienced the actual physical sensation of plaiting and weaving together innumerable threads...' She means in syntax, in imagery and in all the euphony of spoken poetry as it arises from the groundwork of scholarly effort.

Off went DLS to Somerville College, arriving in 1912. This setting will be described in a later chapter on friendship, but for the few years between that arrival and the start of the Great War in August 1914, once again, hard academic study filled much of her time. She did work hard and play hard, and the intellectual demands were extreme; she had to have extra teaching from a 'crammer' because she had to have a basic knowledge of Latin and Greek in order to pass what was known as 'Responsions' (the initial tests on an undergraduate degree) in order to continue on the honours degree pathway.

This was not the only academic demand on her time: she also had to pass 'Divvers' which is shorthand for Divinity Moderations, this meant reading and translating from the Gospels. At this juncture the modern reader is apt to feel a certain level of brain fever, as still more linguistic pressure was applied. In the term after these applications to classical languages and the Bible, she then had to take German classes.

An informative insight into Oxford arrivals at this time is to look at Beverley Nichols, another aspiring writer who arrived at around the same time. His biographer Bryan Connon describes the situation:

> What set him apart was that at Oxford he did precisely what he intended to do, with the combined skills of modern practitioners in public relations and in marketing ... He was an amiable and considerate host and attracted the attention he wanted ... from this circle, he instigated the Psittakoi Society, dedicated to the discussion of a wide range of topics but with an emphasis on

the arts ... he got the editorship of The Isis, a virtually defunct weekly magazine.

The contrast is enlightening: Nichols was determined to forge the first step of a career, whereas DLS was simply being herself and loving her friendships and her social intercourse. Both writers in the end found that the Oxford life they made did play an integral part in the first steps to literary success Nichols with his editing and DLS with her first two poetry publications, from Blackwell's printing department.

The sheer amount of learning and intellectual discussion at this time at Somerville is enough to make the brain ache. One indication of this is the announcement, in 1928, of 'Vacation Term for Biblical Study' which includes this explanation:

The eighth vacation term for Biblical study will be held this year from July 23 to August 13 at Somerville College ... The object of the term is to give students of the Bible who feel the need of more scientific and intelligent study, a special opportunity of becoming acquainted with the results of modern Biblical scholarship ... The scheme is on a Christian basis, and lecturers are invited without respect to their denomination.

In the three weeks of lectures, there was one female speaker: Miss C.C. Burne. The theme running through the talk was 'The presence of the Spirit in the Hebrew theocracy and in the Christian Church.'

One interesting perspective on the Oxford life that DLS came to love so intensely is that she had so many family members and friends living there. She had been born there, of course, but there were cousins, aunties and various contacts all there, including male and female cousins who were students at her stage of progression. Not only did she meet the close circle of friends who were to become known as the Mutual Admiration Society, but she also had cousins to dine with or go to concerts; she had the essential female friends but also some flirtations, and affairs of the heart were increasingly evident in her life. She notes that she was more 'sociable' than scholarly (which is probably nonsense), but there is no escaping the fact that she behaved like the 'advanced woman,' which was a phenomenon very much present in the contemporary media and in the Zeitgeist. This 'new woman' is a theme running through the novels, of course, but there were real-life instances of her attraction to certain male types, and one of these is of special interest – Hugh Allen.

At school, the pin-up for DLS had been the actor, Lewis Waller, who was famous on the London stage and who had worked with some of the great figures in the theatre. He later became an actor-manager, but in his years of fame he was a celebrity of the Shakespearean productions of the Edwardian years and earlier. His major roles before 1900 included Oswald in *Ghosts*, Lövborg in *Hedda Gabler* and Solness in *The Master Builder*.

But at Oxford, along came Hugh Allen, who was 42 and the organist at New College when DLS met him in 1912. Later, he was to become Sir Hugh Allen, Director of the Royal College of Music, and a major figure in British classical music in the twentieth century. As far as DLS was concerned, Hugh Allen had the right kind of presence, theatricality and charisma to attract her imagination. There is more to this phase in the student life of DLS than simply a tutor-student relationship, however; Allen enjoyed the company of young ladies. He sometimes spent time with them in the organ loft. Having stated that, one might jump to certain conclusions, but in fact, it appears that everything in their friendship was above-board, open and spoken of to friends and parents. Barbara Reynolds concludes that the tutor-student relationships he had were 'more fatherly' than anything else. DLS flirted, and revelled in being feminine and adult in his company; Reynolds sums up that perhaps DLS emerged with a sense that she had 'played a dangerous game'. It is surely a case of a mild flirtation and some shared fun.

Sir Hugh Allen was to die as a result of being hit by a motor cycle in Oxford in 1946.

The First World War intervened in DLS's life, as it did for everyone. Ironically, DLS and two friends decided to travel to France just a few days before England declared war with Germany. They were stuck in Tours as the French army was mobilising. After being cocooned in academia DLS saw first-hand a nation preparing for a cataclysm, and then, back home, the problem of how to help the masses of Belgian refugees coming to Britain. The Belgians were helped right across the land, and they certainly had a cultural impact (not least with the creation of Hercule Poirot by Agatha Christie, who gave him the backstory of time in the Belgian police). Everywhere, the Belgians were accepted and assisted, and Somerville became a war hospital; it was close to the Radcliffe Infirmary, and so the arrangement made a great deal of sense.

DLS was active for a while in helping with the settlement of the war refugees, and in one letter she explained:

I helped to see a family of nine Belgians … into a house which the Bursar and Miss Philpotts … Elise and myself had furnished in a week with borrowed furniture. It was a humorous job. You should have seen Lady Mary Murray's cook explaining the kitchen range to us in English.

Student life went on as normal for DLS, but only for a short time. It was still a regime of study and the discipline of keeping to the demands of the college in attendance and behaviour. Plenty of students did go to serve in the war of course, even though studies were not all suspended, and some of her friends were called up. Her studies would end in 1915, after she was awarded first class honours in her final examinations, though she was ineligible to be awarded a degree at that time (but would later be among the first women to have their degree officially awarded, in 1920).

DLS needed something to do, some contribution she could make, but after some enquiries, she stayed to do what she could in Oxford. She filled in some time with friends in London, and then made a decision to teach. After taking advice, she decided on applying to the Hull High School for Girls, at Tranby, a few miles west of Hull, towards Beverley. In a letter, she wrote about her interview, and a certain Miss Elliott spoke to her, 'She said that the High School in Hull had been run by the same H.M. with no ideas for 26 years … and that I was the sort of person she wanted … that she was starting off with practically a whole new staff of young, qualified women.'

Here we have a fascinating situation regarding the history of modern English literature. DLS arrived in Hull in January 1916, the time of the Zeppelin raids along the east coast. These attacks had begun at Great Yarmouth and King's Lynn. Then, between 1915 and 1916, there were raids on Lincolnshire and the East Riding. People died and many were injured; newspapers were filled with casualty lists. In this atmosphere, DLS went to lodge at 80, Westbourne Grove in Hull, just a short walk from a military hospital – Brooklands Officers' Hospital – where J.R.R. Tolkien was being treated. Hull was well populated with writers in the early twentieth century. Only fourteen years earlier, the poet Stevie Smith had moved from De La Pole Street in Hull with her mother and sister to live in London. It is also worth mentioning that the Holtby family lived in Cottingham from 1919, just after DLS returned to Oxford, Cottingham being just a few miles from DLS's lodgings.

Hull, with a population at the time of almost 300,000, exported around 57,000 tons of coal, so of course it was a principal target for the enemy. Tolkien was a private in the 11th Lancashire Fusiliers who were based by the Humber at that time, being billeted at the village of Roos when not receiving hospital treatment; his work around Hull included logging communications along the estuary. There was certainly panic in the streets when a raid was imminent. By the time DLS arrived in 1916, both guns and searchlights were being planned for immediate use.

In the war chronicles published by the Canadian magazine *Post*, a famous citizen of Hull, Sir Alfred Gelder, who was a businessman and councillor, made a speech which included this:

> I remember a year ago that there was a certain raid on an East Coast town [names were omitted for security reasons] which did very much greater damage than the Press Censor ever allowed to be published. I was near enough to hear the cries and shrieks of the people and I never want to be in such proximity again. I thought it my duty to do everything I could to meet this difficulty …. The matter was in the hands of the Admiralty for nine months and at the end of that time there was another raid of a very terrible character.
>
> [...]
>
> There was a man who was on a flat roof of one of the hotels and a bomb dropped within thirty yards. That man was a soldier, and he said, 'I have been in the trenches in France – I have been under the thickest shell fire, but I never felt so hopelessly helpless and weak as I felt when this shell dropped near to me and I had no power of reply.'

DLS would have had to travel out to the school, and so would meet ordinary Yorkshire folk, and hear plenty of local talk. Readers might recall the Yorkshire dialogues of the Grimethorpes in *Clouds of Witness* and this encounter:

'Ah Mr Grimethorpe,' exclaimed Wimsey cheerfully, 'there you are. Awfully pleased to see you … Must be off now. Bunter and I are ever so grateful for your kindness. Oh and I say, could you find me the stout fellows who hauled us out of that pot last night…'

'Dom good thing for unwelcome guests,' said the man ferociously, 'An tha'd better be off afore ah throws thee out…'

DLS was also in Yorkshire later, with her friend Muriel Jaeger (also known as Jim in the Mutual Admiration Society which DLS and friends had formed in Somerville) and of course her discoveries and impressions of the locality would have been used in *Clouds of Witness*.

The Zeppelin raids were something entirely new and very frightening. W.N.P. Barbellion, author of the modern classic, *The Journal of a Disappointed Man* (1919) writing from London, noted 'We heard guns going off, and I had a fit of trembling as I lay in bed. Many dead of heart failure owing to the excitement.'

DLS wrote to Muriel Jaeger after one raid, describing her landlady's state during the ordeal: 'I had thought she would be ill … I had never seen fear before believe me, it is brutal, bestial and utterly degrading I should say it is one experience which is neither good for man nor beast.'

DLS clearly made an impact in Hull, where she worked keenly on putting the French language into a prominent place in school, and naturally, she also injected the regime with plenty of her sparkling personality and a touch of likeable eccentricity. She joined the Hull Vocal Society, with a Miss Biggs, and although trying to enjoy normal life, the war was percolating into every area of life. This hit her sharply when she learned that an organist had heard of his son's death in the war, just before the musician had been due to play in a recital.

She was critical of the educational system around her and, as is often the case when new brooms come to sweep certain things clean, there is criticism expressed. She wrote to Muriel Jaeger that the 'unhappy children' had 'never been allowed to use their brains'. That was certainly something she had been pressed and encouraged to do, and in so many ways. She was at work with the Hull Vocal Society when there was a raid in February, and she wrote home: '...we all had to bundle out and crawl home in the pitchy dark'.

As will not surprise the reader now, DLS was also writing, and she had a project in motion. The booksellers and publishers Blackwell's, in Oxford, were engaging at the time in the enterprising project of printing poetry and other literary forms, and indeed DLS was sending some of her work to them. Her enthusiasm was making a worthwhile contribution to school life at the time, though, and she used her forte for drama by writing and performing short plays and dialogues with her students of French. As the learning methods were traditional by rote and repetition this activity must have been great fun for the Hull students. But regarding teaching itself, and any related thought of a possible career in that, it was not on the cards at all. She made it clear to friends that teaching was not for her, and her thoughts turned towards Oxford again. Blackwell's accepted a collection of her poetry for publication and this was to become her first book, entitled *Op. 1* poetry collection. By April, 1917 she was living in Long Wall Street, Oxford, and had taken up an opportunity to work at Blackwell's, learning something of the printing trade and of bookselling generally. Barbara Reynolds quotes a response to the life of DLS at this time, and the words seem to sum up the product of those tough years of determined study and hard life-experience; the words are from Doreen Wallace, teacher, writer and country lover:

I have never known anyone so brimful of the energy of a well-stocked mind: even at 24 ... she knew an enormous amount about all sorts of subjects ... There was, however, a lighter side to this impressive character. Long and slim in those days, small head held alert on slender neck she loped around Oxford looking for fun.

Here she was, then, entering the world of work, finding energy to learn and understand anything that came her way. She had even talked a Hull printer into showing her some of the technical side of his trade, in preparation for the job at Blackwell's. But at that point, with some teaching behind her and a slim volume of verse ahead, the decision to be a writer was made. She had always read fiction and drama, and in several languages; the scholarship she adored perhaps stood in uneasy opposition to the skills of popular narratives in the novels of her day, but she was flexible enough in her imagination to grasp, and with alacrity, the knowledge and abilities required to succeed in the world of literature. She was profoundly, to use a phrase coined by Iris Murdoch to describe herself in her autobiography, *A Word Child,* and the massive stock of resources for writing in her brain was to find an outlet in her formative years as she learned her true occupation.

Using the phrase 'in her time' implies any number of contextual themes and references, but the words 'may you live in interesting times', sourced to Ernest Bramah, the author of the Kai Lung books which DLS enjoyed so much, have so many applications. How the world had changed between her arrival at Oxford and the completion of her Peter Wimsey novels was reflected in a special issue of the *Morning Chronicle* in April 1935. The issue covers 'four crises' which embraces the Irish Rebellion of 1916, the Great War, the General Strike and mass unemployment. On the credit side, there are features on 'Women win their place in the Sun' and 'The rise of radio'.

Within a few pages, the issue celebrates most of the strands of the cultural revolution taking place regarding opportunities for women, including a photo of the first radio broadcast done by Marie Tempest, an image including six women and six men; four further pictures show a woman factory worker, a woman hairdresser, a woman war worker and a female post operative. In her novels, DLS reflects so much of these advances, and in *Strong Poison* she opens with a scene at the Old Bailey where Harriet Vane is being tried for murder. There are three women on the jury, including Peter Wimsey's friend Miss Climpson; it is a normal affair, as there had been women on a murder trial jury in 1921 in the 'Whistling Milkman' trial, in which George Bailey was convicted for the murder of his wife. Women had been allowed to sit on juries since the Sex Disqualification (Removal) Act 1919, but generally sat on juries for lesser offences.

The massive changes in a given era are also in less visible and definable areas of life too; the *Weltanschauung*, the ethos 'in the air' and in the media, plays a major part also. The same *Morning Chronicle* issue also presents some sharp contrasts between 1910 and 1935: in fashion and sports, women are shown playing golf and tennis, with freer, more comfortable clothing; bathing at the seaside, women in 1910 were well covered and the woman in 1935 wears comparatively little.

Around the same time, in an issue of *The Listener* (May 1934) the writings on social problems positively spill over from the prose: images of Clydeside unemployed on the march are shown, but in the same issue, there is an anonymous communication on a report by the Women's National Liberal Federation:

The Memoirs of the Unemployed published in these pages last summer contained two pieces ... by an ex-businessman and an ex-army officer which gave some indication of the plight of the middle-class unemployed man, who receives no unemployment benefit, no Public Assistance, and who is often kept, by pride and independence of spirit, from giving any indication of the stress he suffers.

DLS had her finger on the pulse in this respect, understanding the equivalence of a certain identified female group in society also, and this is found in the first explanation of Miss Climpson and what is jocularly spoken of as the 'cattery' of Lord Peter: in the account of the female social group concerned in *Strong Poison* we have a sisterhood of spinsters doing useful and interesting work. Maybe DLS was partly influenced by the French tradition on the 25 November, of Saint Catherine's Day when unmarried women over the age of 25 wore yellow hats and dressed in matelot uniforms or other garb; it might be that DLS, with her deep interest in French history and culture, was being ironical in the 'cattery' because in France the tradition was that the women should pray: 'Give me, Lord, a well-placed husband. Let him be gentle, rich and agreeable.' She was depicting a very different breed, and in fact surely her Climpson set were a humorous but perceptive element in the contextual reach of her fiction: 'There were retired and disappointed school-teachers; out-of-work actresses; courageous people who had failed with hat shops and tea parlours, and even a few Bright Young Things, for whom the cocktail party and the night club had grown boring.'

In the France of the interwar years, Saint Catherine's Day was enthusiastically celebrated. *The Daily Telegraph* reported in 1923, 'Nowhere is this feast of unmarried womanhood observed with greater enthusiasm than in the neighbourhood of the great couturiers' salons in the Rue de la Paix.'

The advent of the New Women with a career – and at least the opportunity to pursue one – was one of the most prominent advances of the post-Great War years, and DLS saw and enjoyed the sheer irony of young women on both sides of the Channel actually celebrating their spinsterhood by working at something worthwhile and meaningful. The *Morning Chronicle* special issue also used two very telling photos: one of a Victorian 'Nippy' (waitress in a restaurant) and another of a young waitress in a fashionable tea room of the 1920s, the latter looking good and the former appearing as little more than the lowest domestic servant.

As a coda to the Saint Catherine contrast, it must be noted that *The Telegraph* report stated that: '…there was little else to suggest that the ladies concerned did anything but rejoice in their spinsterhood.'

Of course, at the time of her beginning the Wimsey novels, DLS herself was one of the Climpson generation, though soon to marry, after some false starts in the romantic side of life. Through the progression of writing the fiction, she repeatedly uses imaginative reference to her more internal, personal life, and DLS was never the one to shy away from using good 'material', always with an eye to maximising depth of feeling in her characters with the workable contrast of a similar depth of meaning in the authorial voice.

With direct relevance to the Wimsey novels, the theme of the 'spinster sleuth' has been widely discussed, and of course, the most well known figure in the genre in this respect is Christie's Miss Marple. However, DLS was clearly enjoying the character development of Miss Climpson; there is no doubt that she and other writers of her time had found a contemporary theme in the generation of women who, after the immense loss of young men during the war, found themselves in a great schism – cut off from the course of life preordained for them that had unarguably advantageous to a patriarchal society. The 1919 Act might have created plenty of new openings in careers for women, but almost as powerful was the need for those who formed the Climpson 'cattery' to forge new occupations and aspirations, and to recognise the struggles they had to undergo.

In one of her popular and informative *Shedunnit* podcasts, writer Caroline Crampton takes up this subject of the 'surplus women,' and interviews Leandra Griffith who has done academic research on the theme. Here, Griffith gives several useful insights, perhaps one of the most fruitful being this:

Miss Marple is often described as a traditionalist. She's conservative, she's upholding the ideal of separating certain people in society, keeping women in the home, men being quite masculine, men being the breadwinners ... keeping the status quo in check. When in reality ... she is actually finding ways to utilise certain feminine qualities.

DLS exploits this to a high degree, gathering a team of women whose feminine qualities are such that Wimsey is prepared to buy a property and start a business, with the 'cattery' at the hub.

In my previous work on women writers in these years, *The Women Writers' Revolution*, I stressed the importance of the professional clubs for women, which grew from the academic and educational varieties in the mid-Victorian period, through to their real flowering in the first decades of the twentieth century. In such organisations after the Great War, the new women and the 'surplus women' would have found both friendships and contacts. DLS also had her own 'club', the Mutual Admiration Society, and these friendships form a key part of the next chapter.

The women's clubs (in London principally) gave the women in the professions new opportunities to cultivate networks of contacts, but also to listen and learn at dinners, talks and celebrations. There is one particularly notable feature of the clubs too, regarding the women in the arts and commerce: they mixed with and met a cross-section of people from a variety of backgrounds. A typical example is in the case of Hilaire Belloc's sister, Marie Belloc-Lowndes, whose club in South Audley Street, The Thirty Club, was basically for the advertising industry (which of course, DLS would know about when she worked for the advertising agency S.H. Benson in the 1920s) but in one diary entry she noted, on 22 November 1916, 'There were seven at the Thirty Club. I sat between Lady Stanley and Fanny Prothero. Everyone felt uneasy about the

Russian position, but not much was said owing to the presence of the Russian Ambassadress.'

Marie Belloc-Lowndes was the author of *The Lodger*, a bestseller at the time (1915), so it is plain to see that an author could sit and chat with aristocrats and diplomats, and in the lounge of a club for workers in the advertising industry.

This is just one of the many aspects of the cultural shake-up taking place around DLS as she left behind the false starts in teaching in Hull, and briefly also in London. In 1919 she was back at Oxford and starting an entirely new professional life. By the close of 1920 she could put B.A. and M.A. after her name and she had a supportive circle of friends; she had dipped her toes in the teaching profession and had proved herself as a scholar. With her parents' generous financial help she had managed to progress as an adult, with maturity and strength. DLS had also survived some serious illness; she had a tough inner core of resilience all her life, the foundations of which were placed firmly in her personality during the Great War and its aftermath. Now, with pastures new, she had more challenges.

Of course, as with every experience in her life, dipping her toe into teaching proved to be valuable 'material' for fiction. Although she usually stepped up the dialogue from reality to pastiche in some of the speech given to working-class characters, she had lived in a working-class city and she was attuned to the actual nature of life in a context markedly different from that of the daughter of a vicar in a rural community 'down south'.

It is not difficult to find examples of writers who dabbled in teaching as a career, and there is no generalised opinion as to whether or not teaching experience enriches and inspires creative work. But one thing is for sure: DLS never had any reticence in applying her personal projects and preferences as a reader and writer to classroom practice. She was a rare, sometimes whimsical partner in exploring knowledge, seeing the limitations of simply imparting knowledge, as if filling containers.

Chapter 2

Love, Family and Relationships

From quiet homes and first beginning, Out to the undiscovered ends
There's nothing worth the wear of winning
But laughter and the love of friends.

– Hilaire Belloc

DLS had a flair for friendship; she also had a need for social success, and there is in her personality an actor manqué, although she never missed an opportunity to indulge in amateur performance and of course became a professional playwright after her crime writing. Love, emotional closeness and sensuality were matters of the heart, and when these concerns were integrated into her writing, she was always searching for appropriate channels for their true expression. It is surely significant that in the Wimsey/Harriet relationship, and in Wimsey's friendships with other women, there is a constant flow of wit, badinage, quotation, pretence and the adoption of playful roles and voices. It is as if the mind games DLS desired in actual life had been denied her.

Reading the life of DLS one might be forgiven for seeing a number of contradictions, in terms of her outward behaviour as opposed to her inner desire for creativity and the projection of her personality. The latter phrase is centrally important for anyone wishing to understand the contradictions. She could spend innumerable hours studying Old French and translating the works of Dante, but she admitted that her urge for sociability was dominant in her selfhood; she flirted when young, yet had high moral standards; she had several false starts in life with regard to a possible career, and seemed to flit about, unsettled, and yet once she had a project, her resolve to succeed was exceptional.

These contradictions are really the universal descriptors of youthful testing and trying, sampling the water before swimming, or making moves to establish taste by discovering what is not in one's taste. Not only do these traits become endearing to her readers, one should argue, but they also create the integral elements in her greatest fictional character, Wimsey. She was undoubtedly a women with an immense capacity for love and affection, and she followed Dr Johnson's advice on keeping her friendships 'in good repair'. Mo Moulton, in her biography of DLS and her circle of Somerville friends known as the Mutual Admiration Society (in my text following as the MAS) has given a full account of DLS as a friend among those she chose as special, but there are a host of other people in her life who won her affection. One only has to consider the instance of Fraulein Fehmer, her piano teacher at the Godolphin School. Barbara Reynolds points out that after the Second World War, DLS found out that Fehmer was struggling in a life of deprivation in Germany, and she sent food parcels and little treats by using the Save Europe Now organisation. Her publisher, Victor Gollancz, had become involved in this as it became widely known that ordinary German people were suffering hardship in the post-war chaos.

One problem in the attempt to truly understand DLS and her emotional life has surely been the negative effect of her decision to send her son, John Anthony (later known as John Fleming) to be under the care of her cousin, Ivy Shrimpton, in 1924, when he was less than 6 months old. To the casual reader, moral judgements of this action will perhaps emerge. However, biographers have explained that it was a very practical measure which is not essentially much different from the modern situation in which the wealthy employ nannies and have children at boarding school in order to pursue their glittering careers. As DLS proved, affection can thrive at a distance, and absence does tend to make the heart grow fonder.

The heart of the emotional life of the writer who created such scenes as the proposal of marriage at first sight (in *Strong Poison*), between returning to live in Oxford in 1917 and advancing her writing career is in the notion of what we now call the learning curve. Her earliest 'passion,' which went beyond the *Schwärmerei* described by biographers, was that in May 1919 with Eric Whelpton, a young army officer who worked at a school in France where she was to join him. But in the midst of her time in Oxford, there was the advent of the Rev. Leonard Hodgson, who optimistically proposed. This short episode reveals a great deal about the potential consequences of the sociability DLS so much enjoyed. The young woman described by Doreen Wallace would, naturally, attract attention. Her life with the MAS had brought out so many playful, whimsical and delightfully entertaining attributes that she would be noticed in a room packed with people of similar tastes. She also moved around a various overlapping circles, thanks to her musical and theological interests which have to be added to the sparkle of the self she projected into the MAS activities.

Back in her beloved Oxford after the forays into teaching, she met with success as an author with her first poetry collection *Op.1* (discussed in a later chapter), and she had a most rewarding post at Blackwell's to enjoy. This was in May 1917. She settled into the publishing job, working in a small office but going out to learn a number of aspects of the publishing business when needed. She was to spend two years there, until she reached the age of 26, and really made significant steps in writing.

Here, there is a need to back-track in order to describe the MAS, which had been formed at Somerville when DLS arrived and met her new friends. This was a group of like-minded women, all in some way having interests in writing, theatre or social and political issues of the day. The principal members of the group along with DLS were Muriel St Clare Byrne, a specialist in Tudor history;

Charis Frankenburg, later an expert on parenting and birth control/ midwifery subjects; Dorothea Rowe (known as 'D. Rowe') who was a founder of the Bournemouth Little Theatre and English teacher, and Muriel Jaeger (known as Jim) who was a writer, and a fellow novelist for DLS to share conversations with on their art.

They were akin to what Dr Johnson described when he had been an Oxford scholar: a 'nest of singing birds' – in the sense that they were constantly active, involved in discussion and earnest in their participation in both cultural activities and engagement with the world around them, with its tempestuous politics in the midst of a world war followed by a serious economic depression. They started with an aim of being a support group for creative writing efforts, and they took new writings to their meetings. Somerville was buzzing in those years, coping with the war wounded, housing among others Robert Graves and Siegfried Sassoon; the latter had told Graves that the college was 'very much like paradise'.

The words included in the title of Mo Moulton's full group biography of the MAS: 'How Dorothy L. Sayers and her Oxford circle remade the world for women', may seem a little hyperbolic, but the fact is that they each made remarkable contributions to the enrichment of lives at that time. One only has to reflect on the stunningly impressive life and achievements of Charis Frankenburg, Manchester-born social reformer and health guru, to see that the group were outstanding, and in a generation of socially engaged women facing up to the massive social issues of their time. She came from a northern Jewish family who placed social commitment and philanthropy at the heart of their lives' work. Their generation of middle-class women (yes, sometimes the spinsters) understood the profound personal problems encountered by young women of the poorer class in particular, and the need to act, to engage in meaningful service.

Beatrice Webb, the late-Victorian social reformer from the era of the working-class London settlements, wrote that in her time the idea that service had been transferred from God to man was something of an exaggeration, but its truth was clear to see everywhere. In my own research into the period, I met and interviewed a woman who had worked with Dr Collis in Nottinghamshire in the 1930s, opening a centre for women in industrial labour, providing moral advice, social assistance and productive work, as well as a square meal. There was a spirit in the air of social conscience and service to fellow citizens. Charis Frankenburg was prominent in that world of controversy over birth control, the contentious publication of *Married Love* by Marie Stopes, and the debates over childbirth that filled columns in the papers and magazines.

As Mo Moulton has shown, Charis and her circle made considerable achievements in their chosen field: 'Soon they were able to cut out the middle step, when the Labour minister for health released a memorandum in 1930 allowing local authorities to provide birth control information to married women in their welfare clinics.' She was also an author, penning *Common Sense in the Nursery*, which was widely read and had a definite influence on readers. The Society members sometimes collaborated, as when Charis teamed up with D. Rowe to produce a series called *Latin with Laughter,* which was markedly successful.

The Manchester connection with Charis in mind is very significant in the history of the development of the understanding of parenting, childbirth and family planning. Charis and Sydney Frankenburg lived in Manchester, and as Mo Moulton explains, they were, '...a prominent family, part of a close-knit Jewish community that had expanded as a result of emigration from Eastern Europe.' The family roots in Lancashire were in Greengate, Salford. In the first decades of the twentieth century, Greater Manchester contained numerous hospitals and other medical establishments; the area was one which had employed thousands of children in the mills, and concomitant illnesses meant that a range of social and medical support sources were needed. A memorial volume published in 1929 on the occasion of the ninety-seventh annual meeting of the British Medical Association, lists and describes twenty-six hospitals in the Manchester and Salford area, and these places demonstrate the mix of specialisms generated in a social context, such as The Babies' Hospital, the Greengate Hospital and the Royal Children's Hospital. The Greengate Hospital also had the character of an 'Open Air School,' which was intended specifically for patients with lung disease or diphtheria and pneumonia, and part of its aim was in recovery and convalescence.

The 1929 report informs the reader that 'The hospital is equipped for massage and has an out-patient department where ... both adults and children are accepted. There have been 7,726 attendances in the past year. There is urgent need in Greengate for extension of this work...' The Frankenburgs were very busy in this social world, and Charis herself had four children during their time there, so this experience was invaluable when it came to Charis being involved in social work with mothers and children in what is now Greater Manchester.

Obviously, DLS would be drawn to fellow fiction writer, Muriel 'Jim' Jaeger. Jaeger was arguably a very typical working writer, the sort who is always there but rarely noticed in any full sense by the press. She worked at the subsidiary employment of the jobbing writer: journalism, book-reviewing and reading scripts for publishers. Jaeger was at first published by the Woolfs' Hogarth Press, when they were recruiting in part from the journals, and also from word-of-mouth material; they published Christopher Isherwood among others, so Jaeger was in good company. The MAS had started as a self-help group, and the inevitable opening stages of their activities mainly involved members reading their latest work and so opening up critiques. Reference to writing projects always continued, in correspondence, after the initial meetings, and in the letters from DLS to Jaeger one may detect the increasingly public, editorial and promotional elements of creative work, as in this from a letter of October 1918, referring to her poems and the *Catholic Tales*: 'I am glad to find that very few Catholics seem to find offence in the book. I was very glad to have your friend's opinion.' Such offence expressed by readers is always full of difficulties, mostly linked to the need for honest comment and assessment, but it seems that the meetings were genuine and worthwhile. DLS writes in her letters of work done to take along to the Society meetings. But after their return to Oxford, members were ploughing their own furrows and DLS took up first the Blackwell's post and then, after two years, she worked as a freelance and had a taste of the real 'writer's life', when writing for payment was the order of the day.

Dorothy Rowe, always known in print as D. Rowe, succeeded admirably in her own life back in Bournemouth; there, she taught English but her enthusiasm for theatre was irresistible, and from a small group of amateur actors she and friends worked hard to create what would become a successful and highly rated Little Theatre Club. The story of the Club began with a production of *Diana of Dobson's* in 1920, long before Little Theatres were fully established. The landmark date in the Little Theatre history is 1946, when the Little Theatre Guild was established. Michael Shipley, in a history of the movement, notes that 'Attempts in the late 1930s to form a movement of Little Theatres to serve their special and practical needs came abruptly to an end with the outbreak of war.' But after the war, the Guild began, and the aims were stated: 'To promote closer cooperation between the little theatres constituting its membership, to act as a coordinating and representative body on behalf of the little theatres generally to maintain and further the highest standards in the art of theatre.'

In Bournemouth's centenary booklet on its history, the landmark of progress was given: '1931 saw the Club move into its new home to be known as the Palace Court Theatre ... The theatre seated 553 and included a lower floor where rehearsals and one-act plays were performed.'

D. Rowe is there on the website and in the booklet, with George Stone, Gertrude Oesterly and others, and the very beginning of the enterprise is given as in July 1919, when the members planned little more than performances at private residences. But throughout the 1920s there were performances by the Bournemouth Drama and Operatic Society, and the celebratory booklet has a photo of a production of *Make Believe* by A.A. Milne in the 1927–28 season.

Productions by D. Rowe were highly acclaimed; as well as farces and one-act plays, she produced Shaw's *Saint Joan* in 1936. Mo Moulton points out that valuable antiques were used as props at times, and one press report responded with:

> there were no fewer than three lines of cars drawn up in Hinton Road quite half an hour before the commencement of the performance, and at the time of the rising of the curtain there was offered the unusual spectacle of a number of smartly dressed people vainly looking for seats.

At this time, as DLS did everything she could to remain in her beloved Oxford, she settled in digs in Bath Place, and she had sent plenty of time being sociable, organising meetings, musical concerts and even ghost-story sessions. She appears to be exactly the person Vera Brittain remembered at Somerville:

> A bouncing and exuberant young female who always seemed to be preparing for tea-parties, she could be seen at any hour of the day or night scuttling about the top floor of the new Maitland Building with a kettle in her hand and a little checked apron fastened over her skirt.

This was only the deceptive surface of things, though. Something much more profound and important was going on.

When she was not entertaining or playing music, or writing poetry for her second volume, DLS was immersed in a heady mix of flirtation, attractive male company and awareness of the mysteries and charms of sex. Barbara Reynolds points out that a typical minor passion occurred when she was recovering from an appendectomy in 1918. She met Major Whitelock, who was to supervise her, and there was a dalliance. She wrote: 'I love having someone to fool with ... meeting on equal terms, seeing who can joke the other down.' Surprisingly, that was written to her mother.

The memoirs of the time and place, when it comes to Oxford and the women's colleges, testify to the fun often being linked to some kind of drama, some 'show' or presentation. This was meat and drink to DLS. It appears to have been widespread, beyond Somerville. DLS's near contemporary, Edith Olivier, studied at St Hugh's Hall. She had also come via Salisbury, but she and DLS do not appear to have met. Olivier recalled:

A week or two after I arrived, the Hall gave a party to the students of Lady Margaret Hall next door. The entertainment was to be an extemporized play with rather a large company, and when we met to rehearse I found myself in my element. I was used to acting, so I took charge of the rehearsal.

DLS, of course, took every opportunity to dress up, mimic people, and generally entertain, lifting the spirits of all who knew her. She was the perfect person to have in a group of creative friends. Being able to work extemporarily appears to have been *de rigueur* at Oxford; Olivier remembered: 'The actresses became contortionists, twisting themselves about to be in two places at the same time. We enjoyed it immensely, and so did the audience, who had no idea that anything else had been contemplated.'

She was at the stage of sensual discovery. There was no doubt that she had the ability to attract the attention of intelligent and powerful men, and at this time she received her first proposal of marriage. This was from the Rev. Leonard Hodgson, who was later to be Professor of Divinity at Oxford. She met him at the Blackwells' home, and she had no notion of restraint – or even ignoring the unexpected proposal. She wrote home about it, saying: 'I very nearly fainted to the nearest chair – seeing that I've met him four or five times at most and only twice to talk to at any length.' They became good friends; he was to be widely published in theology and he did indeed remain a good friend.

For a few years, at this hiatus in her life between being the young woman who floated aimlessly from teaching to short-term work in Oxford to the aspiring poet, she was exploring attraction and the nature of sex, with its allurement and its entertainment as a powerful force in society and relationships. Of course, sexual talk, writing and discussion filled the pages of the journals and papers; it was the 'Jazz Age' and society was unsettled, populated by chancers, entertainers, freelance artists and the Bright Young People. Somewhere in the maelstrom of all this there was the need for young people to find a partner and to discover what sex was all about. Through Charis and her work on midwifery and family planning, DLS would have been familiar with issues related to the more everyday social issues around the topic of sexual intercourse. Yet, opposed to the worries and stresses of sex within the family or among young lovers who had a destiny of being 'in trouble', there was feminine mystique, and she was fascinated by its expression.

A major phase of this sexual exploration came when she met Eric Whelpton, who was staying in rooms at Bath Place at the time DLS moved in. He was an army officer, and he suffered from polio. Her relationship with him grew and it led to a European experience of considerable influence on her inner desires and aspirations. Whelpton was tall, dark and charismatic, at least through DLS's eyes.

DLS moved to France in 1919, where she assisted Whelpton, who was teaching English at the L'École des Roches in Verneuil, near Normandy. She became his secretary, personal assistant, but also teacher, sometimes covering for him when he was too ill to work. It was at this time that she first began to think seriously about writing detective fiction; there were some aspects of Whelpton that could be seen as influences on the creation of Lord Peter Wimsey. Although she wrote that she loved him, it was not to develop into a romantic relationship, mainly owing to his own feelings. In his memoir he wrote, 'I had a deep affection for her and I did my best not to hurt her ... The disaster for both of us was that she was so physically attracted...'

Upon returning to London in 1920, their closeness ended and Whelpton met another woman. With her infatuation finished, her mind turned to writing. She read lots of the Sexton Blake crime stories and her imagination was assembling what would be the actual Lord Peter. It should be noted some aspects of his character can be seen to have been influenced by Whelpton, who later went on to work as a BBC news correspondent during the Second World War, before writing several books, mostly on travel, including a memoir called *The Making of a European* in 1974. He married another writer, Barbara Crocker in 1943.

There was a definite augury of success and a radical change in her life when she realised that now, at last, Oxford was to give out degrees to its female graduates. She loved the ceremony. It was exactly what she thought Oxford was at its best, with the pomp required of an ancient academic institution. But a new life of the pen was looming.

She wrote home, 'These are desperately hard times for literary people.' It was going to be a case of either relying on scraps of part-time work in any related activity to writing per se, or going for the ultimate triumph of completing the crime novel. The early 1920s were a time in which writing as a means of earning money was opening out. The papers were full of boxed adverts for writing courses. Max Pemberton, the journalist and crime correspondent, had been involved in the enterprising move of creating a school of journalism; small businesses offered courses in everything from typing to short stories. Still, DLS knew perfectly well that writing a novel was the key achievement, and detectives were in the air – and indeed *on* the air. Apart from the popularity of the Sexton Blake stories and the derivatives from Sherlock Holmes, there were detectives seeping into all areas of popular culture. Even the firm of Quaker Oats issued a paperback titled *The Master Book of Detection and Disguise,* and naturally, the reports of famous murder trials attracted many of the aspirants to crime writing. DLS was planning her first book at the very time when what is now termed the 'Golden Age' of crime writing was taking shape.

But first, before that breakthrough, there were emotional upsets and a sense of inner chaos to weather. After the proposal from Hodgson and experience with Whelpton, along came the writer John Cournos, and after that, she was to marry.

Settling in London in 1921, she worked on what was to become *Whose Body?* And she had to pay a typist. Lots of help and support came from Jim Jaeger, who was always there for her. DLS also did a little more teaching, this time in Acton. The priority was to survive in London, so cash had to be earned whenever and wherever until her writing began to succeed. She moved into what would be a long-term address: 24 Great St James Street, which Jim Jaeger had located for her. What becomes obvious is that by 1922 she was making strenuous efforts to socialise and to make contacts. Trying to rise as a writer or artist in a city with media networks of all kinds requires effort on the part of a new arrival to be noticed and appraised. At this time she met the editor and notable booster of poetry publishing in Britain in the first decades of the century, J.C. Squire, and also an agent Andrew

Dakers. Most significant of all was an offer of publication, which came from Boni and Liveright in the USA, and the promise of serial publication. British publishers were taking a long time to consider her submission, and that was frustrating.

Making contacts paid off. Squire accepted a poem for his journal, and DLS also made a friend in the writer Norman Davey, someone who was never going to be a romantic attachment. DLS wrote of him, 'I hope Norman isn't going to get devoted – that would be the culmination of all tiresomeness.' However, he was a useful and interesting person to know. Born in 1888, he went to Clare College, Cambridge; he went to the USA for a while and then, on his return, he became a professional engineer, acquiring a patent for a gas turbine. He was also a writer, and that career began in earnest in 1921 with his book *The Pilgrim of a Smile,* which was highly rated and was to become a Penguin paperback. He wrote short stories and ten novels, and after failing to win the heart of DLS he married twice, first to Violet Ferguson in 1926.

Her other contact, J.C. Squire, who encouraged her poetry, was a major figure in poetry, notably in reviewing and criticism, and was published in the influential 'Georgian Poetry' series produced by Edward Marsh; clearly he was the kind of contact who would lead to other contacts, and so DLS connected to literary networks where the movers and shakers of the book world of the time resided.

Then there was Andrew Dakers, her agent. He was born in Hampstead in 1887, and first had his name in print with a biography of Robert Burns, followed by further works on Oliver Cromwell and Mary, Queen of Scots. Later, he created his literary agency close to the British Museum. He carried on writing himself, in addition to working with his discoveries. At his best, he did very well in promoting the cause of DLS, who wrote to her parents in 1922 that she had asked Dakers to come to dinner and that 'I think he is working very hard for me and looking after my interests well.' She enjoyed his company, and at that dinner she cooked *cotelettes de mouton garnie* with potatoes and a fruit salad for dessert. More importantly, she and Dakers talked business.

Dakers informed her that the deal in America was confirmed, and that she would receive $250 on publication. Serial publication was not yet decided. But this was her first step on the ladder as a professional. Agatha Christie had been much more forthright and assertive in her first dealings with publishers, and others at around the same time were well informed on these professional matters. Ethel Mannin, for example, learned the business after running a magazine single-handed and writing novelettes for a market she found for herself.

It was in the midst of all the networking and entertaining in the literary world, that DLS met John Cournos. He was Jewish Russian, born in Kyiv, and he came to Britain to find work as a journalist in 1912. After work for the government in the Great War, he moved in highbrow cultural circles, and began writing fiction. He began with the éclat of winning the Hawthornden Prize for his novel, *The Mask*. There is no doubt that he had a mesmeric quality, but perhaps not to such a degree that he could be called a 'Svengali'. More likely is the probability that he could engage in theoretical discussion with DLS, and talk with a high level of abstraction, mixed with a heady brew of personal experience and success in the higher echelons of the London society she valued so much.

DLS was in a phase of her life where she was subject to many varied influences; in opposition to the comfort and strong appeal of Oxford, Bohemian London made a special kind of demand. Allied with the purely literary microcosm there were numerous networks linked to the media, and in a new age of mass communication, the perceived new breed of writer and artist were expected to be set apart in terms of their aesthetic. Hence the proliferation of small-scale groups, such as the numerous poets who gathered around Harold Monro's Poetry Bookshop in Devonshire Street, but also the immense world of 'the bookman' in which second-tier writers managed to make a living by taking on any kind of writing work in order to survive and progress. An interesting contrast might be made with the writer Edward Thomas some twenty years earlier. Thomas died in the war, in 1917, after spending most of his adult life as a married man with a family to support, with his chosen means of raising an income being writing.

Like DLS on her arrival in London, Thomas opened up to anything that would earn cash. He wrote potboilers, cultivated a number of influential editors, wrote reviews and essays, and found time to travel so that he could write topography. His real vocation was poetry, and he met a person who would help to show him that, when he made friends with the American poet, Robert Frost. It could have been the opposite of fruitful. Friendships in aesthetics are chancy, and often tend to be transient, with vanity often playing a part. Yet there must be attempts not only to overcome the essential loneliness of writing and art, but to be seen, listened to, or read in some way. In Frost's case, his great influence on Thomas was beneficial; for DLS and John Cournos it was the opposite.

There was still more complication inherent in the relationship. There was a strong physical attraction, and there was a need for sex. In addition to being writers from different cultural sources with different views of what acceptable writing was, there was also the morality issue. In brief, Cournos believed in 'free love' and rather like D.H. Lawrence, saw sex as a deep desire rooted in self-image and animal urges. He saw sexual relations as being desired by all – separate and distinct from marriage. On top of that, he had no objection to the use of contraception, whereas DLS hated the idea. Intertwined with this was the nature of modernity with its growing interest in the pleasures of sex, as opposed to traditional moral values. Much of Cournos's view, within the fabric of these freer cultural attitudes to sex, was expressed powerfully by Ethel Mannin in 1936:

There is a great deal too much fuss made about sexual relations. When I was seventeen Herbert Jenkins reminded me that 'the sum of human experience is not to be found in a bed'. That is true, but all the same a little bit more of going to bed with the right person would be of great value to the majority of women in this country.

'The right man' for DLS was not Cournos, unless he married her. Cournos's desires were thwarted by the hatred of DLS for the 'rubber shop' contraceptives, for lovers who were prepared to indulge in what she considered a wholly unacceptable practice.

There was an impasse, and then there was a break. Later Cournos was to marry someone else, and ironically, DLS went on to have sex before marriage with her future partner, Bill White. The break between DLS and Cournos was acrimonious, and there were literary outlets for the negative experience of both. For the latter this was partly in his novel *The Devil is an Englishman*, the second part of which featured a fictional account of the DLS/Cournos emotional turmoil. Compared to this, we have the character of Philip Boyes, the murder victim in *Strong Poison*.

In his novel, Cournos creates the pair of Richard Thorley and Stella Thurston, and their relationship, through the male eyes, requires a test of the woman's sexual desire and how it relates to moral values. There is sensuality and eroticism between them, which most likely reflects that in real life between DLS and Cournos. The attitude of Cournos is put neatly: 'He wanted a woman capable of giving abundantly, unstinting, thoughtless of tomorrow; if he were assured of Stella being capable of this, he would take her for his own forever. He waited for the generous gesture, for a token of abandonment on her part; it did not come.'

The modern reader, and certainly the modern historian, reads this and thinks about the problems of illegitimate births, illegal abortions and moral condemnation that ran through British society at that time. Cournos, a well-read and highly educated man, chose to ignore such issues as he theorised about free love, which of course, was the most unfree version of sex available in the world before the pill and before the sexual revolution three decades after his book. He failed to consider the condemnation, soul-destroying poverty and risk to life involved in the 'free love' which went along with sex at will. DLS gave the practical and universal answer to Cournos's question as to why she insisted on marriage: 'Because a woman must be careful. A woman with a lover cuts herself off from the world...'

The relationship with Cournos has caused dissent and discussion over the years, and as recently as the 1990s comments on Cournos caused defensive responses. Marcia Satterthwaite Wertime, who wrote in response to words in a review: 'I feel I must respond to Barbara Grizzuti Harrison's remarks ... She says that Sayers "fell in love with a cad" and after describing the details of the Sayers-Cournos love affair... "The moral idiot had put her on probation."' Wertime expands on this, 'What I find distressing is that Ms Harrison is continuing a pattern of criticism when James Brabazon had contact with my father.' What happened was that her father, Cournos's stepson had allegedly said that Cournos treated DLS 'scurvily'. It is undoubtedly a very easy thing to be harsh on Cournos. The diplomatic conclusion on their relationship is probably to note that it was a meeting of two strong-minded individuals in search of something dependable and stable.

Ironically, following Cournos, DLS met a man whom she did want to marry in 1922 – and she had sex with him before they married, resulting in a son, John Anthony. There is something essentially Lawrentian in another relationship, with someone else, with bike-rider and motoring fanatic, Bill White. The intellectual, suffused with ideals and unrealistic perceptions of people was set against the man of instinct, muscle and immersion in the demands of the physical life. The latter won the day. Matters were not as simple as the contrast of Chatterley and Mellors however; Bill met DLS's parents, and he brought out the homemaker and wife in her. But of course there would always exist in DLS the need for 'a marriage of true minds' and to a point that was always something with a quality of mind and feeling that the Norman Davey types provided for her. However, upon learning of DLS's pregnancy, Bill abandoned his pregnant partner, leaving her with the project of raising an illegitimate child alone.

On first reading biographical material on DLS, readers must surely feel an antipathy towards her on learning that she decided to ask her cousin, Ivy Shrimpton at Southbourne, to 'adopt' her son. DLS thought long and hard about this. A glance at the biographical facts will mislead. Ivy was the ideal person to undertake the responsibility, and DLS would pay handsomely for this to happen. In official terms, relevant here is the 1908 Children Act, because this regulated fostering, in the aftermath of the baby-farming scandals of the Victorian era, which had ended with executions of culprits who had exploited situations in which 'unwanted babies' were disposed of. John Anthony was wanted, but DLS was worried about the effect such a revelation as a pregnancy would have on her older relatives, mainly her parents. DLS's situation vis-a-vis her son was entirely protective and carefully arranged to ensure he had an excellent education and a healthy life. It was also an entirely private affair.

John Anthony was born on 3 January 1924 in Southbourne; it was a difficult birth, and extreme delicacy and secrecy were required. As Barbara Reynolds concludes, 'The loneliness of her situation had just begun.' Fortunately, she was earning good money in advertising, and after about six weeks post-partum, she was at work again.

From that point, in February 1925, the DLS known to all was beginning to find the higher gears in her journey towards being a successful writer, she was increasingly well known and encouraged, with a number of close friends. In modern terms, she was a woman 'with baggage', but that awful phrase does nothing to explain the troubles she had endured. Yet within these struggles, there had been an increasing certainty in her that she was to be a novelist, and her dream was ambitious in the extreme when we consider the genre she was to choose. Maybe, after all, something of the ambitious structures and themes of the high culture fiction of her academic years had endured, and perhaps some of the talks with Cournos had led to notions about the detective novel which persuaded her that it was potentially far more than a single-strand mystery with one-dimensional characters. In her thinking about the genre, as she read essays by Chesterton and chatted about fiction with her new contacts, numerous factors came together to create something new, and it was a challenging, innovative concept. Lord Peter Wimsey had arrived in *Whose Body?* But that was merely a slender beginning, tentative yet grounded in plenty of purposeful thinking.

The years of 1927–1929 were momentous for DLS. She married Mac Fleming (father of John Anthony), a journalist and motor fanatic in 1926; in her time with him she was to experience the polar opposite of the life of the mind which the relationship with Cournos had nurtured. At the same time, there were deaths: her father and mother both died, her father in 1928, just after the publication of her anthology of short stories for Gollancz, and her mother in July 1929. In the midst of this, she was working hard at her relationship with Fleming, and they were planning to live in Essex. Any searches for the work of Mac Fleming, or facts about his life, tend to be frustrated by a lack of reference. Clearly there were aspects of the man that DLS liked, but unfortunately, in her letters, he is a shadowy figure, sometimes a burden and usually a responsibility, as his health deteriorated. In between the business of living there was the business of publishing, and in these years there was a landmark in that respect. Mac died of a cerebral haemorrhage in 1950.

It must be recalled that DLS enjoyed her time with Bill White. Biographers have written directly about the impact of this modern man who was outside the world of coteries and publishers' parties; here was a man who enjoyed life through the senses, and one feels that D.H. Lawrence would have approved of him. All the evidence points to the man as a formative influence on one important side of DLS, who had a need for action, for being involved in the world physically and to be a presence in that element of reality that requires hard graft. There is a glimpse of this in the close of *Gaudy Night* when the culprit called the 'Poltergeist' is revealed as a woman working as a college scout:

> You've never done a hand's turn of honest work. You can buy all the Women you want. Wives and mothers may rot and die for all you care … You're fit for nothing but to keep your hands white and father other men's children.

Into the mouth of a manual worker/servant, DLS puts the resentment and sense of injustice she imagines within the working classes. This was not Bill White, but he did seem to represent the element in life of 'getting one's hands dirty and mucking in' with a real communal strength.

DLS knew about hard work. The anthology being planned for Gollancz, *Great Short Stories of Detection, Mystery and Horror*, was to become several books – a sequence that lasted until the contributors became much more than the *Strand* generation or the popular storytellers of the Great War years and beyond, such as Saki, Hornung and Philpotts. In volume six (1934) for instance, she includes a rich assortment, from paranormal specialist and academic, M.R. James, to writers who were not principally known for their tales of detection, such as A.E. Coppard, E.M. Delafield and John Betjeman.

At the same time as planning the anthology – over two years of very hard work – DLS was also completing the last novel for her contract with publisher Ernest Benn, before writing solely for Victor Gollancz.

All this would be enough for anyone, but there was also John Anthony and the question of her will, in addition to the fact that

Ivy Shrimpton was moving house, to live in an Oxfordshire village, Westcott Barton. The will-making was full of difficult decisions: there was the matter of who would take care of John Anthony should DLS die? Would Mac do so? This was complicated by Mac's health, which had not been sound ever since he sustained injuries in the Great War. But a will was written, and a house bought in Witham, Essex, for her and Mac to live in. Barbara Reynolds made a useful point about DLS at this time: 'There is a tough masculinity about her ... She must have been quite robust to handle the heavy motor cycle of the period and she obviously enjoyed the aggressive noise of the engine and the defiant danger of speed.' A close friend of Mac's, Parry Thomas, had died while speeding on Pendine Sands in Wales, a reminder of the perils of motor cars and bikes at that time.

The main concerns in those years were dealing with Ernest Benn and working hard for Gollancz. The two publishers had once been fellow workers, but Gollancz had broken away and started his own firm; he was to become well known for his publication of the volumes in the Left Book Club, which provided political education for the intellectuals of the 1930s who wanted to be informed mainly on European affairs and international politics. But as noted, DLS had to write more works for Benn before she was free to concentrate on what Gollancz wanted.

For Ernest Benn, she applied herself to completing the three novels on their contract, and Benn also published her translation of the narrative French poem *Tristan*, by Thomas. In order to produce the text for the anthology, she had to order and study several old issues of *The Strand Magazine*, to choose the stories for inclusion. The *Strand* was associated with the Sherlock Holmes stories, and with dozens of other popular fiction writers. DLS had always read these genres, going far beyond detection tales and into such literature as fairy stories, old myths and the horror stories which became popular in the *fin de siècle*.

This wide reading, together with her affection for the literary greats of romance and adventure such as Dumas and Orczy, made her the ideal person to compile, edit and introduce the anthology for Gollancz. Published in 2023, the book, *No Comment* is an account of author Jess McDonald's experiences of becoming a detective, confirming it is far from the image one has from those Victorian and Edwardian tales. McDonald writes: 'I hadn't considered the volume of serious crime exposure and the enormous impact it has both emotionally and psychologically until I'm in the midst of it.' Back in the days of Conan Doyle and his peers, a gentleman could indulge in detection of murder – and from one angle it was a game, just as much an adventure story as the likes of *The Four Feathers* or *Beau Geste*. DLS wisely provided Lord Peter Wimsey with a Scotland Yard detective, but the aristocratic gumshoe could operate with a butler and gentlemen's clubs in his milieu.

One further factor in this lifestyle in the years of working at fulfilling contracts and assembling an anthology was S.H. Benson. She finally left the company in late 1929, and it has to be remarked that whatever venture she took on, there was a product and usually there was success. There were unfinished projects of course, as in the biography of Wilkie Collins that she always wanted to produce. Not long before he died, her father had suggested that she propose to write a volume on Collins for the 'Men of Letters' series, whose volumes may still be found today in second-hand bookshops. Collins was undoubtedly an influence on her, and Barbara Reynolds made a very wise judgement on this, referring to the thinking behind *The Documents in the Case*: 'She may have hoped, by changing course, to achieve her long-cherished aim of raising the detective story to the level of the novel of manners, from which it had lapsed since the time of Wilkie Collins.'

Certainly there is always a feeling in the Wimsey novels, that a work of more depth and gravitas is living inside the storylines and characters somewhere. Collins, in *The Moonstone*, had shown that a detective story and one with a charismatic sleuth can successfully work alongside strands of satire, contemporary comment and philosophic reflection without detracting from the Collins principle of 'Make them laugh, make them cry, but most of all, make them wait...'

In *Gaudy Night*, when the reader enjoys the novel with a knowledge of the biography behind it, so much of what is included, in the first eighty pages or so in particular, make sense regarding the notion of the 'novel of manners'. DLS makes a slow pace, with lots of room for dwelling on the human community around the fictionalised Somerville. Of course, the idea of 'trust the tale, not the teller' is always in one's mind, but nevertheless, the gathering of former students at the fictional Shrewsbury College has all the expected ingredients of a tale with a nostalgic potential; far from that though, there is talk and gentle satire that Austen would have liked; there is also the dominating topic of Harriet Vane's being saved from the noose by Wimsey. In the overall development of the story, from the first menacing notes of the anonymous tormentor, DLS interweaves the 'love story' she was always so reticent about in detective fiction. She had always said, in her letters, that including the emotional element of an entanglement of love and desire was a tough challenge in a crime story. Now here she was, with the necessity of taking the reader beyond the cul-de-sac of Harriet and Peter as it was in *Strong Poison*.

Meanwhile, in life itself rather than in the growing challenges of the Wimsey novels there was the Gollancz anthology to produce. From the letters, we know just how much basic engagement with the fiction of the *Strand* was needed in order to apply the process of essential selection. The *Strand* stories had always had an emphasis on adventure and mystery; in November 1927 a heap of *Strand* issues were delivered and she explains the difficulties to Gollancz. The first fundamental choice was whether to separate the crime tales from the horror ones; just before Christmas that year she certainly had her leisure reading as the stories piled up. Of course, it was hardly leisure, though she had always enjoyed these genres. She shared editorial queries and issues with the publisher, sorting out obvious content decisions such as whether to keep to British authors only. After a month of reading and thinking, she made a decision that seems an obvious conclusion that makes sense to fiction writers: she notes that the best stories are written by the best writers. That hardly seems like any great revelation, but, she adds, 'I am still on the track of a few admirable tales which elude me', and this confirms that she was hunting for previously loved fiction; she was engaging in that exercise that every reader and writer knows: re-reading and discovering what endures and what does not.

The reading must have been extremely demanding. In an edition of *Strand* from 1891, for instance, she would have found *The Prisoner of Assiout* by Grant Allen; *Laying a Ghost* by George Manville Fenn, together with Conan Doyle's Holmes stories. The fiction in the issue covered anything from the fields of Empire, male confrontations with anything exotic or alien, and stories by women such as Kate Lee's *Woke Up at Last*. Women writers were very much involved in professional writing, and in her search for potential stories for inclusion, DLS was fully aware of one notably influential author in this respect: L.T. Meade. In Meade's work, there is something engrossingly original for DLS: medical mysteries. Meade had written *Stories from the Diary of a Doctor* (1893).

At the same time, the book that would become *Lord Peter Views the Body* was also being compiled, and that also entailed careful choice and re-reading; there were short stories, and DLS always wrote in that form. Her stories were still appearing as late as 1953, in the popular magazine, *Argosy*. She had dual attitudes to short stories: they were an easy source of cash once she was an established 'name' in the literary world, but in a sharp contrast, they were always (as is the case with most popular novelists) a chance to explore a theme or character with little commitment to extend or develop matters of personality and context.

In early 1928 her mother's brother, Percival Leigh, died in Australia, and he left some money to Ivy. DLS wrote home, 'I'm so glad he has left a bit to Ivy; it will be a great help to her. She seems much happier now that she has a little cottage of her own.' Reading this, with the knowledge of the real situation between DLS, Ivy and John Anthony, one senses the effects of that necessary subterfuge: the son was a secret because too much distress had been envisaged by the possibility of an illegitimate child being known in the family of a man of the cloth. As to her mother, it is stressed by biographers that her delicate constitution would have found that same 'social stain' too much to bear. All the way through the course of the letters to Ivy, and the education and care given to John Anthony, we sense a determined attempt to encase the bundle of genuine emotions in DLS's inner life inside a breezy pretence that works. It works in the sense that a belief, if explained often enough and strongly enough, will become a fact agreed upon by all concerned.

One has the feeling that Victor Gollancz would have published DLS's shopping list, he was such an enthusiast for her work; he had made the kind of client discovery that invites the charming sound of the till opening and notes welling the drawer. He was to turn out one of the best examples of the publisher-author relationships on record, if we measure that in terms of encouragement and support.

Chapter 3

Lord Peter Wimsey

'High excellence' replied the storyteller speaking for the first time.
'It is truly said that that which would appear as a mountain in the
evening may stand revealed as a mud-hut by the light of day'.
         - *Kai Lung's Golden Hours*, Ernest Bramah

There have been many misunderstandings about the first wave of writers whom we now think of as founding what is known as the 'Golden Age' of crime fiction. Much of this narrow reading comes from not enlarging on very useful perceptions, as Christopher Fowler shows in a short piece on Margery Allingham in his *Book of Forgotten Authors*, which incidentally includes several authors who are far from forgotten, including Allingham. He rightly notes that 'The Golden Age writers led readers into closed worlds, the theatre, clubland, village life, London's brittle nightlife, and brought them vividly to life with an insider's eye for detail.' In the interwar years, those closed worlds were important elements in the myth of 'cosy Britishness' that Stanley Baldwin tried to use for political ends, and in which writers such as DLS and her peers saw the immense potential of crime writing in their creation of their detectives and their immediate social microcosms.

Baldwin wrote:

The sounds of England, the tinkle of the hammer on the anvil in the country smithy, the sound of the scythe against the whetstone, and the sight of a plough team coming over the hill,

the sight that has been seen in England … the one eternal sight
of England.

Fowler's 'closed worlds' are in fact fragments of that vision of England,
but with the worm in the apple: murders that take place within the
social structures that seem so comfortable. Hence, in the crime novels
featuring Lord Peter Wimsey, beginning with *Whose Body?*, we have
killings for inherited wealth, humiliation, envy, money, jealousy and
power. We have, in fact, the kinds of murders that civilised life tends
to generate, and with a disguised, built-in version of evil.

In the years immediately before DLS met Cournos and started
work at S.H. Benson, in the midst of childbirth, stress and a sense
of loneliness in a great city, combined with the disappointment of
the Whelpton relationship, there had been a gradual accumulation of
material and constructive thought related to the genesis of her sleuth,
Lord Peter Wimsey – and of course along with that came Inspector
Parker and Miss Climpson, completing her team of detectives. All this
had to be thought through. The results of her conception of Wimsey
were to be clearly delivered in the piece printed at the end of *Unnatural
Death* the 'Biographical note communicated by Paul Austin Delagardie.'

The biographical note provides the essential profile of the character
who became one of the half dozen truly universal detective characters,
known to television viewers as well as to readers of crime fiction. But
before we explore and explain this complex aristocrat with his book-
collecting and tendency to sing and quote great poets, what about the
readership and the context for this genre of popular fiction c.1920s?
DLS must have really observed and considered the trends in popular
narratives of all kinds. One interesting source of her attitudes to the
'market' may well be in the very popular fiction written by Ernest
Bramah, concerning the storyteller, Kai Lung. The question is asked,
'What kind of story is the most favourably received, and the one
whereby your collecting bowl is the least ignored?' The reply opens up

the nature of that fragile and often fugitive set of factors that explain how and why readers and listeners to tales depends on who they are and what their condition in society is. Kai Lung explains:

> The prosperous and substantial find contentment in hearing of the unassuming virtues and frugal lives of the poor and unsuccessful. Those of humble origin, especially tea-house maidens and the like, are only really at home among stories of the exalted and quick-moving, the profusion of their robes, the magnificence of their palaces and the general high-minded depravity of their lives. Ordinary persons require stories dealing lavishly with all the emotions, so that they thereby have a feeling of sufficiency when contributing to the collecting bowl.

The Kai Lung books were a real favourite on the bookshelf of DLS and she uses the books as epigrams to chapters on several occasions. Ernest Bramah was born in 1868, and he struggled to find a publisher interested in the first book in the series, *The Wallet of Kai Lung*, but Grant Richards finally published it in 1900. There followed *Kai Lung's Golden Hours* (1922) and *Kai Lung Unrolls His Mat* (1928). He also had his own detective, the blind sleuth Max Carrados; the conception seems strange at first, but one only has to recall one of the founding figures of detection in the history of crime and police in Britain to think again; John Fielding, blind brother of the novelist Henry. The two brothers developed the Bow Street police court.

In *Kai Lung's Golden Hours*, DLS would have found a very constructive account of readership in stories, and the notions of readers sharing in the fabulations of storytellers must have lodged in her mind from this kind of reading, as well as from the theoretical literature in her French studies. Also found in the Kai Lung stories were the cryptic interchanges which were to be an important part of Wimsey's character. This may be seen in this kind of talk:

'Rather it is said, from three things cross the road to avoid: a falling tree, your chief and second wives whispering in agreement, and a goat wearing a leopard's tail' replied Lin, thus rebuking Wang Ho not only for his crafty intention, but also for the obtuseness of the proverb he had quoted. 'Nevertheless, o Wang Ho, I approach you on a matter of weighty consequence.'

This has everything DLS built into Wimsey's talk: nonsense, mixed with a quote, and then an undermining of the words, with the final surprise of something important being said.

The biographical account of Wimsey, with the fabricated profile of the family tree and the Denver dynasty, make a fair amount of humorous interest for the British reader, accustomed to smiling at the antics of the aristocrats (as in Bertie Wooster), but the conception of Wimsey that matured from the mind of DLS in the years when he was being formed entailed some real people from her life such as Roy Ridley, an Oxford lecturer, and Eric Whelpton (who had similar faces) along with the composition of his habits and passions (cricket, book collecting, poetry and song) and after that there had to be the forensics. He displays a knowledge of pathology, anatomy and medicine, fused with an awareness of police procedure which he has to know if he is to work with Parker.

On top of the basic conception there is the knowledge of the nature of the story, and of storytelling. Barbara Reynolds quotes this from the unfinished biography of Wilkie Collins that DLS had planned:

In order … to gain the reader's attention in the first place, and in order to secure his belief in far more astonishing parts of the narrative, the writer, if he knows his business, will strive for the utmost and most exact realism in the details of everything that happens 'within the reader's own experience'.

She would have learned a great deal from Collins's own early detective novel in which Sergeant Cuff and others act in the process of investigations. She would have learned the various arts of obfuscation, bluff, embellishment and digression, which could all be achieved without losing the pace of the story. Collins, in *The Moonstone*, includes over a hundred pages devoted to the activities of Drusilla Clack who is, after all, a minor thread in the construction. But at the heart of the skills she learned in the Wimsey novels is the tendency of the reader, once committed to the narrative, to look to the end; the novel as a form in general is teleological: that is, it compels the reader, in a tiny part of his or her mind, to be thinking of the end, the closure, from the establishment of the story. The other dominant factor is the sharing of a story once the 'willing suspension of disbelief' has been achieved. This is why the Wimsey novels employ metafictional devices. Metafiction is the ploy of showing the fictionality of the narrative, as in these examples:

'Exactly. He is the Most Unlikely person, and that is why Sherlock Holmes would suspect him at once. He was, by his own admission, the last person to see General Fentiman alive …' (*The Unpleasantness at the Bellona Club*)

'I might be being cut up and analysed by Dr Spilsbury now – such a horrid distasteful job he must have of it, poor man…' (*Clouds of Witness*)

'I don't suppose detective writers detect much in real life, do they, except Edgar Wallace, who always seems to be everywhere, and dear Conan Doyle.' (*Strong Poison*)

There is much more to Wimsey of course. At the emotional centre is his war experience and his 'shell shock', or PTSD. There is an explanation of this in *The Unpleasantness at the Bellona Club*:

one time when something perfectly grinding and hateful had happened to me ... I played patience all day. I was in a nursing home with shell shock and other things. I only played one game, the very simplest ... the demon ... a silly game with no ideas in it at all.

Earlier in the same novel, Mr Munns recounts a severe case of the condition:

I knew a fellow like that. Went clean off his rocker he did one night. Smashed up his family with a beetle. He was by trade and that's how he came to have a beetle [a type of mallet] in the house pounded 'em to a jelly he did, his wife and five little children, and went off and drownded himself in the Regent's Canal.

Here, DLS pulls off an impressive tour de force of irony and emotion, as she often does by using the demotic and dialect of secondary characters.

Perhaps, just when the reader has thought that a comprehensive view of Wimsey has been given, there is more. A typical element of this is his work for the Foreign Office, which features, though only by humorous reference, in *Gaudy Night*, when he arrives from Italy in order to assist in Harriet's sleuthing. He explains, 'I'm the professional funny man of the Foreign Office. You didn't know that? Well I am. Not often, but waiting in the wings if wanted. Some turn goes wrong ... and they send on the patter-comedian to talk the house into a good humour again.' The reader would surely read between the lines here and come to the conclusion that Wimsey has a very rare and valuable ability in the kind of communication that makes a top-notch diplomat.

Wimsey, in the first novel, *Whose Body?* has to achieve what all talented writers must do when they have a clear concept of their charismatic protagonist. Just as Holmes is seen first in a science lab, and Maigret lying in bed as someone hammers on his door, so Lord Peter enters with a bubbling mix of Piccadilly and rare books. In order to establish the scholarly side of what a very rich aristo would engage in, there is even a footnote about Wimsey's Dante collection. It is also essential to establish the man's man, Bunter, and then soon afterwards, Parker the Scotland Yard man. They all immediately share their thoughts on the forensics of the body in the bath. It is the opening of the third chapter before we have a physical account close up as he plays a Scarlatti sonata: 'At no other time had he any pretentions to good looks, and at all times was spoilt by a long narrow chin, and a long, receding forehead, accentuated by the brushed-back sleekness of his tow-coloured hair.'

As mentioned earlier, at the time of starting the novels, DLS was working in advertising, at S.H Benson, and it is helpful at this point to reflect on the world of the new media and the culture of promotion and persuasion which was arriving in life in the 1920s. In a *Shedunit* podcast, Caroline Crampton looks at the influence on advertising in DLS's life. In an essay written in 1937, DLS wrote about the writing she was doing with S.H. Benson: 'In a few hundred words, or perhaps as few as fifty he must arrest attention, hold interest, persuade, confute and stimulate to action. He learns to write in the hardest of all schools, where very word must pull its weight...' She worked principally on two very successful campaigns: those of Colman's Mustard and Guinness, and the artist with her was John Gilroy. Consequently, the phrase 'My goodness, my Guinness' was hers, and with Colman's the triumph was in the creation of the Mustard Club in 1926. She was to have plenty to say about capitalism and morality later on in life, but the awesome power of the new advertising and promotional culture needs to be stressed here.

A productive angle on this is in an important episode in the life of the other main detective writer across the Channel, Georges Simenon. His character Maigret arrived a little later than Wimsey; Simenon began writing some crime stories for *Detective* magazine in 1928, and then a year later, he conceived of Maigret. But just before this, in 1927, there was the strange affair of the 'glass cage'. Simenon had always written for the pulp magazines and he was stunningly productive, earning a good living by writing multiple 'romans' in every year of his early working life in Paris, after moving there from his native city, Liège. Whereas DLS had carefully developed her Wimsey, with meticulous attention to detail, Simenon had, in his early works, written at high speed, working long hours.

But when Simenon made the acquaintance of an entrepreneur called Eugene Merle, what we see in the results of their thinking was indicative of the crazy and creative nature of advertising at that time, when Paris was brimming over with artistic talent, from Picasso to Joyce. What happened, according to Simenon's biographer Patrick Marnham, is something between an urban myth and a recorded fact: as a publicity stunt, Simenon was to write a novel while inside a glass cage. He was to be locked inside, and the subject and characters of the novel he was to write would be chosen by the public; he would be paid 50,000 francs.

Marnham explains:

> The illusion was entirely created by the advance publicity. 'A sensational exploit' said the pre-launch posters, 'one of the best of the new generation of novelists will write a record-breaking novel, a record for speed, and let's face it, for talent, enclosed in a glass case under the constant inspection of the public.'

Did it ever actually happen? Even Marnham has his doubts. The point is that, during the time that DLS worked in advertising, its power was reaching further and further into the realms of fantasy and psychology of mass thought. The days of premature obsolescence were arriving, and the consumer that DLS was being forced to contemplate, would one day be her reader. She must have seen, when the Colman's Mustard Club began to create a social recreational encroachment into leisure time, going as far as influencing fashion and 'going out' for the night, that the power of the printed word outside the often abstract province of Bloomsbury and academia, led to observable influence on minds and behaviour, rather than simply to inner reflection or philosophy. John Cournos would probably have seen his worst fears about popular culture confirmed.

It is one of the many paradoxes in her life: employment inside one of the great communicative engines of the machine of modernity, while at the same time cultivating her interests in the medieval world with its stories of chivalry, romance and faery mystery. But of course, what these have in common is the magical and complex entity called a story. Within that apparently simple word, used in our lives every day, lay both her inner imaginative passions for writing and sharing mystery, together with the profound beliefs she was nurturing about the need for spirituality in the individual.

When she sat down to write the first Wimsey novel, with its body in the bath and its enthusiastic element of ancient texts and modern fun, DLS had wide and deep reading in the history of crime fiction, as well as in Old French romance. As her later writing was to prove, she had engaged her mind and imagination on questions of detective fiction. If one concentrates only on the phase of modern prose fiction in that genre – starting with Edgar Allan Poe in the 1840s – and omits such forebears as Biblical and classical myths and tales, and even the Tudor prose works about criminals such as the works of Thomas Nashe, then many questions emerge about the form and genre she was to make her speciality.

In her later essay, which was part of her introduction to the anthology *Great Short Stories of Detection, Mystery and Horror* (1928), she wrote one of the best accounts of the history and nature of that brand of fiction. Looking at the literature of detection through modern eyes, it is possible to see all kinds of links to the backstory of the true-crime genre too, and how they interrelate. The question of why detective tales arrived in literature so late opens up topics in crime history generally. One central element is the arrival of crime detection. Whereas in the Saxon, Norman and Angevin centuries, crime investigation went from community action (hue and cry, punishment by trial etc.) to the first government officials (the crowner, later coroner), the creation of the assize courts in the thirteenth century and also of bridewells in the early sixteenth century, meant that there was an emergence of a criminal justice system, and with that there were investigators. Since the thirteenth century, magistrates had sometimes done a certain amount of enquiry into suspicious deaths, and so had the crowners, but it was only when the Georgian years, with the widespread fear of loss of property expanded, that villains and detectives began to be an important factor in crime and law.

When the Fielding brothers set up the Bow Street police court and began to work with 'fences' in the London underworld, they were detectives; it is entirely understandable then that Henry Fielding's novels, notably *Tom Jones* and *Joseph Andrews*, were in print around that time (1740s/50s). Before them, there had been what some see as the birth of the real English novel, with Daniel Defoe and his novels of crime and transgression. In a limited sense, Robinson Crusoe on his island detected in the material world. But later, when the first professional police came along in the Bow Street Runners and then the London force in 1829, detection began to take centre stage.

Yet there is a deeper level regarding detection and crime. This was where DLS's interest lies of course. The root of this interest is partly in Thomas De Quincey's unique essay "Murder Considered as One of the Fine Arts" (1827) and in the new world of police after the first detective force was established in 1847. Before that there had been Vidocq in France, a criminal turned sleuth, but now, with detectives as part of the Scotland Yard establishment, detectives were to be a magnet for readers in the popular press. Dickens was on the scene early, with his factual pieces written for his journals about the first detectives and the river police, but in Wilkie Collins's work, notably in *The Moonstone*, DLS found the real attraction of the detective in fiction. Sergeant Cuff in that novel is a celebrity from the start. The whole of England appears to know the name Cuff. Collins makes him far from charismatic, as he has a special presence.

At one point in the search for the lost moonstone, Betteridge, narrating, has this account of Cuff:

> Sergeant Cuff stood stock-still, and surveyed me with a look of melancholy interest. 'Its's always a pleasure to me to be tender towards human infirmity,' he said. 'I feel particularly tender at this moment, Mr Betteridge, towards you. And you, with the same excellent motive, feel particularly tender towards Rosanna Spearman, don't you? Do you happen to know whether she has a new outfit of linen lately?'

This is a man whose mind had leapt ahead, in a train of thought both practical and prescient, but who, at the same time, is speaking directly in a pressing human situation, with an apparent bypassing of the niceties of society, going straight to the word 'tender' being used between man and man.

The detective, then, is an especially superhuman being, but walking around in the sad fallen world of poor humanity. One may see the appeal for DLS here. When she made Peter Wimsey so unique and so appealing, she did so with an eye to the same creative mix. However, there is another dimension to the detective. De Quincey, in his influential essay on murder (one of a number, as he later enlarged on this) we have a focus on the offender, mainly in the story of the infamous 1811 Ratcliffe Highway murder, but in the singular and puzzling quality of that horrendous slaughter of a family and their neighbours, De Quincey was isolating a new variety of murder, one generated by the age he lived in perhaps? His ironic account of murder links well to what one might consider the most powerful of all influences on the later writers on detection – the mysterious criminal of modernity.

Here again, Edgar Allan Poe takes the lead. In his essay "The Man of the Crowd" (1840) he presents the kernel of the modern serial killer, as well as the outsider figure of much classic writing, and the motiveless Moriarty-like figure who is somehow present but invisible to most. In the essay, the man of mystery walks in the crowd and the narrator observes him, sensing a dark importance. The observation is loaded with uncertainty and the monitoring of a string of meaningless actions and strange pauses for thought; then, near the closure, we have:

> And, as the shades of the second evening came on, I grew wearied unto death, and, stopping fully in front of the wanderer, gazed at him steadfastly in the face. He noticed me not, but resumed his solemn walk whilst I, ceasing to follow, remained absorbed in contemplation. 'This old man,' I said at length, 'is the type and genius of deep crime. He refuses to be alone. He is the man of the crowd.'

The importance of this is that as with Holmes and Moriarty, such a new enemy of the rational order of society requires a very special opponent. One of the bases of that security of crime writing in which the transgressor is punished and the person of virtue succeeds and triumphs, has been summarised as the bourgeois illusion of rationality. But there is another layer of interest, and this is where the Holmes/ Wimsey/Poirot figure becomes crucial, the 'outsider' figure is required for that rationality to be preserved. In Jack Schaefer's western, *Shane*, the threat of the enemy of social and family order is faced and defeated not by a person with all the virtues inherent in the social order, but by an individual, a person with elements of personality against the grain. This outsider may well live and move among the social order, as Wimsey does, but his or her working to preserve the fictional illusion of defeat over the criminal has to have the charisma and ability of a fitting enemy of the challenge to rationality.

DLS had a deep interest in narratives from sources other than crime writing, including her reading and translations of Old French and Celtic; she was interested in universal stories from all cultures, about the interaction of good and evil, adventure and acceptance. She adored the notion of 'faery' in fantasy tales, and the elemental, magically compelling narratives in folk culture. All this explains so much of the disparate range of constituents in Wimsey's character. One of the most meaningful insights into how Wimsey sees himself is in *Clouds of Witness*, when he interviews his brother (under the threat of a death sentence) and there is this exchange:

'You'd better leave it to the police,' said Denver. 'I know you like playin' at detectives, but I do think you might draw the line somewhere.'

'That's a nasty one,' said Wimsey. 'But I don't look on this as a game, and I can't say I'll keep out of it, because I know I'm doin' valuable work ... I suppose it's hard for you to believe I feel anything, but I do and I'm goin' to get you out of this.'

As to the exceptional qualities of Wimsey as the man to combat the challenging enemy of order, it is found in a number of rooms in the great, roomy mansion of Wimsey's restless mind. The reader sees it most clearly in this:

Meanwhile, Lord Peter's projected magnum opus on a hundred-and-one ways of concocting sudden death had advanced by the accumulation of a mass of notes which flowed all over the library at the flat … the life of Sir James Lubbock … was made a burden to him with daily enquiries as to the post-mortem detection of such varying substances as chloroform, curare, hydrocyanic acid gas and dyethylsulphonmethylethymethane. [This is a joke!]

She was clearly enjoying the humour of difficult modern science and its puzzling terminology.

In other words, the detective in modernity has to have many of the characteristics of a mental malaise bordering on highly individual intelligence, fused with a radical view of normality. Holmes found this in a lab and in treating the material world around him as an extension of that lab; Lord Peter Wimsey handled his special detective abilities as if they fluctuated between the obsession of a scholar and the formless irrational vision of a Blakean poet.

All this led to that first appearance in some short stories and in *Whose Body?*; just a few novels on, the reader witnesses the incisive mind at work to save the life of the woman he wants to marry, in *Strong Poison*. His marriage proposal happens in the midst of all that forensic work and frantic search for truth. In this, Wimsey has his deepest emotions out for inspection and yet never loses the project in hand. As with so many episodes in the novels, DLS was projecting her actual life into her fictional material. This is seen in the moments after the proposal is rebuffed, when Harriet asks if he would want a wife who writes books? He says, 'But I should; it would be great fun. So much more interesting than the ordinary kind that is only keen on clothes and people.' It is almost as if Wimsey is proposing while in a whimsy.

By the time the Wimsey novels reach this stage, Lord Peter is established as good company, with a structured life and a fixed address in Piccadilly. Paradoxically, deep inside, he is also that suitable arch-enemy of the new criminal: the 'man from the crowd' who will be symbolically infesting the lower and higher reaches of the world the detective knows. The new criminal exists in the many areas in which the 'rationality' is seen and known.

DLS was smart enough to see that if she were to invent a detective to stand alongside all the other derivative figures following Sherlock Holmes, the character would need qualities of extreme contemporary relevance, and also a deep mystery which would be seen only piecemeal, during action perhaps, more than in thought and contemplation. When, in *Gaudy Night,* questions about Wimsey are fired at Harriet Vane, with the opinions expressed and responses to difficult character aspects tackled, a great deal is learned about the great detective. DLS mixes this material on Wimsey with more searching disquisitions on the name of crime and criminals per se. In one part of this, maybe she was thinking of the Poe and De Quincey essays, as these would have been in her mind at the time, when she wrote: 'and, most interesting of the bunch, a girl with a face like an eager flame who was dressed with a maddening perversity of wrongness, but who one day would undoubtedly hold the world in her hands for good and evil.'

The Dean asks Harriet the direct question on Wimsey: 'Tell me ... Lord Peter what is he like?' The replies tell us quite a lot about Harriet's view of Wimsey: 'I met him once at a dog show,' put in Miss Armstrong unexpectedly. 'He was giving off a perfect imitation of the silly-ass-about-town.' 'Then he was either frightfully bored or detecting something,' said Harriet, laughing, 'I know that frivolous mood and it's mostly camouflage but one doesn't always know for what.'

The literary roots of Wimsey are complex. The reading of stories in *Strand* were an influence, along with her wider reading, and there is also, as previously mentioned, the character of Kai Lung. Elements of the new detective combating the 'new' crimes of the white-collar variety, and even the nihilism creeping into literature and art from

European origins, are traceable. Yet there is a fundamental centre of interest in the aristocrat, as he shapes up into far more than the original concept of the chatty brainbox with wit and quotes, who either impresses or irritates the listener. A prominent element in this basic quality is surely Sir Percy Blakeney, the Scarlet Pimpernel, created by Baroness Orczy. The Pimpernel had to play the role of vacuous upper-class cabbage-head so that he would never be thought capable of the necessary heroics involved in crossing the Channel into Revolutionary France in order to save lives.

There had always been another strand of influence on DLS the crime writer, and that was Sexton Blake. This was a character from the Holmes ere, concocted by Hal Meredith, writing as Harry Blyth. Here was a detective existing in the fantastic, the unbelievable dimension, starting life in the world of the penny dreadful; the tales started at the fin de siècle and continued until the Second World War. Blake was, in a sense, one of the roots of James Bond, emerging from the frenetic, astonishing world of the hero-sleuth. As with all writers, DLS took from this what she wanted, and put that in the mix. The remarkable feature of these stories is that they were produced on a syndicate basis, which meant that pairs and groups of contributors were concerned. DLS was thinking of writing for the enterprise at one time.

An early plan of a story entails a Wimsey character being involved in a Blake outline; but as Barbara Reynolds points out, by 1936 when DLS wrote an essay about the invention of Wimsey, she claims that he sprang from her imagination ready to be the complete personality we know. In effect, the reading she did for the anthology with Gollancz demonstrates the nature of that gestation period in creative work which seems to flower when the time is right, and that tends to be when a number of factors all somehow come together.

What DLS patently relishes in the development of Wimsey is the occasional *aperçu* into something deeper. This emerges in places such as the shell-shock scenes, but also in his ability to have words flitting around on the surface of talk, while beneath, the reader suspects the turmoil of emotional chaos and emotions maybe beyond words. Nowhere is this more evident than in the dinner after the meeting of Harriet and Wimsey when the subject of the marriage proposal is faced. When this scrap of conversation comes along, the reader is forced to form some kind of evaluation:

'I take it, Harriet, that you have no new answer to give me?'
'No, Peter, I'm sorry, but I can't say anything else.'
'All right. Don't worry. I'll try not to be a nuisance. But if you could put up with me occasionally, as you have done tonight, I should be very grateful to you.'

The heroic, in terms of the influential fiction DLS knew and felt as a strong presence in her choice of character and themes, is still there, but somehow it is hard to see the decisive and assertive in the lover, and the notion of a one-sided romance starts to feel important; however, this is not the case. No, and neither is it about a sacrifice of what might have been had Wimsey changed and dropped Harriet. It is partly as dry and practicable as a business arrangement, while at the same time it opens up another layer of interest in her new detective.

The earlier detectives, the ones filling the pages of what was to be a sequence of anthologies for Gollancz, were one-dimensional, and DLS was determined to make the fusion of the dashing and enterprising amateur detective have the capacities of a true lover in his nature. The Gollancz anthology idea grew and grew, and there were eventually five collections edited by her. There has been critical attention paid to this work by critic Victoria Stewart, who has looked at the choice of stories and formulated the range of taste in DLS the reader as well as the writer. Stewart has done the arithmetic, and notes that the work entailed 195 stories over almost 3,500 pages. The study leads Stewart to consider the notion that, in the age of Modernism and the ethos of highbrow culture being prized and assessed as more praiseworthy than popular middlebrow writing, there was a need for an equivalent 'canon' of writing.

Stewart develops her angle on these matters, with an eye to the quality and standard perceived by DLS: 'As well as the individual head notes giving biographical information of the author in question, Sayers provided a brief introductory essay ... Here, Sayers indicated that the series could be considered a primer in the form for the uninitiated. She distinguishes the detective story from the "thriller"'. This all in the cause of demonstrating that there is high quality in the best writing selected by the editorial work. Sayers is, in fact, going far beyond the vague statement of Dr Johnson about popular writing when he noted that what sells well 'must have some species of merit'. That was not enough; the best writers in a genre must be defined and accounted for. Stewart isolates the 'masters of style' in the ranks of the writers, along with the innovators.

What stands behind all this is what was to become the rules of detective fiction as formulated by the Detection Club, which was formed in 1930. More will be said about this in a later chapter, but if one takes stock of the writing career of DLS at this point, c.1929, when she is married, busy, has lost her parents and is seeing her son grow up apart from her, one sees a momentous turning point. This is all concerned with a writer's self appraisal, and usually, doubts come with this. She was successful, of course, and her name was known and valued, but there were doubts and uncertainties. One of the most accurate and individual expressions of this crisis in the writing life comes from Robert Louis Stevenson, writing a letter to William Ernest Henley in March 1884:

And yet I produce nothing, am the author of Brashiana and other works: tiddy-iddity as if the works one wrote were

anything but prentices' experiments. Dear reader, I deceive you
with husks, the real works and all the pleasure are still mine
and incommunicable. After this break in my work, beginning
to return to it, as from light sleep, I wax exclamatory as you see.
Sursum Corda:
Heave ahead:
Here's luck.
Air and blue heaven,
April and God's larks.
Green reeds and the sky-scattering river.
Wilins, un seul coup.
A stately music.

Enter God!
['Wilins' here means 'violins'.]

Here is someone who has written several popular and successful works,
still lost and confused, while placing his life in the context of human
experience coping with the suffering of tuberculosis and an uncertain
future. DLS may not have had such challenges as the fight for life itself,
but at that instant of great and radical change in her circumstances –
newly married and suffering a double bereavement – she looked at the
work and felt insecurities. Her next venture was into new territory, and
involved a collaboration, but she must have had a sharp awareness that
she had created one of the most original and enthralling characters
ever made for fiction in English popular literature. For Stevenson, the
enigmatic diary note expressed his lack of ability to define himself as
the writer with a public presence; for DLS, one supposes that she
was generally dizzy with the sheer application to work, but when she
stopped to take stock, as Stevenson was doing, she must have had the
same self-questioning in intense times of reflection.

So many other aspiring writers must have tried to follow the path she chose, and their trajectory was more likely to be that described by George Gissing in 1903:

> Innumerable are the men and women now writing for bread, who have not the least chance of finding in such work a permanent livelihood. They took to writing because they knew not what else to do, or because the literary calling tempted them by its independence and its dazzling prizes.

DLS had been well aware of the prizes, and had always had that essential self-belief the artist knows or feels to be reliable and viable. In spite of the hard work and the success, her letters still express some doubts as she saw the last novel in the Benn contract completed. She would have found meaning in Stevenson's doubt that all his work was successful – or even had significance for himself.

These feelings are likely not uncommon in writers who have a very high educational attainment and turn their attention to a popular market, hence the basis of her unique success, because, one might argue, her wide-ranging knowledge and linguistic erudition found a way through into the constituents of the narrative writing, and the result was something startlingly new.

In the context of the most successful crime novelists in Britain, by the end of the 1920s DLS was one of the establishment – the peer of Agatha Christie, Ngaio Marsh and others. The inevitable happened in the era of clubs, societies and professional collections of friends and practitioners of this genre, which by that time had become a massive success story in the milieu of fiction publishing. There had been the Crimes Club, formed back in the time when Arthur Conan Doyle and professional friends wanted dinners and talks in order to promote their identity and success, as well as enjoy each other's company and make contacts in the trade, as it were. There had also been the Medico-Legal

Society since 1902. In the ranks of both societies there had been fiction writers. Now there was a society which would not only be the public presence and image of the art of detective fiction, but would have its own rules regarding the writing itself.

There was an oath to be taken: 'Do you promise that your detectives shall well and truly detect the crimes presented to them using those wits which it may please you to bestow upon them and not placing reliance on, nor making use of Divine Revelation, Feminine Intuition, Mumbo Jumbo, Jiggery-Pokery, Coincidence or Act of God?'

DLS was in that select group of writers who conceived of this body, along with such major figures in literature as Christie, Freeman Wills Crofts, Baroness Orczy and G.K. Chesterton. But there were lesser lights involved also, such as one of the prime movers, Ronald Knox, who played a part in the famous guidelines which are known as Knox's Commandments – even though they are guidelines, not hard and fast rules. The club and the guidelines were, of course, primarily concerned with the sub-genre of the whodunit.

Ronald Knox was born in 1888 in Kibworth, Leicestershire; he became a Catholic priest in 1918 and was a chaplain at Oxford between 1926 and 1939. He wrote on many subjects in the fields of philosophy and literature, and was, like DLS very much an Anglo-Catholic in his beliefs. In his most lasting achievement, one might argue, the literary genre of crime writing, he wrote that the mystery in a detective story must 'have as its main interest the unravelling of a mystery; a mystery whose elements are clearly presented to the reader at an early stage in the proceedings and whose nature is such as to arouse curiosity which is gratified at the end.' In more earthy and commercial terms, this is all about reader engagement in a narrative, a commitment by the reader to share in the story told. But the writer must not ruin the enterprise by withholding crucial information or by using literary devices or breaking accepted practice such as not having the detective be the criminal. The most significant rules are: the criminal must not be mentioned in the beginning of the story, that they must not be anyone whose thoughts the reader has been allowed to know, and that all supernatural or preternatural agencies are ruled out as a matter of course. Most of the other rules are matters of minor elements in plotting such as scientific explanations in the closure, or the detective not referring to clues discovered.

A photograph exists of the Detection Club at dinner; though she cannot be distinguished, DLS was there. She had attained the status that most writers only dreamed of, and all her hard work had paid off, at least in terms of her creative self and her desire for a professional life that allowed space and potential for her outstanding abilities as a storyteller; she had taken the time, using her scholarly abilities, to learn a great deal about forensic science, the history of true crime in British society, and police procedure. After all, she had to learn dozens of different aspects of the criminal justice system of her time, and though her beliefs (such as the support of capital punishment) clash with later morality applied to crime and punishment, she was remarkably au fait with the needs to keep up with the types of crime (and especially murder) found in modernity and the rapidly changing world which was heading for another world war.

The detective novel was being taken seriously, and the members of the new Club must have reflected that the words of G.K. Chesterton the previous year in his essay 'On Detective Novels' were having an effect. He wrote, in defence of the standing and nature of detective fiction: 'Any such discussion, clearly conducted, will soon show that the rules of art are as much involved in this artistic form than in any other; and it is not any objection to such a form that people who enjoy it cannot criticise it.'

As for Wimsey himself, the reader who determinedly follows his progress through the novels will be continually surprised at the richness and variety in the seam explored, and in *Gaudy Night*, when he appears to save the day and apply Sherlockian deduction to the situation in the college, the extended courtship chapters with him and Harriet take us on a roller-coaster of emotions, and in the course of this, such revelations as this appear:

> He had tried standing aside. 'I have been running away from myself for twenty years, and it doesn't work.' He no longer believed that the Ethiopian could change his skin to rhinoceros hide. Even in the five years or so that she had known him, Harriet had seen him strip off his protections, layer by layer, till there was uncommonly little left but the naked truth.

In the same novel, we also see Wimsey as he was in the war, a major – and a man who very nearly died. Padgett, the Somerville proctor, greets him as his officer and with the nickname Winderpane, and the reader has a vivid picture of Wimsey as a suffering casualty, and what becomes undoubtedly clear is that Wimsey was never, and never will be, the kind of upper-class drone that the scout hates in her rant when captured in *Gaudy Night*. Throughout the novels Wimsey has no problem in doing any variety of manual work when necessary, and his experience in detective work includes being sunk in a Yorkshire bog and taking out the coal in a working-class household.

If one had to choose the most telling insight into the complexity of DLS's ace sleuth, it would be in Harriet's reflections at the opening on Chapter 21 of *Gaudy Night*. Here, she finds her own words for the negativity under the facade of his playfulness and song:

> she saw him with new eyes – the eyes of women who had seen him before they knew him – saw him as they saw him, dynamically. Miss Hillyard, Miss Edwards, Miss de Vine, the Dean even, each in her own way had recognised the same thing: six centuries of possessiveness, fastened under the yoke of urbanity.

The phenomenal success of Wimsey – one that puts him alongside Holmes, Poirot and Marple, is that he is fashioned individually in the mind of each reader; the reader in the best fiction is not only invited to share in the story as it advances, but also to make their own story as a spin-off, as a personal fabrication, which will ultimately either see the fictional creation as something as 'real' as the people walking around in the reader's version of reality, or as a confirmation of a set of values lumped together with the unavoidable human failure that goes along with their genius: the detective trade is a *mystery* in both senses of the word – a profession (as in the 'mystery plays' done by trades people) and at the same time a bundle of skills and arts which make for enigmatic success in a tough, complicated moral world.

In Wimsey, DLS demonstrated how the detective pays the price of the sparkling intellect, the eccentricity and the difference from the average person who is deep in routine and order. Poetry in the soul helps to intensify the sleuth's personality and create ambiguities and false trails. The fact is that, as in the antique shop scene in *Gaudy Night* when Wimsey plays the spinet as the owner wraps the chessmen for Harriet's gift, our detective is a skilful musician who could perhaps have followed another career. Wimsey could easily fit in when Bloomsbury or the Senior Common Room call, and he could have been engaged in a fistfight with the egregious and bullying Mr Pomfret. Here is the essence of the new detective, after Holmes, Le Coq and earlier, Vidocq. He is the one whose 'plain clothes' duality extends into a wonderful and entrancing metaphor; the personality as something elusive and fluid, rather than fixed and predictable: he or she is the one worker in the new world of dizzying modernity who is able to survive and adapt wherever they may be. Maybe he or she is precisely what we all dream of being or knowing: safe and content in the knowledge that change and shock will never unseat our reason, though we might have to be crazy to survive.

Often, the academic search for the origins of a famous fictional character are no more than a fruitless pursuit of a most insignificant detail in the writing skills evident in the story. In the case of Peter Wimsey, there are so many forebears which had an impact on DLS's imagination that the search is the only way to understand the genesis of this stunningly original creation. On first reading a Wimsey novel, the elements of his character depiction are hard to take; some of these clash, as we apply the kind of accustomed logic expected in character-building in a genre novel. The letters written by DLS during her formative years show convincingly that there are literary roots, and a significant one which comes immediately to mind is Sir Percy Blakeney, the titular 'Scarlet Pimpernel' of the novel by Baroness Orczy, published in 1913.

In *The Scarlet Pimpernel*, the reader has very few words to go on regarding Sir Percy's nature and habits; he is described as being dull, physically immense and rather stolid. But a few pages into Chapter 12, there is this:

'All done in the tying of a cravat,' Sir Percy had declared to his clique of admirers.

> We seek him here, we seek him there,
> Those Frenchies seek him everywhere,
> Is he in heaven? Is he in hell?
> That demmed, elusive Pimpernel

Sir Percy's *bon mot* had gone the rounds of the brilliant reception rooms. The Prince was enchanted. He vowed that life without Blakeney would be but a dreary desert.

The Pimpernel gave DLS several elements which suited her conception brilliantly: the ruse of a deceptive surface personality; he appears to be scatter-brained and sometimes childish in normal social intercourse; he has a playful imagination which deflects from the purposes of the immediate subject of interest, and finally, he has an irresistible charm. In spite of his aristocratic and effete nature, he is rattled by nothing, and his affectations attract rather than repel. He even has a looking glass, to compare with Wimsey's monocle.

Source hunting is always fun in literary matters, but here, there is also the challenge of seeing how influences knit together. DLS gave Peter Wimsey the whimsicality his name hinted at, and mixed a potent brew of other influences in order to make his enigmatic. The reader tends not only to forget the strangeness and the oddness, and even overlook the probable impossibility of his being so many things, from spy to expert bibliophile. But in the end, he is utterly convincing, and he rises above any slot made familiar by what we today label 'cosy crime'.

Chapter 4

In Her Time

Unreal city
Under the brown fog of a winter dawn
A crowd flowed over London Bridge, so many.
I had not thought death had undone so many.

– T.S. Eliot

As DLS settled into her life as a famous and admired crime writer, still writing Wimsey novels, she entered the 1930s with a keen awareness of both the moral changes in progress and the decline of the formerly steadfast elements which had kept macro-economics a dominant feature of the wider world beyond the literary marketplace and the study. There are seams running through the fiction between *The Documents in the Case* and *Busman's Honeymoon* which reflect this stable world under threat. Crime writing, naturally, has always embraced these broader – often global questions, and although the British novelist had never, at this point, equalled the European and Russian counterparts in the universal thematic treatments of crime and transgression, it did not turn away from radical change at that time of the growth of extreme nationalism and the challenge to the rational order of democracy.

At the time DLS was writing fiction, there were rumblings of upheaval across the world, but she would have agreed with J.B. Priestley's comment: 'I will never be one of those grand cosmopolitan authors who have to do three chapters in a special village in Southern Spain and then the next three in another special place in the neighbourhood of Vienna.' He also added, with no real concern for the kind of challenges to peace of mind that crime writing presents, that 'Not until I am safely back in England do I ever feel that the world is quite sane.' Priestley seems not to be aware of, say, the horrendous poverty in South Wales at the time, being chronicled in such journals as *Fact*, with its special issue on the subject. Neither does he appear to have allowed his trips across the land to disturb his peace of mind back in his study. If he had read James Hanley's book *Grey Children*, which was published three years after Priestley's *English Journey* and dealt with the poverty of the South Wales mining communities, he would have felt the need to take a more 'European' view. For Hanley, as he absorbed his subject and decided on style and the selection of content, there was also the poetic response to the miners' situation. That situation was impossible to miss. The media provided the details, such as the fact that the effect of the 1926 General Strike, followed by the Wall Street Crash three years later, caused a massive recession, and this claimed the attention of the world when, in February 1935, 300,000 people demonstrated in the streets of Wales.

A glance at the 'European' view soon shows the English difference regarding writing about crime in the context of greater, macro-economic issues. In *Berlin Alexanderplatz*, a novel by Alfred Döblin, published in Germany at the same time as DLS's fifth crime novel was published in Britain, there is an account of a man released from Tegel prison walking, fearful and lost, into Berlin. The author chose to wrap his tale around social stresses and strains, and he found that, as poet and translator Michael Hoffman wrote, 'In 1928 his monthly stipends were finally stopped by his publisher, Samuel Fischer, who had some time before been warned that his author's talent exceeded his ability to manage either it or himself, in other words that he was likely to prove difficult and unpopular.' European fiction tended to embrace philosophic and social questions with a strong sense of mankind existing outside the kind of value systems tending to have a presence in British writing. This arguably stems from the long British sense of a unified state and culture, as opposed to the political instability of many European countries.

For DLS, her 'time' was one in which comment could be made within the entertainment and distraction of fiction. Her friendship with Charis had made her fully aware of the huge and pressing social problems facing working-class families in the North, but she chose to take a more sweeping view, allowing for the undercurrent of morality also to have a place. This is present in *Gaudy Night*, when Harriet has a conversation with a servant at Shrewsbury College. The dialogue hinges on attitudes to women, both in the 'advanced' world of high culture such as Oxford, and in traditional marriage roles. Much of the roots of this talk might be found in G.K. Chesterton's challenging remark: 'I suppose if we strangled the children and pole-axed the husbands it would leave women free for higher culture. That is, it would leave them free to begin to worry about that. For women would worry about higher culture as much as they worry about everything else.' The college worker, Annie, starts the talk simply as a chat, but then she says, as they speak about children, 'You ought to be married and have some of your own, madam', adding: 'All these unmarried ladies living together. It isn't natural, is it?' Then before the conversation ends Annie says, 'But I always think of what it says in the Bible, about "much learning hath made thee mad." It isn't a right thing.' DLS is boldly addressing the undercurrent of an important theme in the lives of women, one that runs through most of the novels but is particularly prominent in *Gaudy Night* and in *Strong Poison*. There is no doubt that DLS, as she always did, was using the novel form and potential to examine the thinking behind marriage and spinsterhood.

The phrase 'in her time' suggests the interplay between the writing and the changing ideologies or preoccupations of the period in question. For sure, the question around sexuality and gender were prominent. The generation born just before and during the Great

War in particular came to maturity at the time when matters sexual were notable issues and former attitudes were being eroded. One only has to look over to Europe at the time, and at Berlin specifically, to see a striking contrast – one that tempted W.H. Auden, Christopher Isherwood, Stephen Spender and others to live in and experience Berlin for some time. One of the key figures in early-twentieth-century Germany was Magnus Hirschfeld, a Jewish German physician and sexologist who ran an institution presenting topics of sexuality in culture, and writer Anna Katharina Schaffner, reviewing a new work on the man, gives a flavour of life in Berlin during this period: '...Hirschfeld's text remained the most successful ... It depicts a flourishing gay subculture populated by cross-dressers, drag queens, sporty dykes, blackmailers and prostitutes, who establish contact with one another via intricately coded classified ads...'

In 1929 DLS corresponded with a mysterious character called Robert Eustace. The eventual outcome of this friendship was to be the non-Wimsey novel, *The Documents in the Case* (1930), a new departure and a daringly different piece of work in many ways. Eustace, as Caroline Crampton in her *Shedunit* podcast has stressed, is rather enigmatic; she looked into the genealogy of the man and his family, as reference material gives contradictory statements, such as different dates of birth. His real name was Eustace Robert Barton, and after qualifying as a doctor he travelled, and then served in the Royal Medical Corps in the Great War. He died in 1943. While doing all this living and travelling, he began writing, and his first impact on the publishing scene was in collaboration with the amazingly prolific writer L.T. Meade, who produced almost 300 works in her career. Together they produced medical mysteries, and, as explained in the previous chapter, this sub-genre formed a special element in the anthology work undertaken by DLS. Eustace also teamed up with the series *A Master of Mysteries* in *Cassell's Magazine*, but with Meade, they hit on a successful approach, with Eustace providing esoteric and interesting scientific and medical information which would play an integral part in Meade's plot and character development. This partnership was taken up by the editor of the *Harmsworth Magazine* in the 1890s, and one story will show what was done.

In *The Story of the Man with the False Nose*, we have a situation in which a young married man in debt is in trouble after losing – or rather being robbed of – a precious quantity of jewels. All investigation seems impossible until Meade's female sleuth, Miss Cusack, is on the case and her work takes place 'off stage' until the climax, when the mysterious potential criminal gets to work again on board the train, and this follows:

> Upon the floor beneath the seat was a small white substance, which for the moment I thought was merely a lump of chalk, but as I touched it my fingers experienced a feeling as if they were burned with some powerful corrosive ... It was a piece of solid gas carbon dioxide...

One may sense the words provided by Eustace in the explanation:

> The rush of fresh air when the villain burst open the door rendered the gas in the carriage sufficiently diluted for him to effect his purpose.

Between the spring of 1928 and early 1930, DLS and 'Eustace Barton', as DLS knew him, corresponded and an idea related by the doctor concerning a substance called muscarine (a substance taken from mushrooms which was inorganic, and made from asymmetric molecules) was developed to the point at which there was an exciting sense of a truly staggering variety of murders, linked to physics and to organic chemistry, creating a very workable mystery novel. In the letters, the reader sees exactly what the Meade/Eustace relationship must have been like.

The period and context were just right for science and literature to come together. The impact of H.G. Wells and others, at the beginnings of science fiction in the last decades of Victorian Britain, had started the ball rolling; now, after the Great War, there were such hot topics as genetics and eugenics, and the impact of Aldous Huxley's *Brave New World* (published in 1932), in which his dystopian society's children are created outside the womb and embryos are manipulated with chemicals and hormones, was immense. There had also been translations of the works of Sigmund Freud, and psychoanalysis and the unconscious had made its strong influence on Modernist writing and art.

In fact, given the world-shaking advancement of science in the first twenty years of the twentieth century, it is not surprising that ironies occur. For instance, when DLS was studying in Somerville College, Harry Moseley was working on advancing the theories of Bohr, on the structure of the atom. Bohr had seen that an electron inside an atom may jump from outer to inner orbits, so something radically new was learned about the atom. Moseley, only in his twenties when working in Oxford, died at Gallipoli in 1915. What had been learned about hydrogen gas led to the notion of the quantum.

J. Bronowski, in his seminal work, *The Ascent of Man*, explains the importance of this: 'the quantum ... led gradually to a systematic classification of the types of stationary binding of any electron in an atom', and as Bronowski concludes, 'this leads to the formulation of the laws of nature to considerations of pure numbers.'

The excitement of a momentous discovery faced DLS in 1928. At first she had been intrigued by what, on the surface, seems dull. She wrote to Eustace: 'Please forgive my long delay in replying to your most interesting letters concerning polarised light and the Assymetry of Inorganic Products.' This was the letter about muscarine. When a beam of polarised light is sent through the molecule of anything asymmetric a spiral effect is made, but the point was that the result of the light moving would be an optical action. Suppose there was no optical action, and nothing polarised? Then if muscarine had been used, from mushrooms, there would be no proof of poisoning.

But this science meant far more than this. DLS, whose religious beliefs would have been startled, saw that life was perhaps linked to the asymmetry of matter; that life existed because there was an asymmetry of molecules in the state of matter – inorganic compounds have symmetry in their state. Eustace put the important point in all this, clearly, to DLS, and confirmed:

> It is known that light is circularly polarised by the light of the sun from the surface of the sea and it is probable that when this occurred, when the vapour of the atmosphere condensed, and formed the first seas, an asymmetric agent became present on the face of the earth and by decomposing one antipode rather than another, gave rise to the first asymmetric molecule from which all living tissues emerged.

The words on 'decomposing an antipode' means that an opposite is effaced, so the asymmetry no longer exists, and there can be life. DLS was utterly startled by the apparent insight into the beginnings of life on earth; she knew it would form a fascinating centre of her next novel, and she had the confidence to construct a successful human context for the mystery story that was offering, if handled well enough, to present something entirely new in the genre.

It was a complicated piece of biological material to transmute into any variety of fiction, let alone a detection novel with the necessity of knitting into a murder story a thread taking in deadly poison in fungi – as well as creating a cluster of interesting characters living in Bayswater. Yet there were several assets behind her when she set out to write: she had always been interested in the 1922 murder case of Bywaters and Thompson, in which both Frederick Bywaters, the killer, and Edith Thompson, the wife of the murder victim, were eventually found guilty and both hanged. DLS uses this in *The Documents in the Case,* her two people having an affair are Mrs Harrison, the wife of the fungi expert who is killed, and the artist Lathom. She also had the newly discovered potential of the tales of medical detection she had found in the work of Eustace and L.T. Meade.

The Bywaters' case made a profound impression on DLS. Here was a remarkable instance of the dangers of extreme fantasy in a relationship of sexual desire; it was an example of a passion as extreme as that of Othello or Catherine Earnshaw, planted square in the heart of suburban middle-class London. The common feeling among writers and artists of the time was that submerged, dangerous passions for possession or escape were deeply located under the apparent conformity of diurnal duties and chores.

The scene at the core was a ménage-a-trois consisting of married couple Edith and Percy Thompson, and Freddie Bywaters. Crime historian, Oliver Cyriax gives a succinct summary:

> Edith Thompson, an unhappily married bookkeeper, lived with her husband Percy in the London suburb of Ilford. He beat her, but one day in June, 1921 young Frederick Bywaters a good-looking laundry steward on a P&O ocean liner came to stay between voyages. He was a schoolmate of Edith's brother and the families were long-standing friends.

Here was an emotionally explosive situation, and when Percy was murdered in the street, by Bywaters, the murder trial and investigation opened up a cache of romantic letters from Edith to Freddie which eventually led to her conviction as accessory. It was 1923: she would hang. In the interwar years there were several hangings of women, including criminals from various social classes, and there were various death sentences on teenagers (the latter not carried out).

Imagining the life, emotional turmoil and desires of young Edith seeped into DLS's inner life where narratives were engendered, or often left simmering, waiting for the right outlet. The Bywaters' case was a huge sensation, and lies embedded in *The Documents in the Case*. If we want to see how deeply the case cut into popular culture we may peep into a piece written by Beverley Nichols for his 1926 book, *Twenty-Five*, in which he described a visit to Edith's father. Nichols writes, on this visit in which he had to interview Mr Grayson, he quotes the old man:

> he threw out his hands and cried in a broken voice ... To think that this should happen to us! ... It was the universal cry of humanity. Why should it happen to *us*? There were five hundred little houses, all exactly alike in this desolate crescents ...Why had God picked out this little house out of so many?

But the scientific revelations from Eustace also expanded in the novelist's mind, with the Thompson and Bywaters' case providing a foundational setting and emotional core. The same murder case was also to inspire F. Tennyson Jesse as the basis of her novel, *A Pin to See the Peepshow* (1934).

It was a daunting prospect for her imagination. On the one side there were some mind-blowing observations about the consequences of a certain variety of action linked to the polarising of light; on the other hand there was a tempting possibility of a truly rare if not unique ploy to put in place in a detection novel. It was pressingly contemporary also; she could see that she needed a group of characters who would be intellectuals and whose questions and beliefs would come up against an awesome problem. Her instinct told her that an ordinary couple, with certain pretentions, placed in juxtaposition with some very 'modern' minds, would provide the essential quality and feeling for the right kind of development. The result might not have pleased DLS herself, but numerous readers have said complimentary things about *The Documents in the Case*, including Libby Purvis, who wrote the introduction to the 2016 edition: 'Dorothy L. Sayers was, above all, a peerless entertainer, a creator of page-turners so fine you return to them again and again even when you know the ghastly or triumphant outcome.'

The novel is also intensely and provocatively contemporary. Great issues and debates of the time are woven into the letters in this intellectually rich epistolary novel. The crime novels of the interwar years were taking on several roles traditionally in the preserve of the novel of the social world in the Victorian and Edwardian years. Critic Peter Keating, in his study, 'Agatha Christie and Shrewd Miss Marple', has a lot to say about this aspect of Christie, for instance. The writer Rohan Maitzen we have this: 'the world her [Christie's] novels portray is not at all the "cosy" unreal England her detractors suppose. Keating reads Christie's wartime novels as "allegories of European society in the late 1930s and terrifying confrontations with evil".' In other words, the often argued defence of crime fiction as potentially as rich and multi-layered as much literary fiction is exemplified there, and the same could be said of DLS. In *The Documents in the Case*, where there is no Lord Peter Wimsey, there is a novel of ideas worked alongside a mystery genre. There is something of the conversational novel of ideas as in the work of Thomas Love Peacock here, infused with a story as embedded in the time and place as Orwell's early work.

In fact, the setting is made strongly present and creatively active in the flavour and reference of the letters, and at one point, there is the poet, John Munting's account of 1930 suburbia, very much akin to Orwell's in *Coming up for Air*:

> They believe in respectability. They'll lie, die, commit murder
> to keep up appearances. Look at Crippen. Look at Bywaters.
> Look at the man who hid his wife in a bath and ate his meals on

the lid for fear somebody should suspect a scandal. My God! Those people are living, living with all their blood and their bones. That's reality in the suburbs life, guts.

If we set this alongside some Orwell, there is much to explain the core of the DLS novel: Orwell wrote, in *Coming up for Air* (1939): 'The stucco front, the creosoted gate, the privet hedge, the green front door. The Laurels, the Myrtles, the Hawthorns … At perhaps one house in fifty some anti-social type who'll probably end up in a workhouse has painted his front door blue instead of green.'

DLS must have thought long and hard about how to generate suspense and tension; she had no Wimsey in the book, and so the son of the dead man, Paul Harrison, becomes the investigator looking into his father's death. At the very heart of the fictional challenge there is the puzzle of how to make abstruse scientific experimentation, and a theoretical concept, integral to the crime narrative.

After the body of the murdered man is found at The Shack, his Cornish retreat where he can study mushrooms and paint watercolours, the reader is engaged in nothing more than speculation. Then the real talent of DLS comes into place as three learned men of science discuss life itself; if we add to this the interview with the expert, Leader, then there is ample space given to the education of the lay reader, who may not even have a GCE in biology to his or her name. Paul Harrison needs to prove that Lathom had poisoned his father with synthetic muscarine; the assumption made by the forensic brain, Sir James Lubbock – who appears often in the Wimsey novels – is that, as Munting puts it most clearly for the reader:

And you can't expect a jury to accept a vague possibility … if there was any analysable difference between natural and synthetic muscarine, then, of course, you would have something genuine to go upon. Because it would be quite impossible to eat synthetic muscarine by accident except in a laboratory, but apparently there is no difference.

The killer, having learned of the nature of synthetic muscarine, carries out the poisoning in the belief the difference between natural and synthetic muscarine is undetectable. DLS tightens the tension until the last few pages, and the reader waits for the results of Lubbock's test to see whether or not a synthetic poison has killed.

DLS had her finger on the pulse of society at a time of political unease and simmering social revolutions; she knew that the new sciences were playing a prominent part in such accelerated change. She has Lathom discuss Einstein and relativity in his letters to his 'Bungie', and we discover later that when he travels to learn about poisons, he has a basic but active interest in science and knowledge. In *The Documents in the Case*, DLS juxtaposes artistic types and bohemian culture with the everyday working-world of ordinary citizens in a modern city. She enjoys her usual delight in having working-class characters (like the blackmailer and her son), but she also uses the Bywaters and Thompson affair to bring out the malaise in the rigid class stratification of the culture around her. Lathom isolates one crucial aspect of this is his words on his married mistress: 'It's this damned awful suburban respectability that's crushing the beautiful life out of her. When you see what she was meant to be, free and splendid and ready to proclaim her splendid passion to the world and then see what this foul blighter has made of her.'

There is also another very contemporary presence: Sigmund Freud. His work had been translated into English since c.1900 and its impact on the intelligentsia was no doubt all around DLS in her student years and in her literary talk at dinners and events. She gives much of the Freudian talk to her character of Agatha Milsom, who is a force for disharmony and aggravation in the Bayswater house. In her letters to her sister there is a rich Freudian vocabulary, sometimes very direct: 'We had a very interesting little talk about repression, and I have lent her my handbook to Freud. It is so important to get a healthy angle on these things.'

Recent research by John Forrester and Laura Cameron, in their book *Freud in Cambridge* (2023) makes it clear that Freud's thinking had definitely permeated into the worlds of university and Bloomsbury. In a review of that work, Ann Kennedy-Smith wrote, 'Freud had a wide cross-disciplinary appeal. For the Irish scientist J.D. Bernal he was a youthful infatuation, that, the authors suggest, "went hand in hand with her personal grappling with the problems of sex."'

It is also clear how widespread was the reading of Freud and the discussion of his ideas on the subconscious; W.H. Auden's father was a doctor with a strong public presence. In the Second World War he was involved in the promulgation of public health issues, but he was always an enthusiast for Freud also. Historian Richard Davenport-Hines expands on the Freudian importance:

> Psychology was a way of knowingness, of superiority. But it was also fun. Auden's contemporary, Graham Greene, also became interested in psychology when young ... The young Greene, who had discovered Freud, 'would leave the bacon cooling on his plate as he listened with the fascination of a secret detective'.

Auden acquired the habit of 'playing detective regarding other people's motivations'; Davenport-Hines defines the result in Auden's life, and one suspects that these words could apply to the ways in which DLS uses Freudian ideas in her novels: 'but it is certain that he acquired a knowledge of human motives and passions ... that was rare at that time.'

In the end, the one non-Wimsey novel in the Sayers canon is a work which has divided opinion. It is a difficult read, but rewards patience; Barbara Reynolds rightly and sensibly comments that the use of the Bywaters and Thompson case as an influence on the lovers in Bayswater is never satisfactory, and was not so to DLS herself. There was also a scare regarding the science at the base of the murder plot: that the polarisation testing would not relate to any successful practice. Although Eustace worried about this, the knowledge behind the murder plot was later verified, and so the novel stands as a considerable achievement.

The infamous case of Bywaters and Thompson not only inspired F. Tennyson Jesse to write *A Pin to See the Peepshow*, it also had a wider impact. Laura Thompson's 2018 book *Rex v. Edith Thompson* shows. Writing about the book in a review, writer Mark Bostridge summarises: 'As Laura Thompson (no relation) emphasizes, Edith was one of a new aspirant class in the world of post-war Britain. She had a good job as a buyer with a firm of milliners in the City, earned more than her husband, enjoyed a varied social life and remained childless.' This was exactly the kind of profile of a woman in the new age that would appeal to DLS. At the same time, over in Germany, there was a definite concept of *die neue frau* the new woman, and this figure also provides a type from the DLS imagination. She was, in the words of critics Stephen Lamb and Anthony Phelan, 'a woman with independent income, assiduously following the latest fashions, reading women's magazines and dancing the newest American dance styles … her androgynous look … reflected a widespread desire on the part of aspiring independent women to match men in terms of opportunities and achievement.'

If we turn to more forthright and combative engagement with the restless world of the 1930s, the variety of contexts and materials is very impressive. Much of this surely has to be pinpointed in her time with the advertising agency of S.H. Benson and also with the recurrent theme of women and marriage that inhabits the novels. Life in the 1930s is easily understood by the modern reader if we reflect on the consequences for the generation born during the First

World War; by the time they matured and started working, fascism and communism were spreading fast. From one viewpoint, the world c.1935 was a frightening place; so many young people went to fight in the Spanish Civil War, or travelled in order to learn how their own little corners of a declining empire might fare if there was another world war; the generation reaching maturity around the early 1930s found a great deal to criticise in the actions and opinions of their parents and grandparents.

In that world of so much change, one of the major challenges to the novelist was to be sure of the capacities and specific virtues of the novel form. There is no doubt that after the close focus on the murders at the heart of the first novels, there was an opening out in scope, while at the same time, in the novels from *Murder Must Advertise* onwards there was room made for handling several layers of social reference in addition to the crime investigation. What was a novel exactly, then, in DLS's mind? Of all available definitions of the form, the closest in this respect was given by Joseph Conrad in his memoir, *A Personal Record*:

> What is it that Novalis says? 'It is certain my conviction gains infinitely the moment another soul will believe in it.' And what is a novel if not a conviction of our fellow-men's existence strong enough to take upon itself a form of imagined life clearer than reality and whose accumulated verisimilitude of selected episodes puts to shame the pride of documentary history?

In plainer language, Conrad is asserting that the serious novel has the potential to offer more profound insights into the human condition than any careful assemblage of facts. In an age of documentary, DLS avoided anything too openly fashionable and followed her own vision of society as she knew it. How we understand a period, a context or the Zeitgeist – the spirit of the age is working through the secondary streams in the novel's central flow. DLS uses her detective fiction to examine her own values and experience, but also to find interesting insights into the microcosm she knows best: Oxford and scholarship. This takes centre stage in *Gaudy Night*, but is often running through the work. We are talking here about a writer of a very popular genre, so these are high claims indeed. The point relates to crime novelist Ian Rankin, who argues that crime writing has the potential to inspect and describe contemporary life and ideologies as well as, or sometimes better than, serious literary fiction. Much of the reasoning hangs on the notion that when humans transgress, records and testimony of the society at the time give the reader unique insights into situations which otherwise would never be logged. A productive way to check this out would be to search a sample of criminal cases online at the Old Bailey Sessions Papers online.

DLS obviously delights in giving the insights into the world around her by use of the 'tea-tabling' approach that E.M. Forster describes in his *Aspects of the Novel*, in which everyday seemingly trivial talk is actually significant for understanding the characters, and also in the kind of asides and reflections included in the tapestry of a novel, such as this, from *Gaudy Night*:

'Young ladies,' Padgett was heard to say, 'will 'ave their larks, same as young gentlemen.'

'When I was a lad,' replied the foreman, 'young ladies was young ladies. and young gentlemen was young gentlemen, if you get my meaning.'

'What this country wants,' said Padgett, 'is a 'itler.'

The challenge to order as it was seen in the 1930s was a melange of class, traditional values and late imperial restlessness. Yet deep in all these factors is a personal vision of the individual artist's witness to life, and so all the strivings and struggle of one life become a grand, perceptive response to forces at work against past certainties.

These certainties extend into the society DLS knew in her formative years. What history has created in stereotypes, clichés and accepted features of the 1930s has to be examined both in the 'macro' and in the 'micro' approaches. DLS makes a compelling interplay of these, with the 'macro' the broad social forces covering everything the media chooses to feature. From the late 1920s it is clear that documentary became a prominent concept in all kinds of art and writing. It is at once a category and a method. The crime novels DLS wrote throughout the decade preceding the Second World War have these features of contemporary commentary, often done in a restrained, nuanced way, and what strikes the reader of these is that they echo the mainstream fictional critique of that England of the imagination, a landscape of the mind as well as of everyday art which features highly in the post-1918 poetry for instance, and in the popularity of books on the topography of England. DLS, born in 1893, knew that immediately pre-1914 world intimately of course, being at Oxford when the young people went off to war, as recorded in the books of Vera Brittain. One only has to consider the settings and older residents of the Wimsey novels to see how she enjoyed placing the two generations side by side and waited for the fireworks. *The Unpleasantness at the Bellona Club* epitomises this past world of gentlemanly ease, with servants and the beck and call, and routine as fixed as the memorials and speeches about the England they had all fought for.

Peter Parker, biographer and period specialist, in his account of this context and of the life of A.E. Housman, paints a relevant picture – one which could be placed in any of the rural villages featuring in the first Wimsey books and describes the immense popularity of looking at the England being lost; and of course it could be today.

There were all manner of practical things people wanted in the 1920s and 1930s in a country still reeling from a devastating war and beset by unemployment, industrial unrest and the rise of fascism in Europe, but equally they needed reassurance and a sense that the essential nature of England persisted in spite of such upheavals and threats ... Publishers were keen to tap into this renewed sense of what England stood for and how it should be appreciated.

Above all else, the theme that runs through the writings is women and marriage: the individual life of the mind and independence as opposed to the notion of the fulfilled, 'good wife'.

What was this debate and what lines of thought were involved? Two postcards, both printed in 1914, perhaps crystallise matters:

Postcard 1: A mouse stands in the centre of a white space. Beneath the image are the words: 'Put me among the girls!'

Postcard 2: A young woman dressed either as a waitress or a young wife sits before a table set for afternoon tea. She pours tea from a white teapot and smiles rather coyly. Beneath the image are the words: 'Come and have a cup!'

The first refers to the Cat and Mouse Act, enacted the year before, in 1913. This allowed for suffragettes who were weakened by hunger striking to be released from prison, then to be re-arrested when they were recovered.

The second presents an abiding image of what was referred to in mid-Victorian times as 'The Angel in the House' - which came from a poem by Coventry Patmore, written in 1854. This is one of the key statements:

Her disposition is devout,
Her countenance angelical.
The best things that the best believe

Are in her face so kindly writ
The faithless, seeing her, conceive
Not only heaven, but hope of it…

In a number of contexts throughout the crime novels, there is an accumulation of cameos, debates and confrontations which relate to the issues around the place of women, the confrontation between traditional female representation and the 'modern woman'. This takes centre stage in *Gaudy Night*, and one explanation of this is that the novel is part of a prolonged examination of a life chosen and a life rejected. As the criminal investigation into the poison–pen threat continues, we have a series of glimpses into the celibate life of the mind, such as an answer to the question of what do female dons do when not teaching? DLS takes us through a series of activities, including:

Miss Shaw had taken five of her students for a reading party …
Miss Pyke had spent an enthralling time assisting the curator
of a local museum … Miss Hillyard was really glad to be back
in Oxford; she had had to spend a month at her sister's house
while the sister was having a baby.

With such a light touch, and the semblance of a passing reference, DLS describes the desire to be useful and keep the life of the mind active with the fortune of Miss Hillyard, who has to serve the maternal when needed. The reverse would, of course, never be a factor in life. Her sister could never take on some tutoring for Miss Hillyard.

Harriet returns to her old college in the novel, and much of the flavour of the setting and atmosphere dwells on that bittersweet mix of nostalgia and depression which tends to dominate such journeys into a happy past-life. The examination of exactly what has changed in those years is a topic forever present in discussion, such as the Dean's pronouncement and the following talk:

'You can't exercise the old kind of discipline in these days ... it's too bitterly resented.'

'The modern idea is that young people should discipline themselves,' said the librarian, 'But do they?'

'No, they won't. Responsibility bores them. Before the war they passionately had College Meetings about everything. Now, they won't be bothered.'

In this world in which old values live on as shadows and sometimes as empty ritual, Wimsey is aware of the contradictions in his personality and it helps Harriet, in the extraordinary scene with them together after the punting on the river in Chapter 14 of the novel. Wimsey says, 'I'd rather live at peace and lay my bones in the earth. Only I have a cursed hankering after certain musty old values, which I'm coward enough to deny ... I never go home if I can help it.'

Set against all the passing critical references to the women scholars' lives is a truly remarkable description of precisely what it is that a celibate scholarly life offers a woman like Harriet. This is in Chapter 11, when 'the college is empty' at the end of April. She is tired of London, but is not tired of life, merely wanting to have something of the special peace of her alma mater. Then DLS dwells for a few paragraphs on some prose description which would challenge any occasional poem with an elegiac flavour for sheer excellence of composition. The vocabulary almost vies with the meditation of Gray's famous 'Elegy written in a Country Churchyard' in this kind of expression: 'No clamour of young voice echoed along her ancient stones: the tumult of flying bicycles was stilled in the narrow strait of the Turl; in Radcliffe Square the camera slept like a cat in the sunshine...' (The Turl is a narrow thoroughfare from Broad Street to High Street.) DLS adds to this with the reflection that there is: 'no press of traffic upon the shining reaches; the mellow bells. Soaring and singing in tower and steeple, told of time's flight through an eternity of peace.'

Regarding the scrutiny of the oppositional stances taken by women at the time, in the discussion between Harriet and Wimsey that wins him over to her emotional life and is a turning point for them, Wimsey goes straight for the jugular and is so honest and direct (as he often is) that Harriet's preoccupations are out for inspection:

My dear, what are you afraid of? The two great dangers of the celibate life are a forced choice and a vacant mind. Energies bombinating [*sic*] in a vacuum breed chimaeras. If you want to set up your everlasting rest, you are far more likely to find it in the life of the mind than the life of the heart.

Surely this was the result of the dialogue between DLS and her alter-ego and constant ghost of a life never lived, the consequences of a fundamental life decision. So much of the material the themes of the crime novels is latent with powerful consequences for women making such far-reaching choices. Harriet, in returning to her old college and tasting the joys and satisfactions of Oxford, is like someone returning to a comforting first joy of childhood from the standpoint of a troublesome maturity. Then here is this man still offering marriage. The puzzlement has to be resolved in her mind, as the continuing questions and uncertainties never seem to abate. Now here he is again, perhaps about to save the day and catch the villain in the college who is placing a current of fear into the everyday stream of life.

Women's lives and the dilemma of celibacy or marriage is virtually always centre stage through the novels; in *Gaudy Night,* which eventually leads to Harriet's acceptance of yet another proposal of marriage from Lord Peter, has this debate running all the way through the text in several ways. DLS provides layers of interest here, from the discussions in the Common Room gatherings of the scholars, to the long section covering Wimsey's return from his Foreign Office work, through to the resolution and the uncovering of the culprit. From the punt on the river, by way of conversations at dinner, what is provided is a narrative of courtship from several angles. Included here is the surreal experimentation with strangling at the corner of a field; the purchase of the dog collar that saves Harriet's life, and the more prominent appearance of the Wimsey nephew, Viscount Saint George. In fact, one might imagine some readers being far more interested in this strand of love and courtship than in the investigation into the crimes. The expectation and tension are intensified, and when the acceptance comes, it is at the end of a lengthy section of reflection.

DLS keeps the central oppositions in focus, notably when Wimsey criticises himself and his behaviour since his first proposal, mounting to this: 'My talent for standing in my own light amounts to genius, doesn't it? … it was I who asked you to take a dispassionate view and I who told you that of all the devils let loose in the world there was no devil like devoted love…' He adds to this a more pernicious self-flagellation: 'Oh God, what have I done, that I should be such a misery to myself and other people? Nothing more than thousands of women.'

Harriet is more prominent as she emerges through a long passage of what can best be described as a visit into the soul. She had had in her mind for some time the statement by the Dean: '…you can point out that womanliness unfits us for such learning; and if we don't, you can point out that learning makes us unwomanly.' What could be more ironical, then, than the wording of Harriet's acceptance, with the use of the words used in the award ceremony at graduation in which '*Placetne, Domina?*' is answered with '*Placet*'. The 'it pleases' in Latin implies that there is an equality of the scholarly life and the married life, at last, for Harriet.

What has led to this, apart from debates on marriage and celibacy, is the issue of passion. At one point, Wimsey says 'How fleeting are all human passions compared with the massive continuity of ducks'.

His usual use of bathos and humorous shock serves to appeal to the reader as well as to the immediate situation.

DLS had on many occasions written about the difficulties of incorporating 'love interest' into a novel of detection. For years she had thought of the problem as peripheral to her notions of the story of detection, as in the Gollancz anthologies, but now here we are with something very different from any traditional romance. If she worried that the Wimsey-Harriet situation, after his saving her from the noose in *Strong Poison*, was ever going to work out satisfactorily given the natures in combat, she surely had no problem here. After all, Harriet, student detective, does many of the right, sensible things in her attempts to be the person Wimsey would have seen as his apprentice. But the crimes build up gradually, so that by the final attack on Harriet and her head injury, matters have escalated steadily up to the point at which, as Wimsey sees, the offender actually 'hates' the victim. The parallel intensification of the emotional oppositions and the boiling of the hatred to danger level work extremely effectively, so dual closures are achieved.

There was never to be any slackening of DLS's interest in the position of women at this time; when she looked across to Europe, she could see what National Socialism had done. In *Gaudy Night* we have a reference to Miss Barton's book, 'in which she attacks the Nazi doctrine that women's place in the state should be confined to the "womanly" occupations of *Kinder, Kirche, Kuche* [children, church, cooking].' So much for the *Neue Frau* in the Weimar period. But there is a much wider basis for an enquiry into exactly what kinds of commentaries emerged in the 1930s literature regarding the morality as well as the politics of women's place that the gradual reshaping of social ideologies were creating. One view which is relevant to DLS's position here is in a study by critic Benjamin Dabby, *Women as Public Moralists in Britain* (2017), in which he expands on the notion that the new woman had a high level of 'sympathy and moral intuitiveness' and who saw themselves as 'empowered successors of the bluestockings'. In a review of the book, Rohan Maitzen explained one point which is close to some of the issues dealt with in *Gaudy Night*: 'One of his most valuable points is that too often women writers are assessed based on the narrow measure of whether they are for or against feminism.' Dabby also puts forward an important lexical point: that using the term 'progressive' instead of 'feminist' will be productive and closer to the meaning.

However we tend to develop the oppositions that run through *Gaudy Night* and other novels on the theme of women's dilemmas vis a vis celibacy and marriage, the fact remains that the subjects were media 'hot' at the time. In 1931 the *Evening Telegraph* put contrasting views of men and women on the question of whether marriage was worthwhile. Marie Lohr, actress, wrote that the new woman 'had to create for herself an attitude of mind which will allow her to carry on with her business, and which excludes any mental attitude of sex.' In contrast, the writer Peter Cheyney said:

> When a man marries he gives up his freedom and takes upon himself certain responsibilities which the law will soon make him shoulder should he endeavour to evade them. He must keep his wife; he must keep any children of the marriage. Up to a certain point of law the country is there to ensure that he shall be a good husband.

DLS avoided all this, going her own way, as a mother in secret and as a scholarly, creative independent woman with a secret. She was a representative woman of her time, though most would never have known it.

Linked to this was the issue of the divorce. In a feature in the *Nottingham Evening Post* in 1931, on 'friendly divorces' one lawyer commented, in response to the possibility that desertion after three years would become grounds for divorce, 'this provision will open the flood-gates to many more divorces than we have at present. A good many people will seek to obtain divorces through this means rather than on the existing ground.'

One final topic around DLS in her life and work regarding the social context on the 1930s remains: her time with the advertising agency of S.H. Benson. Her novel *Murder Must Advertise* features Wimsey undercover, in the guise of Bredon, copywriter at the Pym advertising firm, and DLS has fun with all kinds of playful scenes using his disguise as a source of subversion. The effect of creating Bredon, with Parker, now his brother-in-law, in the background as a plot concerning black-market drug transactions and the crazy subculture of the Bright Young People of the decade succeeds effectively as a series of snapshots running alongside the everyday working habitat of the advertising staff. In one brilliant passage in Chapter 11, she gives the reader a vision of a modern purgatory while at the same time as providing Wimsey with a revelation which would sit well beside much of the 1930s documentary works:

> He had never realised the enormous commercial importance of the comparatively poor. Not on the wealthy, who buy only what they want when they want it, was the vast superstructure of industry founded and built up, but on those who, aching for a luxury beyond their reach and for a leisure forever denied them, could be bullied or wheedled into spending their few hard won shillings on whatever might give them ... a leisured and luxurious illusion.

Her time in Hull had played a part in her vision of the Britain she was learning to see more wholly. Conrad's quote of the novel, helping us to see 'the strength of other men's convictions' and knowing our own sense of reality was strengthening in her creative mind.

The novel has layers of material and focus, as she had now learned to provide, with assurance and interest: we see and share in Wimsey's esoteric knowledge of pencils for instance – the equivalent of Holmes's arcane documentation of tobacco ash; in the child character Ginger Joe, she indulges in some fun concerning her fascination with the old Sexton Blake stories, and then, as a firm strand of social insight, we have advertising itself. This now extremely powerful arm of the persuasion mindset, post-Orwellian stealthy control, was then new. The novel faces this boldly in the depiction of the office staff. Wimsey puts things succinctly: 'Now, Mr Pym is a man of rigid morality except, of course, as regards his profession, whose essence is to tell plausible lies for money.' Garrett's words add to this: 'They don't know of our existence … They all think advertisements write themselves. When I tell people I'm in advertising they always ask whether I design posters, they never think about copy.' The cynicism thickens with every conversation at Pym's: 'And by forcing the damned fool public to pay twice over – once to have its food emasculated and once to have the vitality put back in, we keep the wheels of commerce turning.'

On the positive side, DLS, using her experience at her agency, is aware of the real creativity involved. When there is the discussion of the line, 'It's a far, far butter thing', Miss Rossiter says, 'He'll make a copy-writer … He's got the flair, if you know what I mean. He'll stay all right.'

The bonds uniting the world of advertising to some of the dominant elements on both modernity and Modernism are many and varied. A very subtle example comes in an advert for 'Genasprin' from publications in the first years of the Second World War. One has a line drawing of two middle-class ladies having afternoon tea in a comfortable lounge, and the copy has this:

Mary is a success-girl. What is it that makes her advice so good? She judges simply by results but there are good reasons for those results. Genasprin is absolutely pure and therefore absolutely safe. It won't hurt your heart or digestion.

If this is placed beside a typical ad of c. 1900 we find this:

F.H. Shubrook: speciality: shirts to measure. Perfection for fitting and comfort.

What was happening by c.1920s was that advertising had discovered *narrative*. Today, narrative fills every tiny square centimetre of advert space; stories and micro-stories occupy whatever place may be discovered, uncovered or created for selling and promotion to find a home. DLS herself made one of the most successful narrative advert sagas when she helped create the Mustard Club. Colman's mustard was a Benson client. She started at S.H. Benson in 1922 and worked there for nine years. At one point she writes home to say that she was struggling to find anything interesting to say about Colman's starch, but when it came to mustard, she hit the jackpot.

As Barbara Reynolds comments, the Mustard Club 'was a household joke all over the country'. DLS sensed the potential of this generation of narrative fragments. The thinking was a precursor of famous adverts that would come much later, featuring creatures of fun and surreal images such as the 'Ovaltinis' or the 'Munch Bunch'. The Mustard Club even had a prospectus, and the characters had humorous names such as Miss D-Gester or Baron of Beef. A recipe book was printed, and there were leisure activities across the land. A typically wacky instance was the creation of the Harold Lloyd Knockabouts, who were described by the local paper, under a photo of them posing with 'MUSTARD' printed on their fez-like hats: 'Young ladies employed at one of the principal drapery establishments in Derby, who, in the role of members of the Mustard Club, form a versatile concert party.'

To look at DLS 'in her time' then, is to form a clear notion of exactly what aspects of her age impacted on her consciousness and of course, in her writing. There is no doubt that she understood, and was attracted to, that age of the Bright Young People (who figure in *Murder Must Advertise*) and looked for a number of images of her age which would resonate with readers. One of the most captivating, and one that actually could be extended into a powerful metaphor for her life at the time, is in an account of being in a motor car, from *Murder Must Advertise*: 'She was getting tired of Tod's hectoring. She was keyed up just enough and not too much. The hedges flashed and roared past them; the road, lit by the raking headlights, showed like a war-worn surface of holes and hillocks, which miraculously smoothed themselves out beneath the spinning wheels.'

DLS knew about that feeling. Bill White had opened up that life of dizzy speed, and a very contemporary thrill, straight from the age of Bluebird and of too-frequent car accidents. It is an easy matter to transfer that thought and plant it in her life c.1925–30. How she managed to hold together the productivity of novel-writing with the work at Benson's, and to cope with the John Cournos episode and other entanglements of the heart, is a subject of difficult speculation. But hold it together she did. At times we find in the Wimsey novels echoes of more typically 1930s writers such as Orwell and Hanley, but she always had her own signature: a hallmark as fanciful and ever-changing at the Wimsey coat-of-arms.

By the time it came to the last crime novel, and Wimsey's honeymoon, there was a watershed approaching. The dual focus of her own life and the closely monitored life of her son, who was loved, and with the pain of distance, it would be a watershed reaching fast and deep, because unfolding before her was a world war, and for a decade she had been without her parents behind her, giving encouragement as well as cash when needed. There were her friends and correspondents of course. Her energy had been expended on a series of innovative and staggeringly different literary enterprises, with characters inside her mind forming a family of friends in that strange make-believe of the world of a novel series. Readers had grown along with Wimsey, Harriet, Miss Climpson, Parker, Bunter and the rest; miraculously, in between the pressures, strains, disappointments and joys of the emotional life she filled with so many demands, there was to be a new DLS. Time was needed to slough off the skin of the novelist; there were loose ends and addenda, but she was a woman of the interwar years, and she would have understood W.H. Auden's lines:

Starving through the leafless wood
Trolls run scolding for their food;
And the nightingale is dumb,
And the angel will not come.

There are, one might argue, different levels and applications of 'contemporary'; often, in popular genre novels of the 1930s, the modern reader sees the context through occasional aperçus, but conversely, some writers seamlessly work a contemporary thread into the tapestry of the work. DLS is able to apply any and every method, sometimes making a contextual element in plot or setting as important as the theme, which she does in the depiction of the Bellona Club. Other writers are perhaps more subtle, largely because their contemporary reference is forthright and central.

Laura Thompson, in her essay, 'Taken at the Flood' for instance, challenges the view that Agatha Christie worked in a '... dark panelled interior... preserved in an aspic that began to set during the reign of Edward VII and gelled at some indeterminate time between the two world wars.' Thompson's challenge to this comes in a discussion of Christie's novel *At Bertram's Hotel*. The heart of the ruse put in front of the reader who expects the usual plot and texture of storytelling in a novel set in a comfortable hotel is that 'The miraculously unchanged

Bertram's of 1965 is, in fact, the headquarters of a national crime ring, and its *ancien régime* solidity is the supreme deceptive cover.'

This essay was backed up by response in the letters page of the *Times Literary Supplement*, when Aleks Sierz wrote to point out that 'Agatha Christie was a quiet radical. In *The Mousetrap* (1952) she included two characters who were certainly gay.' Sierz also added that there were people in the play who were 'a young woman of manly type,' and a 'neurotic young man'. One could make a case equally for many of the secondary characters in the Wimsey novels: modernity seeps unpredictably into development of the fiction, as in this point made in *Unnatural Death* in 1927 when the courts were soon to hang Edith Thompson for a part-fantasy involvement in her husband's death: '"When a woman is wicked and unscrupulous," said Parker, "she is the most ruthless criminal in the world – fifty times worse than a man, because she is always much more single-minded about it."'

This powerfully shows exactly how varied and elusive the notion of 'in her time' is when applied to any author. In the case of DLS, the more prominent aspects of a fictional setting may well be a startling and effective foil to something more subtly present, as in the Bright Young People in *Murder Must Advertise*, set against the apparently routine-imprisoned occupants of the Pym agency. Any reader who has ever worked in an office will recognise and appreciate the antics of the staff at the advertising agency: the games, the in-jokes, the whimsicality, the failed humour, the petty jealousy and the constant, irritating prying into the private life of any one member of the staff. All this DLS knew from her nine years at the desk working for S.H. Benson.

The DLS who fits with the idea of her being 'in her time' then, is one we might recognise in any writer who has seamlessly used an aspect of the life around her by projecting it into a fictional frame. Other writers of the interwar years may have followed the kind of approach expected of them in an age where the 'other England' of the manual workers was more and more fore-grounded. In the left-wing journal *Fact*, for instance, published at the same time as the first few novels of DLS, the agenda and intentions are explained in an editorial describing the forthcoming issue:

> Our first subject will be a small mining town, and our chief investigator will be Mr Philip Massey, the well-known statistician and economist. He will spend a considerable time in the chosen town, with various assistants ... but the name of the place must at the moment remain private. We hope to follow this up with a portrait of a farming village.

In an age of documentary and a hunger for facts about the previously submerged lives of most English people, the crime novel, probably more effectively than any other genre writing, opened up enlightened perceptions of some dark corners of life, both leisurely and industrious. The Wimsey novels demonstrate exactly how the deeper levels of insight and understanding might work.

Chapter 5

Poet and Scholar

There were crimson roses on the bench; they looked like
splashes of blood.
Strong Poison, D.L. Sayers

In planning this account of the poetical works of DLS, I was keenly aware that some readers will have degrees in the arts or have studied poetry to the level of the analysis of structure and technique, while other readers will perhaps never have been informed regarding the constituents of many poems at the heart of the canon of English literature. I felt that my chapter should cater for both groups, and so I make no apology for the inclusion of some explanations here which may seem basic to some readers.

As explained in the chapter, DLS was a determined scholar of poetics and of the mechanics of poetry (mostly in French) from her days at school; when she became an Oxford scholar, her knowledge of forms, notably in medieval verse, became extremely impressive. One also has ro recall that, as she was taught classics by her father when she was very young, she also had some knowledge of the principal poets writing in Latin and Greek.

This is the formidable brain that set to work as a novelist of crime and detection. The knowledge of foreign literature gave her not only a strong basis of characterisation when she made Lord Peter Wimsey, but it also gave her the resources to use quotation as an element in her themes when she began to use her knowledge of the topography of Oxford in her fiction. She also projected into Harriet a great deal of her own introspection regarding the less definable sources of writing poetry. In other words, as I show here, she was just as capable as a 'maker' in poetry when she used free verse as she was when she enjoyed the discipline of writing in metre.

In this chapter, I freely use my own experience of writing poetry, just as I would had I been teaching the elements of verse in the classroom. I am confident that this will help any beginners in the art of poetry who might be reading my book. DLS fully understood that some elusive factor goes into the creation of poetry; it is not simply a practical, manageable concept as if one were manufacturing a trowel in a forge. There is an X factor, as in all the arts, and this is referred to in all kinds of contexts in the fiction as well as in the theoretical writings that DLS produced after her main career in fiction.

Whether or not the reader is acquainted with the elements of verse, I feel sure that this chapter will enhance the reader's enjoyment and appreciation of reading the corpus of poetry in the immense bibliography under the name of Dorothy L. Sayers.

In his essay on Omar Khayyam, written at the time of DLS's most productive period as a popular writer in the 1930s, essayist and novelist Llewelyn Powys wrote:

> Scholars are of the opinion that he composed his celebrated poem at intervals throughout his life, a rubaiyat or quatrain being regarded in Persian literature as a completed isolated unit, as it were a single jewel, a turquoise let us say, from the mines on the hillside above Nishapour to be polished and repolished for its own signal beauty, before being strung with others into a necklace of great price.

The phrase 'polished and repolished' hints at the textual and intellectual pleasure DLS must have felt as she embarked on a translation. If one pauses for a moment to reflect on exactly what would be the degree of confidence required for a modern poet to set about writing a new translation of the ultimate classic of Italian and world literature *La Divina Commedia* by Dante it is hard to find words of sufficient plausibility to explain the adventure in language that this demands. Part of the answer may lie in T.S. Eliot's notion of the emotional and intellectual appeal of the Italian language, which he said he deeply enjoyed before he could fully understand it. Another explanation could be that the knowledge of Latin and Old French DLS had acquired by the time she started the Dante project would have boosted her confidence in her ability to complete the task. Whatever the answer here, the fact remains that DLS the poet was phenomenally talented and never, ever short of confidence. The composition of formal poetry, as Powys explains in the quote, may easily lead an individual writer, as it did for Omar Khayyam, to accept the project as a lifetime occupation, something that will never have a satisfactory completion.

To modern lovers of poetry, it seems to be the case that 99 per cent of that body of readers quite naturally respond to the emotional power of a poem, and that the poetic technique beneath the surface of the words may be just as complex and impressive as the work of Dante or Khayyam, but the appeal is still one of immediacy. We often reach for a poem instead of a prayer, and accept a facile rhythm because that pulse of meaning and feeling is as effective as a song or a hymn. All this is to explain that we live in an age which has experienced the arrival of 'free verse', and even a concept known as 'prose poetry', and that those two concepts would more than likely have provoked in DLS a critical response and not a little sense of refusal to accept such items as poetry, within her definition.

Nonetheless, as the twentieth century moved on around DLS and figures such as W.H. Auden, T.S. Eliot and the Surrealists, the new versions of realism in verse and the arrival of deep introspection, as in the work of Robert Lowell for instance, created an expanding definition of what was 'poetic' and poets such as DLS found a place and a readership at once nuanced and sometimes elusive in a historian's search for pattern and influence in this regard. To put this plainly: DLS wrote her own brand of poetry, and the fact that this had its roots in the technically precise and exact forms which were defined by intricate metres and techniques (such as subtle assonances in *The Song of Roland*). In spite of what may now be sounding esoteric and 'difficult', the kind of poetry many of us experience when tackling A-Level English set texts, there is still a place and a readership for the kinds of poetry DLS produced.

Poetry came easily and naturally to DLS. Time and again, poetic cadences and phrases are given to characters, in particular to Lord Peter Wimsey; but language reaching on tip-toe for effects as natural and meaningful as the best lyric verse is constantly at her command, in prose, poetry itself, and in stage works. The habit came early, in childhood, when she affectionately mimicked the tales of derring-do and fashionable éclat in the adventure stories of the nursery. The poetry also arrived with the impetus of being dramatic, of presenting, expressing, with high emotion, and with the aim of catching the eye and entertaining anyone who would listen.

To the general reader in 2025 though, perhaps the skills of poet and translator are distant and theoretical, with a 'niche' readership. English studies at school now do include some material on rhyme and metre, but DLS, born in the 1890s and reading her first serious poetry when she was in her teens, would have found formal poetry to be the essential element in all her poetry reading and tuition. Until perhaps the 1940s, poetry was learned by heart and recited by pupils. Even today, in my own teaching to adults, I often find that there is a common attitude that poetry has to have lines that rhyme.

As DLS became a student and reached adulthood, she was knowledgeable on the structures of poetic writing, and her affection for French and Old French led her to acquire a broad and profound knowledge of medieval and Renaissance literature. Her tutor at Oxford was Mildred Pope, a highly rated scholar of French literature. She had a doctorate from the University of Paris, and was a reader in French after her period of Oxford lecturing. She taught the celebrated scholar Eugène Vinaver, and of course, DLS. Something that had an impact on DLS was Pope's founding of the Anglo-Norman Text Society, and DLS was to keep up her translation activities and scholarship later, after her fiction writing, being a contributor to the journals of the Modern Language Association.

The love of textual scholarship was deep in DLS, and with this in mind, it has to be asked why her poetic imagination was drawn to Old French literature and the chivalric culture which produced *The Song of Roland,* which she translated in 1957 for the Penguin Classics lists? First, it is a matter of verbal harmony and the power of rhyme and metre; we must add to that the layers of interest born of her affection for the creation of a euphony of effect, and a love of an intellectual challenge.

Anyone who has written or attempted to produce one of our own English popular forms will appreciate the satisfaction derived from shaping a poem in a given metrical structure. DLS revelled in solving and resolving. This could mean a difficult murder case in her fiction, or a poem with a complex formal composition. The point here is that if writing a traditional poem, in a conventional form, was no more than a classroom exercise, then we have to ask if DLS's poems deserve to be in print. But of course, there is much more to her work than just a technical exercise. She was a natural storyteller and a wordsmith, with a sharp sense of the sharing of writer and reader in a text – that means a text of any category or genre. She carried her repertoire of language skills across from form to form, and prose to verse. Never for a moment did she lose the sense of her reader. The time she spent writing copy for S.H. Benson was an experience with productivity and a learning curve across her entire skill-set.

Every poet has their own procedure in writing in a set poetic form; for myself it is a matter of beginning with a prose draft and then working on a key line with the required metre. Sometimes the key line

ARGOSY

Contents for January, 1952

Vol. XIII   **No. 1**

Printed in England by WITHY GROVE PRESS LTD., MANCHESTER, and published on the 10th of each month by THE AMALGAMATED PRESS LTD., The Fleetway House, Farringdon Street, London, E.C.4. Registered for Transmission by Canadian Magazine Post. Subscription Rates : Inland and Abroad : £1 0s. 6d. for 12 months, 10s. 3d. for 6 months. Canada : 19s. 6d. for 12 months, 9s. 9d. for 6 months. ADVERTISEMENT OFFICES : Tallis House, Tallis Street, London, E.C.4. Sole Agents : Australasia, Messrs. GORDON & GOTCH, LTD. ; South Africa, CENTRAL NEWS AGENCY, LTD. ; Northern and Southern Rhodesia, Messrs. KINGSTONS LTD. ARGOSY is sold subject to the following conditions, namely, that it shall not, without the written consent of the publishers first given, be lent, resold, hired out, or otherwise disposed of by way of Trade except at the full retail price as shown on the cover ; and that it shall not be lent, resold, hired out, or otherwise disposed of in a mutilated condition or in any unauthorized cover by way of Trade ; or affixed to or as part of any publication or advertising, literary or pictorial matter whatsoever.

One of Dorothy's later stories, in the popular short fiction magazine, *Argosy*. (Author's image)

Founders of the
Bournemouth Dramatic and Orchestral Club

Founders of the Bournemouth Dramatic and Orchestral Club D. Rowe is bottom left. (Courtesy of the Bournemouth L.T.C.)

15th JUNE, 1931, at 7.30 p.m.

Opening Ceremony

BY

ST. JOHN ERVINE, ESQ.

which will be Presided over by

ALDERMAN PERCY M. BRIGHT, J.P.

Mayor of Bournemouth

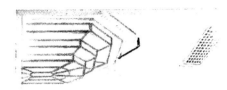

INTERIOR OF THE LITTLE THEATRE.

Celebrations from Bournemouth 1931. (Courtesy of the Bournemouth L.T.C.)

Left: An image of the great poet, *A Shadow of Dante*: M. Rossetti

Below: Anonymous drawing of Victorian female Oxford students. (Author's image)

Right: The author L.T. Meade, who worked with Eustace Barton. (Wikicommons)

Below: 'The Harold Lloyd Knockabouts' from 1938. (*Derby Evening Telegraph*)

HOT STUFF.

A map showing the routes of Zeppelin bombings. (Author's image)

Above left: A spin-off from Dorothy's mustard campaign. (Author's image)

Above right: An image of a Zeppelin raid. (*The Great War,* 1919)

Right: The cover of Dorothy's first publication. (Author's image)

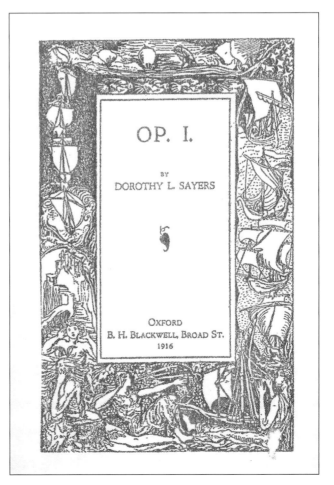

One of the hospitals in Manchester connected with Charis Frankenburg. (Author's image)

A clear view of Oxford at the time Dorothy studied there. (Author's image)

Above: The location of the 1920 ceremony awarding degrees to women. (Author's image)

Right: Ephemeral publications from the 1940s on religious and moral education. (Author's image)

A O H

ARE SEX RELATIONS WITHOUT MARRIAGE WRONG?

DR A HERBERT GRAY

112 CITY ROAD LONDON E C I

Salisbury Cathedral, an important place in the Dorothy's life. She was confirmed there. (Author's image)

MURDER BY SIX EXPERTS

Six famous crime writers have committed the perfect murder—in print, of course—and Supt. George Cornish, late of the "Yard," has brought the murderer to book—when he can!

This exciting scheme is presented in "SIX AGAINST THE 'YARD,'" a super crime serial, which starts in "The Daily Mail" to-morrow.

Here are the authors, every one a guarantee of first-class reading:

Margery Allingham,
Anthony Berkeley,
F. Wills Crofts,
Father Ronald Knox,
Dorothy L. Sayers, and
Russell Thorndike.

This feast of entertainment for every amateur detective and every lover of stimulating reading, begins in to-morrow's ___

Press report on one of Dorothy's literary events. *Gloucester Echo*, 22 July 1938, p.3. (British Library Newspapers)

The cover of the 1949 edition. (Gollancz)

A scene from the religious play *The Zeal of Thy House*. (Author's image)

Right: The blue
plaque at the
Godolphin School.
(Courtesy of the
Godolphin School)

Below: The
Chapter House
at Canterbury
Cathedral, where
the Festival plays
were performed.
(Courtesy of the
photographer, Ian
Osterloh)

Dorothy at the time she knew John Cournos. (Courtesy of the Houghton Library, Harvard University)

Dorothy as a young adult with four women, outdoors. (Used by permission of the Marion E. Wade Center, Wheaton College, Wheaton, IL)

Dorothy at work. (Courtesy of Seona Ford, The Dorothy L. Sayers Society)

Above left: Young Dorothy. (Courtesy of the Houghton Library, Harvard University)

Above right: Dorothy outside, when a teenager c.1910–1913. (Marion E. Wade Center)

St Mary's, Bluntisham. This was the parish church of Dorothy's father, Henry. (Courtesy of Debbie Rudwick and

comes first. After that, I follow the feeling or reasoning, allowing for the struggle needed to ensure that there is an authentic 'flow' in the syntax. This means that effects such as enjambment or caesura have to be smoothly integrated. The popular form of the Shakespearean sonnet is helpful here. I wrote this example as a teaching tool:

A Sonnet Looks at Itself
I begin like this, all full of myself
With plenty to say to make you think,
Like taking just one book down from the shelf.
You read me before you've time to blink.
A sonnet little but with a great heart
And perfect in my way: quite beautiful,
An advert for the poet's craft and art,
Making his approach dark and dutiful.
I'm a poem with a strong purpose, a quest;
To show the love of rhythmic lines and rhymes.
You need to work to make me look my best
And write me in your deepest loving times.
I end with joy, wonder, power and passion.
Amazingly, I've never been out of fashion.

Every poem DLS wrote would have presented its own structures. In this case, the end-rhymes fall into these sections, as the letters show: ABAB/CDCD/EFEF/GG. The lines have a stress pattern with ten syllable sounds in each line.

Early in her writing life when she was still at school, DLS was working hard to master the skills of poetic form and structure. But in her more mature verse, there is a fascination for the reader in tracing her development. Thanks to the editorial work of Ralph E. Hone, in compiling and editing her poetry, it does not take long to see how her abilities in this regard developed. His book begins with juvenilia and progresses to poems from the Christian writings, covering the work in her two collections on the way. These were *Op.1* and *Catholic Tales*, published by Blackwell. She began with occasional poems (poems for specific occasions, not poems written now and then). Naturally, the Great War had a phase supplying subjects for these.

What about the fundamental act of composing poetry? DLS has left a very enlightening account of this, included in *Gaudy Night*, Chapter 11. In three pages, she takes us through the kind of creative process that writers of all hues will know. Harriet is in Oxford, returning there after several years, and the mood is set with the words:

> Mornings in Bodley, drowsing among the faint, musty odour and tarnished gilding of Duke Humphrey [Duke Humphrey's Library] ... in a canoe under Magdalen walls and so by the twisting race at King's Mill ... then back, with mind relaxed and body stretched and vigorous, to make toast by the fire.

It is idyllic, and could be from any of the memoirs of Oxford learning, and even from Housman. But then the prose and the mood switch to a paragraph in which the line of a poem emerges; there are echoes of G.M. Hopkins, a poet who spent time right next to Somerville College, 'looking over the spires of the city, deep-down, fathom-drowned, striking from the round bowl of the river-basin'.

The iambic line comes into Harriet's mind, 'echoing out of nowhere: To that still centre where the spinning world/sleeps on its axis.' Her mind starts to search for end-rhymes, and she sees that it could be the heart of an octave (in a sonnet) so the work begins, with false starts, but she perseveres, and the lines begin to form as she feels 'at home'. But although the full poem does not form through her work, she has the octave, and DLS writes: 'she had got her mood onto paper and this is the release that all writers, even the feeblest, seek for as men seek for love; and, having found it, they doze off happily into dreams and trouble their heads no further.' As the reader takes a few seconds to read on, harsh life intervenes in that dream of creativity, and the subject is the suicide of Annie, the servant's husband.

Nonetheless, something had led Harriet to write, albeit with no defined frame of any stylistic nature. Wallace Stevens wrote on this unknown element:

> While there is nothing automatic about the poem, nevertheless it has an automatic aspect in the sense that it is what I wanted it to be without knowing before it was written what I wanted it to be, even though I knew before it was written what I wanted to do.

This is exactly what DLS highlights in the account of the partially completed formal poem.

This is a successful mix of the formal and the mystical; and this word is the 'factor X' when it comes to the nature of poetic composition. There are unexplained factors playing a part. Behind this account of the creative process the reader feels an acute sense of the authentic poetic enterprise in DLS, and we know now, thanks to Ralph Hone's collection, that from a child, DLS was skilled in writing entertaining and exact metrical pieces; combined with her musical ability and her love of performing and declaiming, we can now see that throughout her life, poetry would be her entrance gate into that vast palace where stories were generated in her mind. This acquisition of an assured poetic voice led to her very first book. She had worked for Blackwell's in Broad Street, Oxford, and learned the trade, and of course also made contacts. When Basil Blackwell, the son of the publisher, started a list of poetry volumes in 1913, he called it *Oxford Poetry*, and the aim was to discover and encourage the young poets around the colleges. The imprint was to include such future greats of English literature as Aldous Huxley and Tolkien. As mentioned previously, her first book had the brief title of *Op.1*, clearly meaning 'Opus 1' or 'work number one' as used by classical composers, which of course hints at much more writing to come from the pen of the author.

The book was included in a series which was an offshoot of *Oxford Poetry*, headed *Adventurers All*. A writer's first book entails much material to consider and understand, mainly in the nature of a contract and all the practical topics of print-run and editing. She wrote to Muriel Jaeger, with the thrill of success: 'I shall be a real published author at the cost of £5 to myself, which is paid back to me as soon as the sales cover the cost of production ... If there are any profits, Blackwell and I share them in proportion to the risk taken by each.'

By June, 1918 there was a second volume: *Catholic Tales*, and she wrote home, with a sharp awareness that her father, the Rev. Sayers, would need to know something of a book with that title, 'Some people think it "wonderful" and some think it blasphemous. Of course, it may fall quite flat. You won't mind being the parents and aunt of a notoriety.' Obviously, the Great War was a shadow over most of the writing going on in her life at the time, as with the work of most other writers, but DLS works into much of her writing some of her favourite themes and images from the chivalric Old French that she loved, both as a scholar and as an aspiring writer.

Before an attempt is made to give an overview of the work collected in the Ralph E. Hone edition, it is profitable to look at the edition and translation produced by DLS for Penguin Classics in 1957. In this work, *The Song of Roland*, she had to do what every editor of a classical text needs to do: explain origins, editions and previous study of the text. But the long-standing affection for the world and stories of the Age of Chivalry are at the heart of her work here. Since Ezra Pound's interest in the troubadours of medieval France and the popular children's tales of King Arthur, there had been interest in tales from the knights, even stretching back to the work of Sir Walter Scott and then the 'serious' novels of Sir Arthur Conan Doyle. Popular tales of chivalry were always there during DLS's formative years, and her childhood love of 'dressing up' was a part of this. Then, as a student at Oxford who had always been fluent in French, she came face to face with Old French and the literature of the period of the Crusades and the Angevin kings.

The nature of Old French literature is a scholarly affair. A recent survey of medieval poets from the North of France, edited by Jacques Darras, extends to 500 pages and aims to revise opinions of the poetry written between the eleventh and thirteenth centuries – DLS's period, by and large. Reviewer Richard Sieburth summarises the basis of the revision: 'Although the Northern *langue d'oeil* produced such narrative masterpieces as the Anglo-Norman lays of Marie de France, the romances of Chretien de Troyes ... Darras argues that its rich tradition of narrative verse ... has been largely overlooked.' It may be seen from the kinds of works that Darras concentrates on here that the texts DLS was drawn to for study form only a small part of the overall oeuvre.

But the corpus is massive and in need of a revisionary look. This is exactly what DLS saw in her age: then she saw that the impact on works such as *Tristan* and *The Song of Roland* had a notable impact on later literature and saw that, at the time when the Modern Language Association was shaking things up in medieval scholarship, new translations could have a powerful effect on building a readership for the modern times.

It is interesting to note the literary context as well. Not long before the Roland project, there had been the advent of Pound and Aldington's Imagism, and Pound's advocacy of Asian literature; this was part of a growing interest in such varieties of writing as work taken from oral tradition and from earlier romantic works which were often part of a nationalistic movement, such as Schiller's writings with oral tradition and balladry behind them. Within DLS's own specific interests, there were also aspects of her reading which were relevant here, such as her love of the writings of Andrew Lang and his 'Fairy Books' series.

Also interesting, as a cross-reference, is the fact that DLS was reading in Italian, long after she worked on French texts. Barbara Reynolds points out that she read Boiardo's *Orlando Innamorato* and was 'enthralled by his simple enjoyment of marvels, particularly the underwater realm of Fata Morgana and the enchanted garden of Orgagna.' All this is testimony to the fascinating feature of her creativity: what appears at first glance to be work which spreads across disparate areas of interest, on most occasions actually interrelates. In a sense, her poetic translations from Old French and the research behind the work show that in European writing and art, so much interweaves and so many popular narratives have a life-cycle in which the stories fade for a while and then later re-emerge, usually in a new form, very much like the history of the key works in traditional folk song.

Her *Song of Roland* makes an ideal introduction to the writing from these times, and the reader is soon aware of the individuality of the translator. In her notes on the verse and her translation, she explains the rhythm and movement of the poetry: 'The best way, if it can be managed, is to take a few *laisses* and declaim them aloud in the bathroom.' Her attraction to poetic form, from the viewpoint of a practitioner as well as that of a reader, comes through in her account of what makes the unit in each segment. Readers new to poetic composition may note here that the word 'stanza' (Italian for 'room') is used for each division in the form of a poem. DLS defines this particular form of stanzas in *The Song of Roland* in such a way that she clearly loves the *laisse* – the stanza. Her account is technical and hard to follow if poetry is unknown to the reader in the kind of analysis we used to have in school English lessons. But essentially, each *laisse* has to have a rhythmic pattern, as it would be recited aloud, as Chaucer's poems were, at the court of Richard II. The poem is an account of the great emperor Charlemagne's confrontation with the Moslem forces in the area of the Pyrenees in the eleventh century.

What fires the power in the narrative poem is the central position of the heroic knight Roland and his closest friend Oliver. Those two names echo through the social and cultural history of England through the centuries: in *As You Like It*, Shakespeare's comedy set in the opposing milieus of court and wild woods, has references to the names, and the male protagonist is called Orlando, the Italian version of Roland; the phrase 'a Roland for an Oliver' was common through the years, meaning 'tit for tat'.

The basis of the story in *The Song of Roland* is actions supposed to have taken place at the Battle of Roncesvalles in AD 778. but as DLS explains, history was transmuted into epic myth as time wore on. The enemies of the Christian knights are called 'paynims', which is linked to the Latin *paganus*, meaning a pagan. The term came to signify a heathen opponent. The power of the long poem stands on a number of rich set-piece episodes and descriptions which are rooted in the techniques of the great Homeric epics, *The Iliad* and *The Odyssey*. These include accounts of physical appearance of the fighters; the horses at war; the weapons used; and then more importantly, the manner of a combat and the grisly accounts of deaths in the saddle. A typical instance of such poetry is this, describing Oliver dying:

Oliver's face, when Roland on him looks,
Is grey and ghastly, discoloured, wan with wounds,
His bright blood sprays his body head to foot;
Down to the ground it runs from him in pools

The fights, woundings and deaths are handled as if the poem is dealing with gods; one of the closest genres to the poem is the modern superhero film or pictorial novel, as the fighters take a long time to die. As in Homer and his battle scenes from the war at Troy, all the combatants are heroic except for those involved in betrayal or who are on the wrong side morally; but at the heart of it all, the poem is the notion of chivalry, and that concept provided a great deal of material for DLS the poet. She was fascinated by the trappings of the warrior both in battle and in peacetime, and gives a neat definition:

'the general tone of the poem, and the behaviour of all the characters, is chivalrous, disinterested and governed by a strict sense of military propriety: nobody wastes time, as Homeric warriors so often do, by stopping in the middle of a battle to strip the corpse of his adversary.'

The words of the Prelate perhaps exemplify the qualities which drew DLS to this genre:

> Soon, very soon we are all marked to die,
> None of us here will see tomorrow's light;
> One thing there is I promise you outright:
> To you stand open the gates of Paradise

The *laisse* stanza attracted DLS with is capacious reach: in stanza 105 may be seen most of the features that allow for the kind of flexibility her tone of voice demands, mainly with an assonance on the ends of lines 1, 4, 6, 8 and the final one. This allows for the overall sounds which here has to suggest the impact of a deadly scrap and creates the anticipation in the ear of the listener.

Even when everything has to be concluded, and a mass of facts communicated, the fluency and movement of the *laisse* continues, as in stanza 271 which includes this:

> In the old Geste 'tis writ for all to read
> How Carlon summons vassals from all his fiefs,
> Now in the city Aix-la-Chapelle they meet,
> It is a high day, a very solemn feaste

The pulse through the entire work is sustained. The tale of Roland and the pass of Roncesvalles became one of the defining works of what became known as *chansons de geste* – songs of (great) deeds, and as we know from English literature, knightly narratives continued, but one interesting sidelight on the notion of chivalry is in Chaucer's profile of his knight in the Prologue to *The Canterbury Tales*. In the first lines, we have:

> A knyght ther was, and that a worthy man
> That fro the tyme that he first began
> To riden out he loved chivalrie,
> Trouthe and honour, freedom and curteisye

But, as critics Francis King and Bruce Steele have explained: 'Although, as an ideal, he may be a reproach to all those who fail in their duty, the vivid reality of the world in which he is placed makes him something of a melancholy anachronism ... He is a figure from an attractively simple imaginary world.'

Another medieval poet, John Gower, has a more forthright address he wished to make to the average knight:

> Oh knight, who goeth far off
> Into strange lands and seeketh only
> Praise in arms, know this:
> If our country and your neighbour
> Are at war themselves, all the honour is in vain

But this is of course what drew readers to chivalrous tales, and the criticism that in reality they might be dreamers and wanderers, nonetheless, they make wonderfully attractive heroes. The reality still fits: Monty Python star and historian Terry Jones has pointed out that 'These knights of the eleventh century were by no means aristocrats. A recent study has shown ... that many of them were often of lowly or even unfree origin...' but none of this matters when there is a noble battle to fight and the *chansons de geste* have to contain something significant.

Naturally, this is exactly what DLS would have found so appealing as a subject for poetry, and the imaginary knight of chivalry has definitely lived on in films and fiction. DLS was drawn to the literature of that great period in French literature in which several poets made significant contributions to the whole of world literature. She was the kind of scholar who revels in the textual mosaics that build narratives; even at her Hull school, she must have been an exciting and atypical French teacher, as she writes in a letter: 'I've only time for a line this evening. I'm awfully busy preparing an experiment for the VIth Form. We are going to make texts, whole families of them – and see how they work out.' She must have provided the kind of creative shock that Robin Williams's students had in *The Dead Poets Society* when he jumps on a desk to talk about viewpoints in creativity.

Her scholarship is most evident in her connections with the Modern Language Association. This body was formed in 1883, and it seems likely that Mildred Pope was involved in DLS becoming a member. Whatever the facts, surely they would have welcomed her into their ranks, as she was translating most of the *Tristan* written by Thomas back in that same period of the flowering of chivalrous themes and tales; the editor liked the translation so much that the submission was published in two issues of the journal, *Modern Languages*. DLS had always read widely in the early narratives of European cultures, from Celtic to Old French; she could apply herself to sustained work. The famous dialectologist Harold Orton once said that 'a scholar never works at his or her leisure.' DLS could burn the midnight oil in this context. She could bring stories alive in the retelling, and in a number of channels.

Barbara Reynolds wrote in her biography: '...the young Dorothy L. Sayers already characteristics which will make her a compelling lecturer in later years: an orderliness of mind enabling her to perceive a pattern in seemingly shapeless material, as well as an engaging desire to communicate delight.' The research, collation and the developed delivery of the formal completed body of work all demand the same degree of attention.

Poetic form is at the core of the varieties of work we may read in the collection of her verse collected and edited by Ralph E. Hone. Perhaps what needs to be stressed here relates to the probable trajectory in the career of the average poet. Of course, the latter concept may not exist, but conventionally, the early poems are called 'juvenilia' and this phase entails experiment; the poet works to try out set forms and to find his or her own voice, in the sense of a tone and style that mark out their individuality. This assumes the kind of poet who follows a set pattern which has been established by tradition and convention, and relates to the educational aspects applied to the poet's life. In this respect, surely DLS was an exception.

Hone's collection shows the development of the poet Dorothy L. Sayers, as opposed to the DLS of popular crime writing; yet there is not necessarily a structural or logical progression, as we might find in Tennyson or Wordsworth for instance. What we do find is a logging of a writer's fascination with established forms, and approaches to poetic form. However, there is another thread to this interest. Take for instance the *Lais* of Marie de France. DLS knew these of course, as the text is a standard prescribed work in French studies. These narratives were written in the late twelfth century, and the author is unknown, in spite of the name 'Marie de France'. Basically, apart from topics such as metrical elements and devices, the themes of the Old French tales and narrative poems often contained examples of universal stories which draw together universal morals and values, behaviour and relationships. One of the *Lais* is particularly important for DLS, and her life with her 'hidden' son. This is *Milun*, a work in which Milun visits his damsel in a garden near her bedroom, and there she confesses that she is pregnant. The tale then has this (translated by Glyn Burgess and Keith Busby):

Milun replied that he would do whatever she suggested. 'When the child is born,' she said, 'You will take it to my married sister in Northumbria, a rich, worthy and wise lady ... She should see that it is properly brought up ... I shall hang your ring round its neck and write you a letter.'

Apart from these types of moral dilemmas which are the stuff of the great medieval texts are made, through to Chaucer in the late fourteenth century, the textual challenges and the concomitant fun of creation account for the appeal of the literature to DLS.

The most useful way to look at DLS's interest in and use of poetic form is to concentrate on one specific poem. It would be tedious to analyse every work in the collected poems. A stanza from her lengthy poem on Oxford, *Lay* (1916) will suffice. What is a 'lay?' For Victorians, the word would be associated with the successful Macaulay poem, *The Lays of Ancient Rome*, and that is handy in order to have a more recent idiom in the genre than looking only at medieval works. The standard dictionary definition relates the lay to other shortish narrative poems such as a ballad or a *conte*, or even *fabliau*, but 'A short narrative or lyrical poem intended to be sung' provides a basis for thought. DLS gives a definition from the French poet Eustache Deschamps to indicate what she understands by the term, and Barbara Reynolds has given a translation of Deschamps's description; in it we learn that the French poet demands 'a long affair ... there must be twelve stanzas, each divided into two, and the final two lines must reflect their equivalent in the first stanza.'

Looking at the first section of *Lay*, there is this rhyme scheme, using the usual alphabetical listing for the words on the end of each line that make the end-rhymes:

ABABABB.

This is the same pattern in the second stanza. Then a crucial question has to be asked: why do this? To say that it is a metrical exercise is not applicable. The point is, what is gained emotionally or intellectually from any kind of patterning? DLS wrote and spoke about the nature of 'pattern' in all the arts and in the human imagination. Yet still we have to ask that question. The answer is that the poem, opening a XII stanza long poem celebrating the many appeals of the Oxford of 'Dreaming Spires'; in this first stanza the imagery is concerned with opening the thought behind the poem with a stress on change, loss and nostalgia. It makes an appeal that the past has to stay there: 'Mummers! Let love go by' and then the poem closes with 'We've a ragtime tune instead – but yours is already dead.' If we delve inside the poem we may easily find a hinted basis of a lament for a past time of great worth to the poet.

Another worthwhile instance of why and how a form is worth the hard work is in the sonnet, and in 1916 DLS wrote a Petrarchan sonnet, which has the end-rhyme scheme of:

ABBAABBA.

It pays to look at a classic example here, before focusing on DLS's poem *Icarus*. There are variations in the sestet (the last six lines) and the form is usually ABBAABBA in the octet and then usually CDCDCD, or variations, in the sestet.

Here is a very famous Petrarchan sonnet from Wordsworth: *Composed Upon Westminster Bridge* (1802):

Earth has not anything to show more fair: [A]
Dull would he be of soul who could pass by [B]
A sight so touching in its majesty: [B]
This City now doth like a garment wear [A]
The beauty of the morning; silent, bare, [A]
Ships, towers, domes, theatres, and temples lie [B]
Open unto the fields, and to the sky; [B]
All bright and glittering in the smokeless air. [A].............octet
Never did sun more beautifully steep [C]

In his first splendour valley, rock, or hill; [D]
Ne'er saw I, never felt, a calm so deep! [C]
The river glideth at his own sweet will: [D]
Dear God! The very houses seem asleep; [C]
And all that mighty heart is lying still! [D]...................sestet

Most of the other basic features of a metrical arrangement are seen here also:

Enjambment or 'run–on' where a line carries on to the next one no punctuation used.

End-stopped lines: where punctuation provides a 'barrier' or pause. Then caesura is a pause in the line for meaning or emotional effect. DLS loved to use all these techniques and discusses her use of them in her notes to translations.

A neat way to see most of the basic poetic techniques in the commonest writing is to look at the epitaph of rhymed couplets in *The Nine Taylors*: the first two lines provide the rhythm, to set the tone for the lines, all in <u>pentameter</u> (five metrical feet/ten syllables):

Here lies the body of SAMUEL SNELL
That for fifty years pulled the tenor bell

Then the next two lines show <u>enjambment</u>:

Through changes of this mortal race
He laid his blows and kept his place

Then, in the third last line we have a <u>caesura</u> with no punctuation, after the word *mute*:

His clapper mute his metal crackt

Leaving aside the medieval studies and writing, an account of Hone's anthology repays attention in order to reveal DLS the poet. This was always in her. The poetic voice is always breaking through the fiction, but when she set herself to work on set forms and traditions, she revelled in the challenge. Reading her collected poems is like seeing a mosaic assembly taking place, images reflecting both her inner creative landscape and the important people and places in her life, from Arthurian legends and tales such as *Peredur* from the Welsh *Mabinogion* cycle, to the elegy on Oxford, the war poems in tribute to people she knew, and through to the free verse of her 'cat poems'. These free verse poems and exploratory verses, such as *Target Area*, the long poem to her former German teacher Fraulein Fehmer, whom she clearly loved and thought about all through her life.

Free verse works by the stylistic pulses through the lines that make a rhythm, rather like jazz improvisations, and DLS was a remarkable proficient exponent of these forms; one feels that she could have earned a high place in the 1960s with such writers as Lawrence Ferlinghetti or Roger McGough. In *Target Area* she wants to give a comprehensive picture of a woman, but also of a time and place, and of a material world for which DLS herself was deeply fond. The affection works through every line. In fact, the theme is most ambitious, using a powerful paradox: the element of affection and materiality is set in opposition to the war, and the poem begins with the words: 'OUR bombers/were out over Germany last night, in very great strength/ their main target was Frankfurt.'

Clearly, she had accepted that modern subjects required some experiments in free verse, although her concept of poetry was usually based on tight technical expertise. .

The free verse enables an impressive range of insights and descriptions, calling for a succinct visual strand to the approach, such as words on the Fraulein herself:

> Fraulein Fehmer was stiffly built,
> With a strong square face, lionish, slightly blunted,
> As though the hand of the potter had given a gentle
> Push to the damp clay

The quality of her poetry stems from the mix of a specific occasion or theme, and her satisfaction with a rhyme-scheme that reveals the right kind of treatment. Hence the topics covered include work on the medieval material she later translated, along with treatments of themes which flowers well when the decided metrical shapes meet the subject with perfection. Yet in her free verse there is a special quality; the freedom of reflecting inner thoughts, and one of her strengths is found in the poems spurred into form by the Second World War, as in the poem to Fraulein Fehmer. Her work of 1943, *Aerial Reconnaissance*, demonstrates this fusion at its best.

Here she utilises that skill so often seen in the depiction of the workers and ordinary folk – the voices from the depths, as it were, wide of the mark when it comes to large-scale dimensions of life. From this thought, for example, in the first section of the poem she creates a voice that describes something so familiar to twenty-first-century readers and viewers; the aerial depiction of a target destroyed. No direct statement about deaths or victims is included, and so the voice she makes works rather like the ironical voice used so powerfully by her almost – contemporary, Stevie Smith. This first section, closing with 'but of course I am quite convinced/that the destruction was enormous – absolutely convinced – /absolutely.' So that what reads like a passing conversation, barely any kind of official report, hits home with that blend of irony and implied horror.

She changes tone and switches to childhood memory and sharp imagery in the second section of the poem, reminding the reader almost of some of W.H. Auden's perspectives on the 'big history' around him: she also adds the required drive and force here with several lines containing only two or three strong stresses, like blows or stabs of feeling:

> but I know this picture –
> That's real
> Something that means something
> That I can interpret for myself

Overall, an assessment of DLS the poet has to take in all the foregoing areas of activity; for a poet, reading one of her poems is to feel either the admiration of her handling of formal discipline in the writing, or to wonder at the successful way she manages to do what Samuel Johnson said when referring to Metaphysical poetry, that 'heterogeneous ideas are yoked by violence together', but the violence is all in the emotional or intellectual shock for the reader. One feels that readers of this area of her work who have not written poetry would still sense the rhythmic effects and sense the delight taken in the music of the words.

I once wrote to Seamus Heaney to ask about how free verse happens, or how segments of a metrical line happen, he replied:

> I suppose what I write about when I write best is the undervoice of a poet or a poem, that register of sound, that particular musical or sonic pitch which seems to have a carry-over meaning. Not that the meaning can be put into an articulated set of propositions; it's more that in the tone of a writing or in its undervoice that one picks up an attitude to life.

One way of demonstrating this is to consider another Oxford poet, and one whose work is perhaps echoed in DLS's Oxford poem referred to above: Thomas Gray. In his case, the roots and sources of his elegies may be found in classical literature, but also in his own somewhat exaggerated notions of Welsh poetry. His notions of 'bards' are surely very similar to DLS's echoes of medieval writing. Like DLS, Gray has to find a way to inhabit his formal structures with something of the 'undervoice' of authentic feeling which lies beneath the surface of traditional writing. Heaney and others have spoken of a pulse or rhythm which gradually infiltrates the feeling behind a poem and its springboard experience.

Finally, it must be stressed just how much the DLS's poetry avoids a lot of contemporary fashions; not being a member of a group, a clique or even a political or ideological cadre meant that, again like Stevie Smith and perhaps also Alun Lewis, she had something different from a 'voice', a quality more like a weighing up of a shared, broader experience. After all, one world war happening when she wrote her first poetry, and a second world war when she showed her fine abilities with free verse. One way of marking the prowess of a poet whose work tends to be written in response to events as opposed to the poet who always searches for subjects is to consider the back-up feeling to the intentions behind the work. That is, to put it more succinctly, there is the habit of waiting for the Muse to arrive, as opposed to inviting her in. DLS tended to do both, letting the formal demands of what form she chose dictate a string of feelings, so that some poems appear to have the words hung out on a frame, rather than there being words waiting for a frame. She supplies works with the flavour of both approaches, but Heaney's 'undervoice' is not so straightforward as to allow for more potential success in one approach as compared to another. In fact, one might suggest that the undervoice is more of a presence in free verse, and that DLS paid most regard to the more rhetorical or studied diction of the classical principles she admired.

Chapter 6

Being a Writer and More Wimsey

*Five minute's practice before the glass every day, and you will
soon acquire that vacant look so desirable for all rogues, detectives
and Government officials.*

The Nine Tailors, D.L. Sayers

R eading a Sayers crime novel is very much like sitting in a
railway carriage facing a storyteller, while having details of
passing scenes and events pointed out. The novel she offers is
a journey with attractions along the way, and one never quite feels able
to sum up the technique, as there is a spectrum of methods. In *The
Nine Tailors* for instance, for the first seventy pages the genre could be
a fiction of English rural manners and community; then, placed at the
heart of the vicar and the village dwellers at Fenchurch St Paul, there
is also the challenge to concentrate and register arcane material about
bell-changing. As that reader or listener, we summon the required
patience, allow for the entertaining dalliance and digression required,
and yield to the charm of the harmony or disharmony of the voices
collected to adorn the tale.

Anyone who has driven from the south of Lincolnshire, over Sutton
Bridge and into Norfolk, along the base of The Wash, will know that
sense of venturing into Norfolk via Gedney and into Terrington St
Clement, which of course echoes the fictional place, and will be aware
of something expressed by writer W.F. Rawnsley eight years before
The Nine Tailors was in print: 'As we left Gedney and looked back
over the fields the tall and Italian-looking campanile, whose bells,

however, cannot vie with the eight bells of Holbeach, made a unique and memorable picture.'

The writer who was to put that past of England into the said novel was a very different person six years after 1934 when the fictional Fenchurch had appeared. By the years immediately before the outbreak of the war against Fascism, DLS had become famous and influential, and there is no doubt that she was very skilful and adept at playing the role of advocate for, and public face of, crime fiction. There she was, planted firmly at the core of the Golden Age of detective fiction. A sample of media interest and events will show how much of a presence she was by c.1940. One report from the *Daily Mail* has the headline 'Murder by Six Experts' for an event, and explains, 'Six famous crime writers have committed the perfect murder in print, of course – and Supt. George Cornish, late of the "Yard" has brought the murderer to book when he can!'

This was to be a *Daily Mail* serial, and the authors, 'every one a guarantee of first-class reading' were Margery Allingham, Anthony Berkeley, F. Wills Crofts, Father Ronald Knox, Dorothy L. Sayers and Russell Thorndike. This was a read for 'every lover of stimulating reading'.

In 1938 DLS was one of five writers referred to as 'mighty names in the realm of fiction, and they were the major contributors to a publication called *The Book of a Thousand Thrills*, produced by the *Press and Journal*. Why were the top crime writers so highly praised? The report, in the *Aberdeen Journal*, had the answer: 'They are writers who work with consummate mystery on the whole gamut of human emotions, they write with supreme force of love, adventure, terror, crime and romance.' Also in 1938 the DLS detective thriller, *Busman's Honeymoon*, written with Muriel St Clare Byrne, was to appear at His Majesty's Theatre, Aberdeen, and the paper adds that 'Miss Sayers' novel is probably the best of her Lord Peter Wimsey series and has been so widely read by 'thriller' lovers that it requires no introduction.

DLS had 'arrived'. With Gollancz behind her, and a seemingly inexhaustible supply of material for fiction, she was on a carnival ride of success. Where had the phenomenon come from? In *The Nine Tailors* there is a strong presence of her father in the character of the vicar, and something of herself in the character of Hilary Thorpe. This interchange may well have happened at the vicarage when she was a girl; it follows a remark that the girl might make it as a writer, when she is speaking to her father:

'You'll want a bit of experience before you can write novels old girl'

'Rot, Daddy. You don't want experience for writing novels. People write them at Oxford and they sell like billy-oh. All about how awful everything was at school.'

Lord Peter Wimsey had more than survived, with all the competition from several very successful writers' pens; he was something of a phenomenon, and at this stage it pays to revisit the character before looking at his 'last bow'. Unlike Holmes, he has a multi-layered nature. The last thing that defines him is a brain in a dressing-gown, and, owing to television, in the popular imagination he is sometimes confused with Bertie Wooster, for obvious reasons. There is a fundamental fact about Wimsey which is not too often stressed: the PTSD. I have already briefly discussed the 'shell-shock' as it percolates into the fiction, but what must now be stressed is just how much this was a contemporary issue of huge significance. Thousands of wounded men came home with the naive belief (not their own fault) that their only damage was to their organs or limbs. But now we really know the truth.

Jon Stallworthy is one of several biographers of Wilfred Owen to convey the evidence and features of PTSD as it was apparent at the time of the war, and here he uses Owen's own voice: 'One became conscious that the place [Craiglockhart Hospital] was full of men whose slumbers were morbid and terrifying – men muttering uneasily or suddenly crying out in their sleep. Around me was that underworld of dreams haunted by submerged memories of warfare...'

In fact, a more recent biographer of Owen, Guy Cuthbertson, has not only pointed out that Owen 'would have had a chance of meeting' with Tolkien and Sayers; he also adds something that immediately contributes to the conception of Wimsey. He writes of Craiglockhart: 'which seemed like a scholarly and gentlemanly place by day but at night was filled with monstrous screams, as, in nightmares, men were sent back to the Front.'

Owen's own poem, *Mental Cases* takes a stance that, if applied to Wimsey, knocks him firmly out of the world of Sexton Blake or Sir Percy Blakeney and into the twentieth century's darkest corner:

These are men whose minds the Dead have ravished.
Memory fingers in their hair of murders,
Multitudinous murders they once witnessed.
Wading sloughs of flesh these helpless wander,
Treading blood from lungs that had loved laughter

Put together, the contrasts and conflicts in what Owen sees, and within himself, may apply to Wimsey, and in doing so, this all reminds us of the daring and innovative achievement of a writer who integrates such things into a popular fictional genre. She must have been aware that the true nature of the 'neurasthenia' which had been in all the media discussions, would seem out of place in a detective novel. But the character of Wimsey, with his mental anguish, has to deal with the scrutiny of corpses on a regular basis, and copes far better in this respect than Inspector Morse, who feels nauseous at the sight of blood.

Wimsey, Gollancz and the war, put together, formed a massive influence (and a boost, of course) to the writing career of DLS. It was an age in which creative writing and journalism were expanding markedly, and opportunities abounded for aspiring writers. She had moved, in a decade, from being the author of stories for *Pearson's Magazine* and Sexton Blake derivatives, to a major figure in popular literature. Along the way, she gave birth to her secret son, John Anthony, in 1924. 'Tony', the son of an unemployed car salesman who left DLS after learning of her pregnancy, went to live with (and was raised by) her cousin and aunt. She also suffered the loss of both of her parents between 1928 and 1929.

By the time she reached Wimsey's marriage, and the adaptation of *Busman's Honeymoon* from play into book, DLS had achieved remarkable feats of fictional subtlety and ambition. She had acquired the ability to create intricate and extensive settings, all interwoven with accuracy and subtlety, as in the (arguably risky) long sections of narratives recalled in *The Nine Tailors*, or in the tortuous ins and outs of inheritance law in *Unnatural Death*, but these moves generally come off triumphantly, and readers who follow the novels largely through an involvement in the ongoing relationship of Peter and Harriet will have to endure absences and trials, gaps in activities and long uncertainties. On several occasions they might ask where is Harriet? Yet the rewards of a devotion to the series are substantial. There are few examples of equally compelling detective series projects in crime literature.

The concept of the Wimsey novels is such that it can cope with wanderings, factual freezes of pace, indefinite lingering on matters which may or may not be important, and so on. Is every apparently trivial chat that Wimsey has with any specific labourer, waiter or taxi driver likely to be of future importance? If so, or if not, does it matter? The writer–reader bond is so strong if the Wimsey magic works. In *Murder Must Advertise* he can be given a female admirer; in *Strong Poison* he faces the hangman in empathic feeling with the love of his life, and in *The Nine Tailors* he tricks death while climbing up a belfry tower in the midst of a terrifying flood. The point is that here is a detective who exemplifies qualities often applied to members of that fragile and volatile profession: the hunger for action and the mortifying dread of inactivity. Wimsey will chase a certain first edition for his book collection one day, and fall into a lethal bog in Yorkshire the next.

To add to her comfortable position as a writer in the mid-1930s there was also the advent of Penguin Books and their interest in the famous 'greenback' paperbacks, which included the primary members of the Detection Club and gave the whole genre a boost commercially. Agatha Christie was part of it, and her works earned a vast sum for Penguin.

DLS's life was full in all sorts of ways. In late 1933 she wrote a note to Ivy regarding her son John, in a letter that reminds readers of her efforts to balance profession and family: 'I can't come on Saturday as I have a committee meeting and dinner engagement in Oxford. I will be along some time on Sunday probably after lunch.'

The busy and fulfilled life was to bring all kinds of pressures as well as pleasures, as usually tends to happen. In a letter to her friend Muriel St Clare Byrne in 1935, after finishing *Gaudy Night* there is an insight into this kind of experience. Not only do readers write to an author in order to point out factual inaccuracies in the novels, they also tend to become deeply enmeshed in the emotional turmoil of fictional relationships, and in the case of Peter and Harriet there were inevitably such topics for discussion. Writing to her friend, DLS said 'I think it quite certain that people will say again, as they have said before, that they can't see what Peter sees in Harriet ... All through the book he is never seen through any eyes but hers.' She also adds that he is 'a catalyst ... that changes everything that comes in contact with it.'

As a successful novelist and public figure in the literary world, DLS was having to search inside her creative centre, and every novelist knows that characters who really 'take off' have aspects in their composition just as mysterious as actual people do in real life. DLS once said that she had no idea where Lord Peter came from. The motivations people argue over tend to emerge and become important when a character has come 'alive' and is dictating motivations. The issue concerning Harriet and Peter stems from the fact that Lord Peter is conceived as the mentally scarred survivor of a wartime shock to his system; on top of that, he is managing to operate in life with a basis of mainstream wealthy persons' experience, such as buying expensive incunabula at book auctions, opposed to his need for the excitement the crime detection gives him.

It cannot be over-emphasised just how intensively the personality of the detective melds into the life 'on the edge'. Since the professional detectives appeared on the scene in 1849, and before that with the Bow Street Runners, the work of detection in serious crime has involved the notion of empathic knowledge. That is, it takes a deviant to know a deviant. Lord Peter's deviance is like a pressure chamber, and steam is released through minor channels, while all the time the personality itself is in danger of disintegration. Holmes has his drugs, his physical prowess and his obsessions; Wimsey has similar obsessive traits and also delights in dressing up, in a similar way to Holmes, who gets a kick out of having another identity. We know that Lord Peter dreads sleep. The PTSD has left him with an existence a few steps removed from normal humanity, and so he relates to Harriet in a way that all readers would understand, making Wimsey novels both intellectually stimulating and emotionally fascinating, as well as compelling.

In the 1940s, Howard Fast wrote a science fiction story, 'The First Men', in which the children become so intelligent that they achieve an existence in a very slight dimensional shift in time; the adults have no way of reaching them if the children move over into that state of existence. This is Wimsey's condition, metaphorically. One of DLS's correspondents, Donald Tovey, a professor who was deeply involved in Peter and Harriet, enjoying interchanges of 'fan letters' which DLS seemed to welcome and enjoy responding to. In late 1935 she writes to Tovey: 'But Peter owes you an eternal debt for having been always kind to his Harriet. He is the kind of person who, while not saying much is, I know, sensitive about people's attitudes to his wife, and appreciative of those who appreciate her.' All the evidence points to this kind of success both with the works themselves, and with the consequences of that surrender to a fictional world we see all through the history of literature within print culture, and that we see expanding in fan culture websites; in the same cultural land of mystified nexus, we have people in the street cursing and reviling the actors whose soap opera characters have sinned.

Before returning to the public world of the literary personality and the coming of war, attention must be given to an autobiographical subject that Barbara Reynolds explained in her biography of DLS. This relates to the interior life of the artist – in contrast to the Dorothy L. Sayers in the papers, magazines and public events. This concerns an unpublished manuscript headed *Cat O'Mary,* which tells the story of Katherine Lammas, who 'after marriage and motherhood will seek fulfilment in the life of the mind'. (Barbara Reynolds). This is a slightly parallel storyline, although it is scanty in the novel, in *The Nine Tailors* to be seen in young Hilary Thorpe, the aspiring writer who has an inheritance at the novel's closure. Clearly, DLS was preoccupied with this case for the defence in relation to the intellectual provenance of a female character who grows and succeeds in this respect, regardless of oppositions. At school, DLS had written a short work using autobiographical material and now here was some kind of development of this theme. Barbara Reynolds sums it up in these words: 'At the age of forty, Dorothy looks back on the child she was and takes a violent dislike to her. Some of the passages are startling in the self-disgust they express.'

The important point is that if this text locates and describes some reasons for self-disgust, then it is evident that the thinking is based on achievement and her related vanity, which she would revise and reassess after so many years, as we all tend to do. The girl/young woman who knew languages, played instruments, wrote wonderful stories and poems for the Mutual Admiration Society, then became a famous author, was possibly too much of a superhuman alter-ego to live with, and the vanity she maybe hated had no choice but to appear in the simulacrum of the person known to the public. Celebrity brings its penalties.

One relevant note is quoted by Reynolds that has a bearing on this: 'I have made a muck of all my emotional relationships and I hate being beaten, so I pretend not to care.' There is no doubt, though, that her Oxford identity redeemed her in the eyes of that inner self; the acceptable persona of Dorothy L. Sayers of the Detection Club and scholar of Somerville was evidence that the early dreams were all of a piece: the tuning fork of the personality had sounded and was consistent. *Gaudy Night* explores much of this. Harriet's time in the conditions of retreat are a spiritual awakening, as described in the foregoing poetry chapter.

Switching back to Lord Peter: he is, in *Gaudy Night*, the 'new stranger', the reclaimed personality who has to change in order to be up to the mark when it comes to explaining his proposal. His remarkable honesty comes across almost like a guide to Harriet's inner confusions and challenges, as if he now has the ability to apply a true and proper insight. DLS has touched on this in her Oxford poem, in the section where she described what is lost in order that the true inspiration that fires the self be admitted:

And though the pole-star burn intense,
Shudders to know how many ships thus started,
Feeling the wrath commence
Of old experience,
And drowned green ghosts that crawl from unsuspected dens.

With all this in mind, *Busman's Honeymoon* has to be seen as a special case, and also a significant change of gear in that intellectual life DLS and her persona had faced and triumphed in.

In her personal life, at the time when *Busman's Honeymoon* began its life as a play (before it was a novel) she brought about the formal adoption of her son, John. She wrote to Ivy that the boy would now officially be John Fleming, adopted by 'cousin Dorothy and cousin Mac'. She also added that 'Dorothy L. Sayers should be omitted from things,' and wrote, 'Explain to him that professional writers want their business and private affairs kept separate.' John's education stepped up, and included a tutor in Kent, so he was travelling in the triangle of Oxford-Kent-London when she went to spend time with him, although he would never live with her at any point. Later he was to graduate at Oxford and was successful in life. He always knew exactly what the situation around him had been, and was well informed regarding his father, and also about the development of his mother's career.

The theatre was now central in her life: *Busman's Honeymoon* was being produced in Birmingham, and she wrote to John, 'I expect it will be on in town during the Christmas holidays, and you and Aunt Ivy will be able to come and see it. It is tremendous fun doing it rather like a grand dressing-up game with grown-up people.'

The play/novel becomes of real interest when one reflects on DLS's statement: 'It has been said by myself and others, that a love-interest is only an intrusion upon a detective story ... The book deals with ... some sort of answer to many kindly inquiries as to how Lord Peter and his Harriet solved their matrimonial problems' (dedication). In fact, one could argue, this misses the point. One doubts whether or not DLS actually saw and responded to something deeper in the culmination of the Harriet and Peter storyline. The clue is in a short interchange about the killing of fowls in *Busman's Honeymoon*. Here, Miss Twitterton is being interviewed by Superintendent Kirk and she refers to the ease with which one might kill a fowl; the conversation was becoming unpleasant, and Harriet is there. We then have, 'Harriet was angry, and her face showed it. Men; when they got together they were all alike – even Peter. For a moment, he and Kirk stood together on the far side of a chasm, and she hated them both.' Just after that, as Peter opens a door, DLS adds, 'she darted a reproachful glance at him, but, as with Lancelot and Guinevere, their eyes met and hers fell.'

This incident is one of the most fruitful insights into the profound theme at the heart of the love story. In fact, to call it merely a 'love-interest' is to reduce the significance and interest of the whole relationship which from the first battle to save Harriet from the noose has been on the surface a roller-coaster ride of emotions, but to dig deeper, there is a theme bursting to come through that finally becomes truly apparent in *Busman's Honeymoon*. The hint about the depths beneath the 'far side of a chasm' could almost be Lawrentian. This is DLS touching on a fundamental, even elemental opposition, as explored in Lawrence's most successful novels of sexual power and tension. He relates such business to identity, and so does DLS.

Also prolonged into the crime fiction is the Arthurian cross-reference; after the comments that Harriet's eyes 'fell', surely the reader senses a deeper area of imagery at work: there is a submission, and in the male sphere of Paggleham, where the old macho unwritten values prevail, down deeply in its history and culture lie the domains of the Dukes of Denver and their ilk. The London man, McBride, comments, 'I wouldn't have believed there were places like this, within fifty miles of London. Beats me how people can live in 'em.' However, the reader will be aware, casting memory back to the intense debates of *Gaudy Night*, that there is the Wimsey oath outside the church. This is notably present in the new life when Wimsey says, 'All right, Domina … Cactus for both and no lotus till we share it. I won't play the good British husband in spite of your alarming plunge into wifeliness. The Ethiopian shall stay black and leave the leopardess her spots.'

The long discussions in *Gaudy Night* have prepared the ground. This concerns a true epiphany on the part of Peter. If one bears in mind the mental state of the detective, the PTSD and its effects, what becomes evident is that Peter's constant need to divert things from the hurt of feelings (even down to his house of cards when they fall out) is most visible when he and Paggleham come together, and at such a vital point in his life. Harriet, in the same novel, reflects that she has 'married England', and the reader is indeed immersed in a place which Peter notes has its own shocks: 'Stir up the mud of the village pond and the stink will surprise you.' DLS has brought the storyline to a conclusion that faces the deeper sense of identity in both lovers.

The 'love interest' is not an adequate definition of what is in the text here. The development of the lovers' relationship has been written to appear somewhere on the cusp of a romantic, impassioned attachment crossed with an unreal *narrative of ideas*. The latter interests the reader constantly, because the various countermoves in their story indicate narratives of the emotions involved from some submerged sphere, out of view from the surface of the novel. Responses to the central relationship here have been mixed; perhaps readers who commit themselves to being involved as some of the early readers and correspondents to DLS clearly were, will either suspend belief and take the characters as 'real' in the fictional sense, or treat Harriet and Peter as pawns in the *whimsicality* of their story.

Writing *Gaudy Night* and *The Nine Tailors*, DLS was aware that there had been a step forward in her fiction, in terms of literary substance; through both novels there is a poetic, lyrical presence of place and people that reaches back to the more comfortable pace and feeling of a Victorian regional novel. Again, one senses the presence behind the words of her admired Wilkie Collins. *The Nine Tailors* in particular reaches towards epic proportions. The Rector, Venables, is very much her father, but also the community of Paggleham.

There is also an intensely contemporary dimension to both novels, with the undermining of the Oxford ethos by the eventually revealed criminal 'scout' in *Gaudy Night*, and in *The Nine Tailors* there are the various elements impinging on the police investigation and the sustained storyline of the sluice and the eventual flood. One of the most apparent to readers at the time, and to anyone interested in crime and law, was the long police investigation and the series of interviews conducted by Inspector Kirk. The novel was published in 1937, when the media were making it clear that there were major police reforms in process, led by Lord Trenchard, and this work was to lead to the 'Report of the Departmental Committee on Detective Work and Procedure' of 1938. The harsh reality of detective work, as opposed to the life of Parker and the way he works with Wimsey, had experienced many years of criticism and examination.

This committee had been appointed in 1933. It is interesting to note that volume four was not on sale to the general public, and the topics in that report were on communication. One significant aspect of this was exactly what we witness in the Kirk interviews: he is a cultured man, swapping quotes with Wimsey; he appears to be some kind of ideal that may be integrated into the humorous heart of the novel, for that is what the play and the book are: quintessentially wonderful, celebratory comedy with Englishness at the core. This is the society that will survive, one might read into it, if and when a cataclysmic war comes along. Kirk, at the centre of the moral initiatives, along with Wimsey. In the conclusions and recommendations of the report on detective work, which cover thirty-three pages of close text, there is one short paragraph devoted to 'Communications between police and public'. In contrast, several pages and dozens of paragraphs are concerned with matters such as police procedure and recruitment.

This lack of awareness and change became increasingly apparent in many of the important serious crime cases through the period 1940–70s. Time and again, notably when Scotland Yard was called in to conduct investigations, there were cases of alarmingly brutal and cavalier interviewing procedures being applied (a massive case here was the Stefan Kiszko case in the 1970s in which this Rochdale man was arrested and convicted of murder and rape when in fact he was incapable of producing sperm and had a sound alibi).

Was DLS including such a 'good cop' as some kind of spark to a debate? Again, we might draw a comparison with Sergeant Cuff in *The Moonstone*. Even in the 1860s the detective was a celebrity. This is all a part of an interpretation of *Busman's Honeymoon* that opens out the nature of the humour though, and here there is more than a hint of this new focus in the fiction. DLS was always like the philosopher friend of Dr Johnson for whom, in philosophic interchange, happiness was always breaking in.

It has to be stressed, however, in the case of *Busman's Honeymoon* just how much of a new departure is evident. DLS had proved herself as a dramatist: the stage version of the novel had done very well and her friendship with novelist and theologian Charles Williams was about to help to change her writing life. Before the religious drama which was to fill her life for some time, there was the life of the theatre. The letters to friends convey the excitement of the beckoning new life. The project of the play seems to have begun when DLS recalled the visit of a chimney sweep to her home, and she reported the comedy of his work to her friends Muriel St Clare Byrne and Marjorie Barber. The performance and speech of the man who was destined to become Mr Puffett in *Busman's Honeymoon* are the core of the theatrical idea.

Barbara Reynolds pointed out that DLS was often at work on two books at the same time, and that she would use different rooms and desks for each specific book. The dramatist in her was emerging very strongly, and she adored the world of the theatre; around this time she also met Wilfrid Scott-Giles, a writer and artist, who was to create the famous Wimsey coat of arms. Her new circle of friends met with the old acquaintances, and the woman of the theatre became even more sociable than she had been previously. Writing for the stage meant the exciting experience of being involved in the 'spadework' that needed to be done, from casting through to readings and then rehearsals. DLS moved around with the company when it came to performances. The subtitle of the play/book is: 'a love story with detective interruptions', and that is exactly right. DLS said openly that 'if there is to be but a ha'porth of detection to an intolerable deal of saccharine, let the occasion be the excuse'.

The novel has a framework of grand ritual with a large dose of demotic speech, as if Shakespeare's essential quality of contrasting the serious plot with the entertainment of the yokels has been extended almost to surreal lengths, and in that statement lies a difficulty. The extended working-class monologues were funny on the stage, of course, working in a way similar to the commentaries of Joseph by the side of the protagonists in *Wuthering Heights*. However, the issue of the nature of such working-class depictions is much more significant to a modern reader than to a 1930s' reader, who was becoming more familiar with 'the labouring classes' in the age of documentary. The novel really goes to town with characters such as Mr Puffett and Mrs Ruddle, together with Crutchley the gardener. DLS had a sound grasp of dialect, but tended to fuse two registers together, putting such things as authentic contractions of words juxtaposed with clear 'send-up' vocabulary. This was much the same as had to be done by, say, dramatist Arnold Wesker much later when he had to represent Norfolk proletarians.

Today, one hears comments when any local dialect is used, about such speech depictions being racist. But the fact is that in 1930s England, on the eve of war, DLS was one of many who risked criticism by putting her dialogues and monologues somewhere between realism and sentimentality. After all, in *Busman's Honeymoon* the aim was for an unashamed proportion of the 'saccharine' she wanted to be there. There is also the topic of social class. Inspector Kirk is placed between

the Wimseys and the Ruddles, and the fact that Lord Peter has the
rare ability to mix with anyone and be a social chameleon, needs a
counterbalance. Kirk has decided opinions on those above him, and
these come out when Sellon suggests that Wimsey may interfere with
the questioning of Miss Twitterton:

> They aint' compounding no felonies nor yet obstructing the
> law. All that's the matter is, he don't like hurtin' women and she
> don't like hurtin' him. But they won't either on 'em put out a
> finger to stop it, because that sort of thing ain't done.

There is a firm expression of the case for the defence here, when it
comes to the demotic of the village: without the accent and dialect there
is no humour. The stage has always required the Eliza Dolittles and
Touchstones in the woods. Without the convincing eternal qualities
there is no exceptionalism. DLS wanted to produce, in *Busman's
Honeymoon* in particular, a sense of the deeply rural, unchanging
nature of that village life beyond the metropolis. The theme was being
exploited at much the same time, with remarkable success, by Stella
Gibbons in *Cold Comfort Farm*.

Reading the various biographies of DLS, one would be forgiven for
thinking that, at the beginning of her career as a novelist, everything
ran smoothly and she had no real struggle. This is not the case. One
has to recall that there was plenty of time expended on planning and
changing lines of thought. Gollancz and the firm of Benn were at the
centre of the eventual success, and Victor Gollancz himself moved
very quickly to back and advance his authors. We know this from
other writers' accounts too. The Halifax novelist Phyllis Bentley was
another of the firm's new intakes in 1928. His first response to Bentley
was to ask her to cut 20,000 words from her first submission, 'The
Partnership'. But then, after a lengthy wait, the first manuscript was
kept in abeyance. Finally, after trying to submit her first work for a

prize, Gollancz concentrated on sales and promotion. Bentley never looked back. She became defined as a regional novelist of great ability and promise, with her critically acclaimed novel, *Inheritance*, being published in 1932.

Gollancz was equally supportive of DLS and of course, their anthologies did very well. The arrival of Wimsey led to a decade of unstoppable success and an expanding readership. Moreover, the novels were not the only fiction. She never wasted an idea, and as with most writers, whether she kept a notebook or not, her mind was capacious and when the kernel of a fictional idea formed, especially if friends were enthusiastic, it generally progressed into a completed work.

Gollancz served DLS well, and his actions in a number of potentially disruptive and annoying incidents were admirable, even down to the complaints of a reader called 'Cranston' who didn't like the fact that a crooked character in *The Nine Tailors* had his name. As Janet Hitchman puts it, Gollancz 'gave the man short shrift'. What strikes the modern reader most impressively about Gollancz is that he published the religious dramas; one might think that this was hardly a commercial move, but the best known, *The Man Born to be King*, has been in print in over twenty editions. Again, in Hitchman's words, Gollancz 'knew what he could sell'. He seems to have survived some rough rides in his business, including times when some of his writers wanted to leave him.

DLS's work was also, just before war broke out, difficult for the public to miss when it came to crime writing; in between the novels there were the short stories, and of course, the airwaves. In 1936 the *Gloucester Citizen* listed in their radio events 'Miss Dorothy L. Sayers on "Plotting a Detective Story" on the National Channel'. Only seven years earlier, the airwave revolution had begun, when *The Daily Telegraph* proclaimed: 'Wireless Music from across the Atlantic', and explained: 'On Friday and Saturday nights "listeners-in" throughout Great Britain had the opportunity of hearing musical programmes then being broadcast from Pittsburg, USA, over 3,500 miles away. This achievement opens up an interesting vista of future possibilities.' They were not wrong. DLS was to find that writing 'for the air' was to be a large part of her future career.

But first, attention must turn to another aspect of her work that was increasingly prominent. The work of Gollancz on short story anthologies has been described; what has not been stressed enough was her ongoing attachment to short fiction. If one talks economics, then of course, short story publication was always a source of income in between books, but now, in c.1940, she could take part in the discussions, promotions and assessments of short fiction in print and on the air.

Announced in the papers in June, 1926 was 'The June "*Pearson's Magazine*"' and a list was circulated which included *The Thrills of Motor Cycle Racing* by Alec Bennett, along with *Training Baby Racehorses* by Cavendish Hope and ... Dorothy L. Sayers a new detective story of Lord Peter Wimsey called *The Dragon's Head*. This was one of many media notices that remind us today that DLS was one of the short fiction writers in print across a wide spectrum, and she produced short stories throughout her writing life, right through to her contributions to the popular paperback format collections of the 1950s which were then on newsstands alongside the lifestyle and fashion magazines.

The short story as a twenty-minute read had come of age in an era when the number of commuters into London had greatly increased, creating a whole new readership of people who wanted a short and interesting piece of fiction for the journey into work. This was the same readership that had created a demand for books such as *Three Men in a Boat* and *The Diary of a Nobody* in the 1890s. The form became central in the context of the boom in creative writing that came along in the Edwardian years and later. When DLS was just getting started with the Wimsey books, the adverts for writing courses proliferated in the papers; the Women's Educational Union in 1922 noted (rather puzzlingly) that 'Every pupil should be taught to write a short story with a view to staging a playlet.'

The press and publishers saw the expanding market; a typical publication in this area, by Cecil Hunt, sums up the attitude: *Living by the Pen*. As one review put it, this was 'an excellent and essentially practical handbook for the aspiring author. No book quite like this has hitherto been available to the tyro in letters.'

Through those years of her busy freelance life, she did what all storytellers do: she went searching for a good plot. One such instance, showing a link between a published story and a possible source, is found in *A Writer's Notebook* by W. Somerset Maugham. This was published in 1949, and recalls a story probably going the rounds in literary circles. It concerns two men discussing a murder story in the papers. A man nearby listened (much as happens in *Unnatural Death* also) and then intervened with thoughts on motives. Maugham continues:

Then without warning, as though he were saying something quite ordinary, he said, 'I don't mind telling you that I committed a murder once.' He told them that he had done it just for fun and he described the thrill. Since there was no motive for it he knew he would never be discovered. 'Someone I'd never seen in my life,' he said. He finished his drink, got up ... and went out through the swing doors.

In 1952 DLS's story *The Man Who Knew How* appeared in *Argosy*. Here again she uses the 'overheard' device, changing it to one man reading, as a stranger talks about murder and, as in Maugham's report, the story opens with a situation in which a discussion leads to the stranger appearing to confess to killings he has committed. The events lead to the ironical conclusion of the stranger being a journalist who enjoys playing his little game of pretend killer to make train journeys interesting.

This illustrates the kind of transmutation from brief idea or influence, through to a finished story. When there is a burgeoning demand for interesting short stories, germs of ideas tend to float around and be picked up, altered for plot purposes, and used. Maugham himself knew all about that process; in the same book, he writes of 'the shilling shocker' and defines a story of a lower artistic order to what he sees as a short story, and his note is clear on DLS's notion of a worthwhile fiction: 'The hours race by. You have defeated time. And then you have the ingratitude to throw aside the book with a sneer and look down upon its author. It is graceless.' The 'short story' as both Maugham and DLS understood it by c.1935 was above the 'shocker,' but as is known from the Gollancz anthologies, the shocker had certain aspects in its appeal for DLS. This all makes it clear that she knew the spectrum of options in the short fiction market.

DLS arrived early on the scene when it came to being anthologised everywhere. As early as 1939 one of her stories, *The Dragon's Head*, was published in an anthology for schools published by the Oxford University Press. The story was a Wimsey one, not reprinted from the *Lord Peter Views the Body* collection. It uses her knowledge of books, and of course, the created volume has to seem convincingly interesting to the Wimsey who spends huge sums on ancient tomes and knows all about variorum printings. The significant point here is that the name Sayers stands beside W. Somerset Maugham, Frank O'Connor, Saki and John Galsworthy in the collection. In the biographical notes she still has 'Mrs Fleming' after her authorial title, but clearly her quality of writing is considered high enough to stand with these other names in a school anthology.

As I researched and discussed in my previous book, *The Women Writers' Revolution*, the interwar years in Britain were not simply the 'Bloomsbury Years'. In these years, together with the Mass Observation initiatives of the war years, the working classes were revealed as interesting and worthy subjects for creating writing, beyond their traditional nature of being one-dimensional servants or rural 'hodges'; the Great War and the industrial strife of the 1920s had provided the first great wave of change in this context. Much more was to come; a wave of documentary writing passed through British literature by the time totalitarianism was on the rise, and influential writers such as George Orwell made the phrase 'proletarian writing' part of the linguistic currency of the arts and literature. Detective fiction had its important place in all this, and as biographers of Agatha Christie have also shown, popular genres can offer far more than the stereotypes when it comes to British social life in this period. DLS might have had a snobbish tinge, but that comes from a sense of the necessary scholarship required for her specific variety of crime writing, and that fact alone explains the focus she puts on the world of scholars and aristocrats. A writer, when all said and done, writes about the microcosm he or she knows well, and imagines everything beyond that province of the experience. Readers accept the make-believe, and as she saw from her childhood melodramas, readers and listeners will enjoy the suspension of disbelief if the pretence is engrossing, whether this is in fun or in serious contemplation of something as extreme as a homicide.

In 1928, a dozen stories have titles which immediately suggest those *Pearson's* publications. Words such as 'adventure', 'farce' and 'affair', suggest the conventions of the Holmes stories in *The Strand*, but having said that, the majority of *Strand* stories and *Harmsworth Magazine* tales have that sensational tenor to the titles. There had been a clear divergence in the short fiction market during the Edwardian years; detective stories had found a home in their own sub-genre, but overall, the well-made literary story, as practised by Saki or Maugham for instance, was often a narrative with an oral feel; a yarn on a fragmentary episode in a life. The popular genre-stories fed the hunger of the new reading public. The more cynical critics had no time for popular fiction, in novels or tales: 'Nine-tenths of novel-writing is a waste of time because nine-tenths of novels are written for old ladies in Buxton or Cheltenham sunning themselves in the bow-windows of hotels with the circulating library's latest novel on their laps.' As one anonymous journalist wrote.

The Wimsey stories were in the tradition of the longer story, as had become entrenched in the solid journals produced by Harmsworth and Newnes. The challenge for DLS was to provide an enthralling plot, add Wimsey at his most brainy but chirpy, and give the story the aroma of the outlandish or challengingly different. Her reading of Sexton Blake had prepared her for all that. Crime writers tend to experiment along all the sub-genres of crime and law, and settle on what suits their disposition; Raymond Chandler, at the same time as DLS in her early phase, was discovering that the famous *Black Mask* detective magazine was where his home lay.

One only has to survey the range of publishers with an interest in short fiction to see that there were many possibilities for aspiring writers. The popular press carried adverts for courses and guidance on writing tuition. Max Pemberton a member, with Pearson, of the Crimes Club was a guiding force in promoting the London School of Journalism. He had himself started out writing short fiction and he wrote that he had 'a letter from the editor of the *Chamber's Journal* who accepted a story of five thousand words to my very great astonishment. He kept the story for two years and sent me eventually five guineas for it.' It was a precarious existence for most, but for DLS it was always 'bread and butter' earnings, as she had the right touch for the market and had found her niche.

The Detection Club was also going strong at this time, and she increasingly enjoyed commentary and explanation of the skills she had mastered. In one instance, she offers an image that will always help aspiring writers:

there is not only a trick but a 'craft' of writing mystery stories … It is almost as satisfying as working with one's hands. It is rather like laying a mosaic putting each piece apparently meaningless and detached – into its place, until one suddenly sees the thing as a consistent picture.

Much may be learned from some reflections on the two story collections *Lord Peter Views the Body* (1928) and *Hangman's Holiday* (1933). With the invention of her other detective, wine and spirits travelling-salesman Montague Egg, contrasts are useful. For a modern reader, much patience is required the lengthy Wimsey stories; some are very long indeed: 'The Undignified Melodrama of the Bone of Contention' would be a *roman* in France and a possible novella in Britain. The Egg stories are perhaps around 3–5,000 words and sharply focused on scene and people. With the Wimsey stories, for someone who reads primarily to enjoy Wimsey's antics and *bon mots*, the DLS approach of finding an unusual *modus operandi* or a rare and bizarre context will find some very extensive explanation and back-tracking of events.

The factor of pace in a long story is important when long explanations are needed; when a complex reversal in time reference is given (as in *The Nine Tailors* with the episode in France and the war) then a massive excess of detail and events will drag, particularly if Wimsey is not figuring in the backwards reference. If one reads an Egg story by the side of a Wimsey one, the contrasts highlight the advantages of the traditional shorter tale. With Egg, the limited range of setting and interaction has huge benefits. This is seen at its best in 'Sleuths on the Scent', which takes place entirely in a room in the Pig and Pewter. Here, the assembly of men (all suspects) are explained and defined by the place and by their words and appearance. The pay-off for the reader is the same as in the traditional, conservative *short* short story, in which a shock or 'turn' defines the closure.

The Wimsey stories highlight one outstanding element in the massive success of Wimsey generally: he needs to be in a story of a novel's breadth and scope. In *Gaudy Night*, his absence abroad intensifies the impact of his appearance, just as the audience for *Julius Caesar* or *Othello* enjoys the expectancy when the protagonists finally appear, after being spoken about. Wimsey also has to have the multiple scenes in which to have elbow-room for the wit, the digressions and the interplay with characters from all slices of society.

DLS's accustomed approach to crime fiction: think of an unusual murder or serious crime, create a complex human context, place Wimsey in the fury of it all, and then commence the muddle. From that muddle the reader will trace and share the very gradual clarification and the denouement. The one drawback is potentially in the explanation. This may be seen clearly in 'The Image in the Mirror', which depends for its fascination and complexity on a difficult explanation, attained through a mix of knowledge, from physiology to genealogy and some human interrogation. After thirty pages of intriguing mystery, one paragraph sets the reader's mind racing and offers some hope of sense and completion:

> Dissimilar twins and some kinds of similar twins may both be quite normal. But the kind of similar twins that result from the splitting of a single cell may come out as looking-glass twins. It depends on the line of fission in the original cell. You can do it artificially with tadpoles and a bit of horsehair.

Here, we are back in the world of Eustace and L.T. Meade. Science always offered DLS some of the most tempting plot devices and motives; in c.1930, in the age before mass television and other screen narratives, when the source of a mystery was identified, the problem for the writer was then to tie things up neatly and quickly. The old cliché of the murder mystery in which the suspects gather in a room, the detective arrives, with his head packed with cool reasoning, and points to the killer, define something of the patience (as well as the structure) involved in a crime narrative in which pace is not a primary factor.

Conversely, Montague Egg, in 'The Poisoned DOW 08', gives us this wisdom in the closure, when the police officer asks why Egg says 'I knew it was Craven the minute he came into the room': 'He called me "Sir" explained Mr Egg ... "Last time I called he addressed me as – young fellow – and told me that tradesmen must go round to the back door."'

As may be so often observed in literary biography, the background to all this is the nature of the professional writer's life. DLS, at the point of imminent world war, was about to have her career take a new turn – and her creativity meet a new challenge, but by that time she had established herself as one of the establishment's voices of literature. For this to happen her output had to keep pace with others in popular fiction, and she had to have a presence in the media; writing short stories had achieved that for her. The war was to prove exactly that kind of occasion for many, as one might see in the career of, for instance, J.B. Priestley. His postscript talks and essays reinforced his status as a writer whose opinions on the most trivial to the most global could be respected. He had fought in the Great War, and so he had the gravitas for broadcasting; this was, after all, the age of *The Brain's Trust* and the role of the BBC as a conduit for communication was as important as the ministries and their initiatives. Creative talents were sought and recruited; even the unreliable Dylan Thomas was hauled in to use his words for the war effort.

In the first year or so of the war, when the Blitz had done most of its worst destruction, DLS's mind was on matters above and beyond fictional detectives; but of course, novels of detection were excellent vehicles for the quasi-propagandist subjects of the 1940s such as the 'Real England' imagery and the determined exploitation of what has been called by Peter Parker 'Housman country'. The rural backwaters in the Wimsey novels were decidedly brilliant instances of the 'lost'

England which had been recently rediscovered through the folk-song collections of Cecil Sharp, the compositions of Ralph Vaughan-Williams and the Georgian Poets. By the mid-1930s, DLS's novels had themes and subjects that could be juxtaposed with such works as *Cold Comfort Farm*, *Keep the Aspidistra Flying* and *Decline and Fall*. DLS's deep affection for minute detail and wonderfully accurate material description stood impressively alongside more overtly documentary books. She had troubled to produce the kind of writing that Orwell described in his 1947 essay, 'Why I Write'. There, he gave as one of his reasons: 'aesthetic enthusiasm: perception of beauty in the external world, or on the other hand, in words and their right arrangement. Pleasure in the impact of one sound on another, in the firmness of good prose or the rhythm of a good story.'

Keeping to the sophisticated levels of voice, style and reference is the one directing factor that maintains the DLS difference when it comes to evaluating the crime writers who have had most impact on the genre.

Chapter 7

Dorothy The Dramatist and Creation

God was executed by people painfully like us, in a society
very similar to our own…
  – The Man Born to be King, D.L. Sayers

The DLS who was to assume the role of dramatist was now appearing, and building a circle of friends and contacts from the theatrical world. But this change of focus was also to bring confrontations and a certain level of stress in aesthetic differences, mainly in the world of broadcasting and the BBC. She would have found this account by theatre critic James Agate (who was not exactly her friend – as his reviews contained plot-spoilers when he discussed her novels):

A slight breeze with the BBC in connection with my broadcast in the Forces programme about the revival of Korda's Lady Hamilton.

BBC: 'Do you mind prefacing your talk with the statement that whereas you hold a high opinion of Nelson's seamanship you have a low one of his morals?'

J.A.: 'Yes, I mind very much.'

BBC: 'But don't you realise, Mr Agate, that you are talking not only to the soldiers but also to their mothers and wives who don't think that their sons and husbands should be told that women like Emma Hamilton exist?'

J.A: 'I don't care a damn what the mothers and wives of soldiers think.'

DLS was to have a similarly frustrating experience with her writing for radio, but first, in the early phase, and her work for Canterbury Cathedral performance, *The Zeal of Thy House,* she was to experience the highs and triumphs, the sheer artistic satisfaction, of writing something entirely knew, exercising talents in dramatic storytelling which she had always had.

The writing for the 'Canterbury Plays' series was to be a crucial transition in DLS's creative life, and it was a commission carrying very high esteem in the literary world. Her religious play on the architect William of Sens was following distinguished works, which included the first one Masefield's *The Coming of Christ*, in 1928, and also T.S. Eliot's *Murder in the Cathedral* (1935) and Charles Williams's *Thomas Cranmer of Canterbury* (1936). It was Williams who was largely responsible for the commission. Canterbury had taken the bold and exciting step of bringing back the old liturgical dramas; there were also occasional 'study drama' readings such as Tennyson's *Becket*, but this new initiative was to be a major step forward, using the Chapter House as the venue.

The standard biographies give the basic events: George Bell was the man responsible for the plays. He was Dean of Canterbury Cathedral at the time, and he was in many ways a strikingly remarkable man. He later became Bishop of Chichester, and before the Great War he had worked in some of the Leeds slums and also with the Board of Settlements; immediately after the war he was active in the World Council of Churches. His time at Canterbury covered the years 1925–29.

But for DLS's involvement, it was Margaret Babington, the Festival organiser, who contacted her about a possible submission; nobody could claim that DLS was a renowned dramatist or poet, such as Eliot and Masefield, and *Busman's Honeymoon* was not exactly a title on everyone's lips. DLS's response was to write, 'it is rather out of my line and there is also the serious question of whether I could possibly find the time'. However, Babington seems to have been determined to get her woman. The correspondence continued, and on DLS's part there was a degree of reticence and modesty: 'I fear ... that mine will be but a simple and unimpressive kind of play compared with the fine verses and elaborate mysticism of Eliot and Charles Williams.' The latter had in fact been well aware of the DLS oeuvre and had put in a word on her behalf. When the story of William of Sens flowered, and the dramatic and emotional potential became evident, the idea was about to develop into something substantial. It turned out that William had fallen and become severely maimed, and into the story came the notion of arrogance and hubris. The chronicler Gervase, writing about William, had stated that 'Either the vengeance of God or the envy of the Devil wreaked itself on him alone.'

Then followed the assistance of Laurence Irving, son of the great actor Sir Henry, and from that the professionals gathered, and there was music sorted out, and Harcourt Williams as a producer. It seemed that the name Williams was uncannily enmeshed in the dramatic work. Harcourt read the script of what was then a story entitled *The Zeal of Thy House*, and he liked it. Others liked it too, including Babington. It was now a going concern and Harcourt in the lead meant that there was someone with vast theatrical experience. He had worked with the famous Benson touring company, led by Frank Benson and his wife, who had put on Shakespeare for the recruits in the huge new army camps where the military training was taking place. Born in 1880, Harcourt made his debut on the London stage in 1900 and then appeared on the Irving tour of the United States; he served in the Friends' Ambulance Unit during the First World War, as he was a conscientious objector. This meant he avoided a stretch in gaol.

Just before the work with DLS, Harcourt had played Hamlet in the 1926 Barrymore production, and later was to direct at the Old Vic. He was considered something of an eccentric, but was 'a fanatical enthusiast for the theatre'. The team of Laurence Irving, Babington and Williams must have clicked and enjoyed the whole project; as Barbara Reynolds notes, 'Harcourt Williams was her guide and collaborator from the beginning' and she had found a friend.

Arguably the most important element in the writing here, for DLS at least, was the boost she must have had from the definite success of the production. The opening performance was on 12 June 1937 and DLS revelled in the occasion, with a special train for her close friends being put on from London. These included her new friends, along with Aunt Maud, and some of the Mutual Admiration Society. DLS had always had 'the theatre bug' but now she was thoroughly smitten with the magic of the boards and the glamour surrounding the acting profession.

Something else turned out to be very significant for her writing trajectory as Sayers the dramatist was born, and this emanated from the thinking behind the play. She had fastened on a relationship between the God she had always prayed to and reflected upon, and her own profession. The notion of creativity burgeoned and her intellect set to work on the theme, as is clear from these words of the Archangel: 'For every work of creation is threefold, an Earthly trinity to match the heavenly.'

DLS wrote to her friend D. Rowe: 'nothing can be more essentially dramatic than Catholic doctrine; but it is all lost if one surrounds it with a vague cloud of let-us-all-feel-good-and-loving-and-God-won't–mind-anything-much'. In the unhappy tone of that string of hyphenated words there lies a tough discontentment. This was to find a place in her leap of theorising and didacticism that was to become her book *The Mind of the Maker*, which saw print in 1941.

First, she was to write another play for Canterbury (*The Devil to Pay*) and then her most ambitious dramatic work. In *The Mind of the Maker*, she works out and spells out the thinking in the Archangel speech. In that play she had persuaded herself that every created work had a three-strand nature, a structure which was definable. In the 1994 edition, the series editor Susan Howatch points out that DLS was offered a Lambeth doctorate in divinity by Archbishop William Temple, but refused it. Howatch gave a well reasoned list of factors which, she thought, supported the need for the book to still be in print. Mainly, she argued, the book is:

> an attempt to describe living truths ... what Sayers has to say about creative artists is of interest to all those who seek to explore the concept of God as Creator ...many people who write about creation have an inadequate understanding of the creative process not only in terms of science but in terms of the arts.

The book at first brings out a less pleasant and likeable element in DLS's nature. Her preface comes from her criticism of the results of education, and she sees the poor attainments of people around her as a block to the understanding of religion and spirituality. She writes in this testy prelude to the argument: 'What is of great and disastrous importance is the proved inability of supposedly educated persons to read.' This might seem like a snipe at the ordinary reader from some conservative bias, but in fact, it matters because poor reading and understanding inhibits the understanding of logical argument, and the ability to distinguish fact from opinion.

The preface could be your most aggressive and frustrated headmistress, with statements such as 'The education that we have so far succeeded in giving to the bulk of our citizens has produced a generation of mental slatterns.' But then she moves to the crux of the book's argument. It is a development of the Archangel's important speech at Canterbury, and here she puts it with care:

> The Christian affirmation is ... that the Trinitarian structure which can be shown to exist in the mind of man and in all his works is, in fact, the integral structure of the universe, and corresponds, not by pictorial imagery but by a necessary uniformity of substance with the nature of God, in Whom all that is exists.

Now, this is a huge leap of logic, but what DLS does is then develop her thesis through the book with a tight logic kept within the frame of reference in that statement. Since 1941 there have been several theories of what creativity in homo sapiens is or may be, but it is difficult to dismiss her argument – whatever one thinks of the logical framework. What is important, and useful, in understanding DLS and her explication of the Trinity, is to consider the 1941 context. In that same year, Penguin Books published *The Gospel for Tomorrow* by the Bishop of Truro, J.W. Hunkin. Like DLS he had lived in the 'lower depths', and among working people; he was a chaplain in the Great War, working at Gallipoli. His book looks at the creeds, and at the importance of the Trinity too. The key through his line of thought is from St Paul in Ephesians: 'Through Christ we have access by one Spirit unto the Father.' This is backed up with a statement close to the creativity DLS sees. It comes from theologian Benjamin Whichcote: 'for God is more in the mind of man than in any part of this world besides'.

DLS's design on which to build her argument on creativity, is in that Canterbury speech:

For every work of creation is threefold, an
Earthly trinity to match the heavenly.
First: there is the Creative Idea; passionless,
timeless, beholding the whole work complete
at once, the end in the beginning; and this
Creative Energy, begotten of that Idea, working in
time from beginning to end, with sweat and passion,
being incarnate in the bonds of matter; and
this is the image of the Word.
Third, there is the Creative Power, the meaning
of the work and its responses in the lively soul...

The sequence 'Creative Idea Creative Energy Creative Power' is, of
course, open to the challenge of being arbitrary. Why not five or even
ten stages in the process? But DLS isolates these from the creative
process she knows, and gives examples to show the universality of the
thinking. In plain everyday language, if one applies this to a poem, for
instance, it entails:

The theme through to its closure. This poem will be about...
The application of brain to form one's abilities strive to create
something envisaged without form, existing only in abstraction.
The study and response of the product does the poem speak as
planned?

The context of this remarkable essay in creativity and theology needs
some explanation. *The Mind of the Maker* is in fact the first volume
in a projected series called 'Bridgeheads'. In DLS's mind, the origins
of this concept were as large-scale as one could imagine. She wrote to
the Guild of Catholic Writers about the idea, using phrases such as
'national reconstruction' and 'creative spirit'. This was at the height

of the Battle of Britain and the Blitz, and there was dark – a sense of foreboding beneath the surface spirit of indomitable resolution. The question of how or what could writers and artists contribute to the war effort was a burning issue. A presiding spirit of DLS's thinking was a seminal essay written by T.S. Eliot, *The Idea of a Christian Society*. DLS was becoming a prominent figure after the Canterbury writing, and a number of people recognised the potential she had to make a definite contribution to the mood of the times, and to a sense of more optimistic attitudes being promulgated. She had a confirmed status in literature and was widely known. She could almost have said the same as Laurence Sterne's Tristram Shandy: 'I have the greatest honours paid me & most civilities shown me, that were ever known, from the Great & am engaged already to ten noblemen and men of fashion to dine...'

In the early days of the war, all kinds of national plans and projects were beginning to form, and DLS, like so many other writers, was looking for a sideways move from crime writing. She was attracted to writing essays which would make some sort of contribution to the social issues emerging from an emergency mindset. It is clear from her last few Wimsey novels that her mind is very much settled on a contribution to what might be called the 'condition of England question', which was a phrase applied by historians to the 1840s. The moral values reflected and expressed in *Busman's Honeymoon* for instance, touch on the kind of everyday Christian behaviour regarding transgression; Mrs Ruddle worries over her petty theft of a little paraffin for instance. Now, Eliot's essays were having an influence on her thinking.

The Bridgeheads series had high ideals: 'We aim at the Resurrection of Faith, the Revival of Learning and the re-integration of society.' She was increasingly convinced that there was in people a 'creative power' which constitutes their real claim to humanity. She convinced herself that her contribution to Bridgeheads was about 'creative mind'. Her letters show that she was excited by theology; as the child of a country vicar, she had absorbed everything in the Christian life and ritual that could be considered food for thought in such an intense intellectual life. DLS sucked in everything in the range of mental stimuli and let it churn until it was mature; her ideas for novels often started with a glint of insight into the potential of a small action or an acute emotion which had the kernel of a narrative.

Bridgeheads never happened, but *The Mind of the Maker* did. It was to be the first in the series, but remained as a solid text, linking aspects of theology to notions of what creativity was, and why it was important. Part of the significance of this rare exercise in cross-disciplinary thinking and writing, DLS takes the option of writing as a teacher teaches, but with a sense of discovering for herself, as if the logic she imposes will work out if she really believes in the foundation of her thought. Theologians were impressed, but opinions from literary theorists are bound to be divided today, after the revolutions brought about by a series of new waves in the philosophy of creativity. However, the book fits comfortably with the thinking about mankind and spirituality in her time. Her friend C.S. Lewis, for instance, wrote: 'God had no need to create the world, but once created he has allowed himself to be affected by us. He invites us to cooperate with him in the achievement of his purpose.' Also, part of Lewis's interest in the importance of myth runs parallel to the creativity argument: 'Man is a poetical animal and touches nothing which he does not adorn.' Lewis's well-known work on what he calls 'joy' is relevant to the idea of what creativity is: 'We want something else which can hardly be put into words to be united with the beauty we see, to pass into it, to receive it into ourselves, to bathe in it, to become part of it.'

Naturally, when developing her thoughts on creativity, she uses creative writing to illustrate the thought. By the side of such a tome as Arthur Koestler's *The Act of Creation* (1964), *The Mind of the Maker* comes across as a unilinear, tight argument. This is her one concentrated, focused explanation of her art and craft. Throughout the novels, the comments on 'being a writer' reappear. In *The Nine Tailors*, for instance, there is this, from Hilary:

'Yes ... You begin to imagine how it all happened, and gradually it gets to feel more like something you've made up.'

'H'm' said Wimsey, 'If that's the way your mind works, you'll be a writer one day.'

'Do you think so? How funny! That's what I want to be. But why?'

'Because you have creative imagination, which works outwards, till finally you will be able to stand outside your own experience and see it is something you have made, existing independently of yourself.'

This is akin to a number of concepts in aesthetics. It explains the heuristic approach to learning, in which a discovery is made which reflects back and creates something new. It also supports the notion of phenomenology: the artist or even the 'user' in media studies, at some point stands 'outside' the experience of the mind working, and so the nature of creation is open to some degree of understanding.

DLS convinced herself that the parallel between theological reasoning about the nature of belief and of how God works or is understood, and aesthetic thought, is a contrast worth pursuing. She sees the nature of the phenomenological as being central here, although she does not use that term. She uses a quote from G.K. Chesterton to make the point:

I mean that I really did see myself, and my real self, committing the murders ... I mean that I thought and thought about how a man might come to be like that, until I realised that I really was like that, in everything except final consent to the action.

The link between God and earthly, human creation is made in this way: 'The writer, in writing his book on paper, is expressing the freedom of his own nature in accordance with the law of his being; and we argue from this that material creation expresses the nature of the Divine Imagination.' The trilogy of idea-energy-creative power, when applied to the composition of a book is something that DLS knew inside-out. But the weight she puts on the 'energy' is really the heart of the thinking in the application to people: 'It is the energy that is the creator in the sense in which the common man understands the word, because it brings about an expression in temporal form of the eternal and immutable idea.' The writing of the book and the expression in material form is what lies behind this.

The autonomy of the story is familiar to any novelist, even with the modern notions of 'plotter' and 'pantster' in mind, which explain those who meticulously plot their story out before beginning to write, and those who follow the lead of their instinctive storytelling. A writer might say, 'the character told me why she was going to London that day'. And so the implication is that the writer follows a phase in the business of creation that is leading the way, and she is merely a typist. But that condition of work is arguably best described as a 'trance', in that the writer follows inner thought, and the words find expression to her satisfaction. Questions then arise about the difficulties of choosing three levels of activity rather than five or even ten. Yet, however a logician might follow that route in an argument, the tendency for that basic old formula of beginning–middle–end keeps returning to discussion and often remains a very helpful attitude in creative writing classes. The concept of 'triune' structure kept on attracting DLS as a winning formula, but of course there is far more to creativity than the old recycled formula.

There is also the question of the 'pantster' approach, which means being led by the story, or, in DLS's words, seeing that the final stage of a story is somehow developed on a 'back-burner', with the narrative taking shape as the author writes; they don't know where the story is going. In DLS's final stage much of this hinges on the teleological nature of a narrative: something in the writer and the reader *looks to the end*; this may be seen in everyday life, when readers early on in a whodunit, began to anticipate the closure (figuring out the villain of course). In a detective mystery, a tiny part of the brain surely begins to think towards a resolution, a synthesis, something that will restore mental, conceptual order as well as reflection of a desired social order. The unpredictability persists as a factor. Biographer Hal Jenson reminded readers of an interesting case here, regarding Virginia Woolf, who:

> invented a contemporary author Mary Carmichael – whose necessarily imperfect novel contained a gem of truth in the little phrase 'Chloe liked Olivia'. From such small, unimpeded steps, Woolf suggested, the female writers of the next 100 years would be able to develop incandescent voices of their own, wherever they might lead.

To build on the notion of an unplanned narrative which is instinct with the creative energy, it has to be noted that there is nothing new in that. Back in 1759, in Sterne's fictional exploration of what constitutes a narrative, we have this:

> Could a historiographer drive on his history, as a muleteer drives on his mule – straightforward … from Rome all the way to Loretto, without ever once turning his head aside either to the right hand or to the left he might venture to foretell you to an hour when he should get to his journey's end, but the thing is, morally speaking, impossible; for if he is a man of the least spirit, he will have fifty deviations from a straight line to make with this or that party as he goes along, which he can no ways avoid.

In other words, as DLS puts it, 'The artist's knowledge of his own creative nature is unknown.'

There then has to be a leap into theology, because the creativity of people and words is most familiar to a professional novelist who has struggled through all stages of apprenticeship through to confirmed success. The link to a theological proposition is put well here: 'This threefoldness in the reader's mind corresponds to the threefoldness of the work ... and that again to the threefoldness in the mind of the writer. It is bound to be so because that is the structure of the creative mind.' 'Jumping across to Trinitarian doctrine,' she says, 'is what we are driving at.' She moves to assert that the structure in the writing work is 'the structure of God's mind'.

Some of this relates to her friend Charles Williams's ideas of ideal aesthetic forms, and that in turn shares some characteristics with nineteenth-century German Idealism. Bringing this down to earth, the proposition is that we are able to see and understand an ideal of beauty in form because it reflects an ideal beauty within God's universe. For Williams, one outstanding instance of this was when Dante the Florentine poet saw young Beatrice, who would become his definition of perfection in the canon of divine creation. In his poems composing *La Vita Nuova* he attempts to described and reason on this perception.

Whatever one's view of this line of thought, unfortunately, as the reasoning progresses, DLS has to include in her material some more generalisations based on little more than observation. A typical assertion is: 'It is because, behind the restrictions of the moral code, we instinctively recognise the greater validity of the law of nature.' One may see in statements such as this the source of her insecurities. She even made statements that undermine her own achievement, writing to her old friend Father Kelly that 'People won't understand it, and will think it silly or blasphemous.'

One open-minded conclusion surely has to be that the book is a success in terms of opening up many questions about creativity which apply across the spectrum, to far more than writing; the argument reveals some fascinating links to theological propositions, and does offer an interpretation of an appealing dimension of the concept of the Trinity. If one presses the demands of logic, then it is an easy matter to see the book as another instance of Procrustes' bed: forcing a belief into a framework, no matter what hurdles stand in the way of the cerebral efforts the exercise entails.

This is the kind of extended essay that makes a thesis, inviting the antithesis; yet given the idea of the Bridgeheads series, there is a great deal to admire and to take away for further thought here. Barbara Reynolds quoted some supporting views from professionals, such as 'I think this is the way theology should be written' came from the Rev. V.A. Demant. What should be mentioned here is a wider application; if the ideas and propositions are considered in the context of c.1940, then what comes to mind is the reaction against mechanisation and mass industrialisation which had fired the Arts and Crafts movement, and then been a main focus in a number of writers and artists such as George Sturt and Eric Gill, along with followers of John Ruskin and to a certain extent, of D.H. Lawrence also.

Turning to the other large-scale project of 1941 and after, the BBC was now ready to call for DLS's help. It was perceived, within the same vision as the planned Bridgeheads, that producing religious drama over the airwaves would be a productive educational manoeuvre. A first glance at such thinking brings to mind Soviet Agitprop or Bertolt Brecht's concept of drama that would entertain and educate with a left-wing direction (his *Lehrerszenen*). This project was to lead to *The Man Born to be King*, a massive success telling the life of Christ to the eager listeners, chiefly to the children's programmes initially aired from Bristol. The whole enterprise began with a letter to DLS from Dr James Welch, Director of Religious Broadcasting, who agreed with the comments and strictures expressed by DLS and the focus shifted to the managers of the Children's Hour Department, and what followed was a gradual slide into fiery disagreement. DLS when roused was a fearsome opponent, and she stood by her beliefs and principles.

Her reputation had been confirmed and raised after the work for Canterbury and now she warmed to the suggestion, agreeing to write a number of short scenes for a set deadline. As the project moved forward, the central bone of contention emerged: the question of autonomy, and the preservation of the script as written by DLS. There was a long negotiation period, in which the Central Religious Advisory Committee had to inspect and approve each of the short plays in the planned cycle; on top of that there was a confrontation with a particular BBC producer, May Jenkin, who seemed to have no notion of an author's right to have control of her script; Dr Welch did his best to be peacemaker after DLS had made it clear that her role as the writer was to sit in her study and write, and she spelled out the conditions of her work with the BBC in no uncertain terms: 'What goes into the play, and the language in which it is written is the author's business. If the management don't like it, they reject the play and there is an end of the contract.'

Never was the gap between a creative writer and a manager more visible. One might add that also never was there more of a misunderstanding about the nature of a successful writer by someone who should have stopped to think about how their two professional attitudes stood opposed.

The Man Born to be King went through twelve printings between 1943 and 1947, and the editions had ample material about the writing and planning of the play. DLS took the opportunity to explain most of the problems and responses involved. Her principal reason for the project is expressed cogently: 'I am a writer and I know my trade; and I say that this story is a very great story indeed, and deserves to be taken seriously. I say further ... that in these days it is seldom taken seriously. It is often taken, and treated with a ginger solemnity; but that is what honest writers call frivolous treatment.' She and the BBC were, after all, taking the foundation narrative of the New Testament and of the gospels and wrenching it out of the church space and the schoolroom, into a mass media context. Material shows just how much the story of Christ's life on earth was in need of being told in a totally different way. As a scrap of autobiography, I can relate that in my own religious knowledge classes in a secondary modern school c.1959, I was taught Bible stories by a man wielding a big stick who then tested us by rote and a certain degree of fear. DLS was well aware of other settings in which this great story was normally told: 'an honest writer would be ashamed to treat a nursery tale as you have treated the greatest drama in history'.

The oppositions to the dramas were, ironically and with a delicious humour, thanked in this introduction: 'I render my sincere thanks to the Central Religious Advisory Committee, standing so gallantly to their guns in the Battle of the Scripts.' The Lord's Day Observance Society was also thanked for their constructive opposition.

What did she achieve in this cycle of plays? Through mixed responses and stubborn resistance to innovation in creative approaches to the Bible, she achieved some truly impressive feats of spare, powerful storytelling for children, and also for those whose general Biblical knowledge was limited, for whatever circumstances. For working people, over the previous century and more, the education on Biblical themes had been assertively present, but it had been effected by parrot-learning in many instances; the Victorian and Edwardian religious crusades, the teaching of religion filtering into the London settlements and the Sunday School classes had all played their part; there had been cheap tracts as well, and no end of speakers on Christian topics in a society that relished parades, talks and gatherings, but had the basic Christian story actually had an impact? DLS's giveaway statements in the preface to *The Mind of the Maker* shows her reservations about general knowledge as acquired through the basic workings of reading. In between her words is the determined attitude of a leader of a crusade. Now, in her plays on the life of Christ, she had the chance to find the right words to appeal to the 'common people', as the historian G.D.H Cole (fellow mystery writer also) had put it.

She had written working-class characters extensively in the Wimsey novels; now here she was, writing for children, and perhaps writing for a great number of children who had left school very young or missed school almost completely. Such was the power of the radio narrative. My own maternal grandmother, daughter of a miner in South Leeds, left school at the age of 14 to work in service. I believe that she probably never read a book at all, and she never referred to the Bible; she was a product of an oral culture, knowing songs and tales from work and play, stories passed down from her forebears, who were mostly farm workers. Listening to the radio telling them about Jesus Christ's life and death must have been several thousand similar children.

Media responses tell us a lot about the responses that the press wanted, but how accurate were they? One mistrusts the headline, 'Voice of Christ on BBC', from the *Aberdeen Journal* in December 1941. It went on, 'Openly risking criticism by religious bodies and possible offence to church listeners, the BBC is, with the permission of the Lord Chamberlain, to present an impersonation of Jesus in twelve radio plays.' In 1938, years before the plays, DLS had written a religious tract which, according to the same paper, 'would make some devout people gasp'. The general tenor of the piece is that DLS decried the weight of 'dull dogma' in church, and the report states that her aim was to enliven the topic: 'It is the tale of a time when God was the underdog, and got beaten when he submitted to the conditions he had laid down, and became a man like the men he had made...'

In the summer of 1938, DLS gave a talk to people who had special interests in drama; this was given at Tewkesbury Town Hall, and, in the topics, she covered most factors related to the BBC plays which were soon to be written. She spoke forcefully and entertainingly:

'Other plays were written because the author thought it would be terribly nice to have a pageant at Diddlington-on-Mud and drag in a bit of ecclesiastical history', adding: 'To get hold of the people one did not bother about the parson and religion, but they should give people a good play in which there was something to argue about and thus their interest would be started.' The audience must have been stirred to think and question; it was a talk to shake things up in the provinces. She lamented attempts to write a play to 'fit a doctrine', and said that 'it was ridiculous that religion should be put in one box and all things in another ... Religion ought to be in everything ones does.'

Her thinking on religious drama was obviously brewing in her mind, and the drama to come was clearly simmering in her imagination. It is useful at this point to branch out into a wider view. In her book *The Lion and the Waste Land*, Janice Brown looks at the work of Eliot, Sayers and Lewis with regard to redemption, and leaves no doubt in the reader's mind that the historical context of their writings was one in which we might identify a Golden Age of Christian literature, something entirely apposite as well as ironic in the case of DLS. The point here, however, is to reflect on the years between c.1940 when DLS was writing her religious plays, and the 1950s, as in those years there was a sense of the 'reconstruction' that had been a keyword in the concept of the Bridgehead series. It is not too far-reaching to argue that from the shadow of the Blitz and the widespread fear of a challenge to the very survival of Britain in the face of the totalitarian threat, there was an emergent Christian literature, from apologetics to such efforts as DLS's creative had far-sighted contributions, to talks and to radio.

There was a massive and determined string of production in these years, from all kinds of ephemera such as leaflets, tracts and fragments of autobiography, through to serious work by the likes of C.S. Lewis and Charles Williams. There was a foundation for much of this in the work of T.S. Eliot, and in an interview on the C.S. Lewis website, she spoke about her book, and there she spoke of the 'Golden Age' which was coined by Adrian Hastings. Brown insists that in spite of their basis in apologetics the real virtue of both Lewis and Sayers were in the creative presentation of the nature of Christianity and belief. The heart of the thinking in the phrase 'fearsome redemption', however, is moving closer to what lies inside DLS and her aims. Brown expresses her recognition of the 'bleakness' at the core in their work, and Brown summarises the situation like this:

> An erudite poet and literary critic found himself patrolling the dark streets and piecing together images of fire and redemption, C.S. Lewis, Dorothy L. Sayers and T.S. Eliot became something they had not been before the war: bearers of a terrible, yet triumphant message that people could not expect to be spared from pain and suffering, but they would be redeemed through pain and suffering.

The situation was dire, and all the resources of the British cultural base were gathered for action; across in Europe, nations had fallen so easily to the Nazi assaults; the narrow Channel was all that separated Britain and the enemy. There was going to be a dire and dogged struggle to stay alive, and people watched London being destroyed every day during a long period of fearsome attacks. The leaders and intellectuals looked to the threat and asked what they were fighting to save. What actually was British civilisation? It had been a nation with a vast empire, and the Anglo-Boer War had shown convincingly that British armies could meet their match. However, the expansion of the German navy through the late-nineteenth century presented a tough challenge to British naval supremacy. Even worse, the wars with the Boers and then with the German and Austro-Hungarian empires had shown how feeble, undersized and unfit our armies were. The Industrial Revolution had also played its part in weakening both body and mind, some argued. With all this pressing for attention as recruitment began and Home Guard assemblies prepared for possible Nazi invasion from the skies, the thinkers and writers made their contribution. The basis is simply expressed: there was a war of such dimensions that our civilisation could end very soon. What is that civilisation, and what are we saving?

There was no doubt that many saw the way to remedy many of the shortcomings was through education, and through religious belief. Hundreds of writers and speakers perceived that there was guidance needed, that mentors could advise, inform and guide. DLS's radio plays were an important part of this quiet revolution, and yes, Janice Brown's thesis was an important element in these matters. There was also the influence of T.S. Eliot, in his play 'for voices' which was published in 1922 as *The Waste Land*, and was formed and edited with the help of Ezra Pound. Here, through a series of bold and fragmentary scenes from imagination and from life itself came a challenging narrative which had at the heart a cluster of images all concerned with spiritual meanness and deprivation. Nothing direct was said; that was for the satirist or the political and social commentators or the speakers at Hyde Park Corner; but at least for adherents of Bloomsbury and readers of the quality newspapers or literary journals, the content was clear: the dreamlike nature of life, so divorced from the network of actions and beliefs in the Christian life, were denuded and eclipsed. Metaphors of drought and sterility reinforced the shreds of poetic description, all creating this 'fallen world' which matches in some respects, Eliot suggested, with the *Inferno* or *Purgatorio* of Dante's great poem *La Divina Commedia*.

After this, there was Eliot's period as a social critic and thinker, and the content of his writing on Christian society, in 1940, had an influence on DLS. His affirmation that he thought of a society of 'ordinary men' rather than 'saints' would have been sound to her mind. His negativity was of course, realist, and this came powerfully

in his words, 'the Kingdom of Christ on earth will never be realised
... the result will always be a sordid travesty of what human society
should be.' Yet he wanted a community, a togetherness, and some
of the well planted factors in DLS's villages in the fiction had been
sure and stable in terms of a morality which stemmed back to Saxon
settlements, one could argue. In other words, there were rooted
traditions and networks of value that she would have seen as having
counterparts or instances in the Christian society Eliot described.
There was also the issue of 'those who have abandoned the world',
and here the social becomes the literary in the Wimsey novels, with
a confident sense that although the metropolis might suggest amoral
abandon, there is always the world of the parish church, the afternoon
tea on the lawn and the village fairs to remind one of stability and
resistance to change of any kind.

George Orwell made his usual strong and clever contribution to
this. In his essay 'England, Your England', he begins with: 'As I write,
highly civilized human beings are flying overhead, trying to kill me',
but in his second paragraph he has a comment that would have caused
tremors in the hearts of some readers when he says of national loyalty:
'In certain circumstances it can break down ... but as a positive force
there is nothing to set beside it. Hitler and Mussolini rose to power
in their own countries very largely because they could grasp this fact
and their opponents could not.'

Moreover, in terms of DLS's life and circle of friends, there was
the moral framework and how this linked with so much in the religious
writings about the true Christian life. Her friend C.S. Lewis had
written reams of advice for ordinary people, bringing together life
experience and intellectual analysis. Yet still there was another strand
in the potential work which could be done as part of a 'reconstruction'.
This poured out in the tracts and leaflets. Topics such as friendship,
adulthood, sexuality, marriage and worship (to take a random sample)
were available in print from a number of sources. The rebuilding after

the trial of war was to be as much about citizenship, family values and the work of the vicar as about anything abstract that might be discussed after a reading from the gospels.

A sample will suffice to show that DLS's talks and broadcasts were happening in this Golden Age of Christian writing. The *Epworth Press*, for instance, printed *Christian Courtship* by Charles J. Clarke. Some of the best advice for a person wishing to 'court' another was: 'Choose a Christian'. Then there was the Alliance of Honour. One of their typical publications was Dr Herbert Gray's 'Are Sex Relations without Marriage Wrong?' And a fold-out leaflet from the United Society for Christian Literature distinguished between 'love' and 'self-love'. In other words, there was far more to worry about, many at the time thought as war accelerated, than the inability to read properly (as irritated DLS).

There was little change in some ways over fifteen years after the 1941 plays. There was always opposition of course, and DLS must have had a good idea of how some of the thinking which opposed her views tended to work. One instance we know of was in poet Stevie Smith, who wrote a great deal about religious belief, and at one time, as her biographers Jack Barbara and William McBrien wrote, 'The pamphlets of the Catholic Truth Society afforded Stevie her best evidence of the cruelty in Christianity, especially its "hideous" teaching about hell.' When faced with an argument that 'hell is what God's love becomes to those who reject it', which was stated at one time by DLS, could never wash with Stevie Smith. The difference between Smith (who always, she said, waivered in belief) and DLS reveals the kind of readers that were assumed to be lining up as part of the 'reconstruction' of values and Christian education.

In the end, any attempt to use drama or myth, and certainly poetry, to play a part in a more general crusade to promote a national communal sense of fulfilled acceptance, will always fail, in a similar way to the kind of failure that Eliot envisaged. Still, the new adventure, into a different kind of 'Golden Age' of writing brought out another side of DLS, and she revelled in the role of mentor as well as of storyteller to the children or partially educated adult. Surely, one has to conclude, the strength and impact of the parable, or the literary allegory, will always pack a punch, and the reception given to *The Man Born to be King* asserts that there was a massive audience waiting for that kind of presentation of one of the oldest stories in the whole of Christendom – and that was a territory under extreme existential threat as DLS sat down to write.

Looking at the events surrounding the 'Golden Age' of Christian writing, as some called it, what stands out is how much there was in reserve in DLS's fertile and restless mind; in becoming a religious dramatist, she could see an extension of the novelist and of the talents known to members of the Mutual Admiration Society, but what she saw when she looked at her achievements as a speaker and broadcaster must have been a staggering revelation. My own feeling here is that there was an almost bottomless well of stored strong opinion, all enriched and fed by the range of her experiences as she had given herself to life at the core, much as Joseph Conrad expressed it in his epigraphy to *Lord Jim*: 'In the destructive element immerse.' She had been such a chameleon, working in advertising and writing novels at the same time, then going from a private, self-contained scholarly discipline to a classroom and the literary life of the aspiring arty hostess in London. This all enriched her palate, as it were, as she set out her abilities to create Wimsey and the rest.

Now here she was, no less a person than the writer who was offered an honorary doctorate, and whose works stood alongside intellectuals within the church; all her life, plunging into the waves of extreme confidence had perhaps never been easy, but it had been adventurous, and had rewarded her with learning experiences which played a major part in making both Lord Peter Wimsey as real to many as Sherlock Holmes, and also made her a household name. In some ways, she compares with Agatha Christie in that she 'bestrode the world like a Colossus', regarding that world of her principal profession, as Christie had done. But DLS moved laterally, and did so quite often. There had to be both challenges and triumphs for her.

Chapter 8

A Noble Note

Some work of noble note, may yet be done
Not unbecoming men that strove with Gods.
- Alfred Tennyson

From the middle of the Second World War to her death in December 1957, DLS was never at rest, never at leisure. Her mind had to have a project and had to be restless with enquiry and a search for resolutions as well as invitations. Moreover, before there was any space between writing projects that might have worked out (such as Bridgeheads) the whole Christian world appeared to want some of her time. Between 1939 and late 1943 it became clear to her that, as she was now in possession of a high reputation as a religious writer, there was an assumption that she could be the populist theologian that so many Christian groups in society wanted. One might apply the word 'faction' here, as there were so many disagreements and differing philosophical positions. The string of requests to speak or write began to intensify when her help was needed to work in the establishment of what became the Guild of Catholic Writers. This was the start of numerous calls to her for time, advice and wisdom.

Some of the appeals gave her the opportunity to speak about, and explain the creativity at the core of, *The Mind of the Maker*, but there were very many other Christian concepts that people thought she could clarify and define. The Guild was functioning beside the Church Social Action Group, and the secretary of that organisation became a friend: Father Patrick McLaughlin. She made the mistake of expressing strong opinions on topics that invited further development, and more than that, opportunities in the media to expand and establish beneficial influence. She soon began to feel the strain. At one point she tried to stress that she was cutting down on religious speaking and writing, saying, 'I spend half my time and a lot of stamps telling people that I have not been giving them a fancy doctrine of my own.'

The already established set of arguments she had propagated about creation in the Trinity and throughout mankind began to hook into another dominating theme across the outlets for debate: work. It appeared to be logical and morally right to DLS that what had been theorised about the nature of work was important. This was that it should be an element in humanity's basic nature rather than as a boxed-in element functioning in one of Henry Ford's division of labour production lines. She saw a fallacy in the view that work was only defined by money-making activity.

A neat way to understand this debate, and how far back the opinions went, is to consider the famous paintings by Ford Madox Brown called *Work*. Produced between 1852 and 1865, the two paintings show muscular workmen in the street, grafting hard in construction, while various social groups look on: some appear to be the leisured class and others are perhaps unemployed; the set on contrasts suggest two strong oppositions, in a work created at the time when various kinds of laborious work were repetitive, exhausting, done in very long working hours, and anything but pleasant or fulfilling. One of the observers is Thomas Carlyle, a writer with a habit of stirring up both the conscience and the humanitarian instincts of the middle-class Victorians. In short, work, for Ford, has to be admirable and for far more than pounds sterling.

There followed from all this interchange of ideas an important event for DLS: a conference at Malvern College in January 1941, with Archbishop Temple supervising. DLS was to be one of the speakers there, and there were two key questions: was the church fighting in the midst of a social breakdown? Then: has the church been too located in moral pronouncements and concerns, rather than in moving closer to the actual economic and sociological issues of the age? Her speech was a notable success, and naturally, this brought more and more potential openings for her to speak and write more on her pet themes. At the centre of her reasoning was her problems with the excess of moral comment in the church's image. She put this succinctly: 'The church is uncommonly vocal about the subject of bedrooms and so singularly silent on the subject of board-rooms.'

Time and time again she saw that many of the flaws and shortcomings in the common appreciation and talk about Christianity stemmed from limitations in basic education. A simple distinction such as the difference between fact and opinion, together with flaws in logical expression, were topics that she saw as leading to dissension. Obviously, as her letters show, to be something of a celebrity in the field of Christian apologetics was hardly what her career plan had made as an ultimate goal of all the hard work at the desk and on the platform.

In addition to DLS and T.S. Eliot, the Malvern Conference had an impressive gathering of theologians. With the 2017 Malvern Conference on her mind, writer Barbara Ridpath explained the significance of the event by listing the topics and relating them to today's issues. As well as DLS's area of the nature of work, she included: the link between the economic activity of man and 'the good life'; political freedom and failing economics; the healthy balance of town and country; respect for the earth; and the sin of man is to put himself at the centre where God ought to be.'

DLS, in a very short space of time, had moved from a crime writer, to turning her hand to Christian drama, and on to become the peer of learned theologians and experts in Christian thought, busy with the most pressing contemporary issues in that world which had a war for survival to fight. She was certainly to be relied upon to deliver a cogent argument, a forceful opinion or a sound piece of reasoning, though she had her unpopular moral views and some of these, such as her backing for capital punishment, were notably against the tide by the early 1950s towards the end of her life.

Then there was the impact on her life as John Anthony came to adolescence; he won a place at Oxford, and entered his college in 1946, ironically with Roy Ridley as his tutor; although DLS appears to have forgotten that years before she saw in Roy Ridley the model for her Peter Wimsey. She backed John Anthony with confidence, advice and cash. Then, in 1950, Mac die, after a long illness. Mac had not been able to contribute much to life for some time, as he was ill for many years and needed care. DLS was embroiled at times in confrontation and controversy, as in her awkward relationship with politician Tom Driberg, with who she had crossed intellectual swords.

John Anthony won a first class degree, and he was shortly afterwards made the sole beneficiary of DLS. Dorothy's keenness to be one of the multiple voices in the world of social and political opinion may be highlighted in her writing for a journal edited by Maurice Reckitt. He was a Yorkshireman with pronounced views on Anglo-Catholic ideologies and left-wing leanings. He wanted DLS as a regular contributor, and this gave her a channel in which to give her opinions an audience beyond the daily press and anyone with a need for sensationalist angle on world affairs. Reckitt was widely published, and much may be inferred from his founding of the National Guilds League: the name hints at a Ruskinian bent, a support for the ideals DLS had expressed previously about the importance of true labour. He had recently published his autobiography when the journal, *Christendom* began appearing.

Then along came one of the truly great works of European literature – *La Divina Commedia,* in which an Italian poet of the High Renaissance imagined a universe and a template of human life within God's organised frame of existence. DLS could have finally written the mainstream literary novel she had thought about; she could have completed her projected biography of Wilkie Collins; she could even have lived a full, rich life as a speaker and perhaps attained the status of literary sage, with profiles of her in the highbrow literary journals. But no, along came Dante Alighieri, the Florentine, and his creation of a narrative poem that towered over almost everything else. There was a task and a challenge, and out came the scholar and the linguist deep in the soul of the crime writer. The sins and failings of her villains and even the vanity of her protagonists were not trivial beside Dante's personnel in Hell, Purgatory and Paradise, but they might have been less complex. That made the challenge all the more inviting.

There was another dimension to spending time and effort with Dante too: the fact that there was something incomplete about Dante studies; that there was knowledge yet to be uncovered. As I write this in 2025, yet another new work has appeared on the great Italian: *Dante's New Lives*, by Elisa Brilli and Giuliano Milani, and as a review points out, (see the bibliography), they demonstrate that, 'One of the most remarkable aspects of Dante's writing is the way it continually reassesses his life and work.' He has a similar status to Shakespeare and Goethe, in that even the smallest fragments and footnotes from the author's life creates more than a stir: it invites revisionist opinion and new scholarly possibilities.

What would draw a detective novelist and religious dramatist to the seemingly insuperable task of translating Dante's *La Divina Commedia* into English, and more than that, also into the metre of *terza rima*? Perhaps DLS's discovery of Dante's great classic was just the kind of challenge she welcomed, or perhaps one should look to influences such as Charles Williams and his seminal work, *The Figure of Beatrice*, as this is generally accepted as a key modern study of Dante.

DLS's response to this gives the modern reader a hint about the direction one must take in order to assess the ways in which reading Dante had such a profound influence on DLS's last project. Barbara

Reynolds fully understood this influence. She was, after all, a specialist in Italian literature as well as a close friend of DLS. She quotes the key statement from DLS, referring to Purgatory in the *Commedia*: 'Was there ever a heaven so full of nods and becks and wreathed smiles, so gay and dancing? ... Surely nobody ever so passionately wanted a place where everybody was kind and courteous.'

Still, one has to come down to earth here and look at the text of the translation DLS produced. She almost completed the gargantuan task of translating all three sections of the *Commedia*; the project was left at her death as the *Inferno*, the *Purgatorio* and two-thirds of the *Paradiso*. But here, the task is not to explain in details the nature of the great Dantean work. That has been done not only by DLS herself, but by numerous academics and Italian specialists. Since the Rev. Francis Cary back in the Regency years produced an influential translation, there have been as many translations as there are opinions about how the work should be 'Englished'. The result is a difficulty in agreeing on the varieties of readership, and what constitutes a 'modern' text.

Translating Dante has always generated criticism and debate. In a useful overview of translations of the great classic, critic Peter Hainsworth wrote: 'Even translators who aim at plain prose are certain to find themselves criticised for mistakes and misunderstandings. What is more, the message or messages of the Comedy are always closely bound up with how they are put.' DLS, approaching the poem as a creative writer with a scholarly ability, was working from outside the academic network and its traditions.

To understand DLS's attitude, one has to consider the notion of poetic diction, as it has been since the Augustan period, in Georgian Britain, as contrasted to the revolutions brought about in various movements in poetry since the first wave of Modernism c.1920s. It is useful to begin with William Wordsworth's influential preface to the *Lyrical Ballads* of 1800. Here, he wrote something which would be

read as a shake-up of the scholarly attitudes about what the language
of poetry was or should be:

> Low and rustic life was generally chosen because in that situation
> the essential passions of the heart find a better soil in which they
> can attain their maturity, are less under restraint, and speak a
> plainer and more emphatic language; because in that situation
> our elementary feeling exist in a state of greater simplicity and
> consequently may be more accurately contemplated and more
> forcibly communicated.

There is an unconvincing strand to the thought here, but the reasoning
is easy to grasp. Wordsworth and Coleridge, writing in a world in
which there was a general idea of diction suitable for the writing of
poetry, added to 'suitable' subjects for poetry.

Ironically, here was Dorothy L. Sayers, famous writer, who had
been delighting in putting working-class people in the pages of her
novels, now changing to the role of translator of one of the most highly
rated poems ever written, deciding not to put her emphasis on 'plainer
and more emphatic language' as the basis of the work. This is not to
say she did not see that forthright words were needed. In the very first
canto of *Paradiso* we have:

> Short time I endured him, yet so short 'twas not
> But that I saw him sparkle every way
> Like iron from out the furnace drawn white-hot

The image might have been something from the world of modern
industry, a Victorian metaphor, but on the other hand, the diction in
that first canto has these utterly conventional features from a poetic
world which reads overall like a text Dr Johnson would have picked

up in St Paul's churchyard: 'Whence she to whom my whole self open was / as to myself, to calm my troubled fit / stayed not my question, but without a pause....' This syntax, together with a style far removed from the language of Wordsworth's 'common men' would be, and still surely is, a poem from the study and the lecture theatre, not from the kind of living poetic diction most of the British poets since c.1950 have worked hard to create. One might compare the above lines with this version from John Ciardi:

> I had to look away soon, and yet not
> So soon but what I saw him spark and blaze
> Like new-tapped iron when it pours white-hot.

The reasons for this are not hard to find: we are talking about a subject that relates to DLS as much as it does to, say, T.S. Eliot, Ezra Pound or any poet with a classical education and a penchant for reading the classics rather than any contemporary text. Our influences, thank the stars, differ, and always will.

The topic here is, in fact, the *life of the mind*. DLS was scholarly from the beginning; her personality had different strands of creativity. One was expressed in the games, dressing-up and rhetorical speeches. This theatricality, in the mature woman, was a natural source of drama across the air waves. The other source was the sophisticated storytelling generated from the germ of a story digging into her literary brain. When it came to translating Dante, it was a case of showing reverence to a classic of classics. If we add to this line of thought her love of poetic form, then it may be seen what *terza rima* had to offer. The basic pattern of the metre here is in a sequence of rhymes, hinging on the power and malleability of the ABA triolet, so we have this rhyme scheme: ABA-CDC-EFE-GHG-IJI. That is, the alternate rhymes, with caesura and variation in enjambment and end-stops, gives a simple frame but 'to the ear' helps maintain the feel of the narrative which, after all, is from the mouth of a man on a pilgrimage, with the great Roman, Virgil, as his guide.

Still, there is the issue of readership. In her essay 'And Telling You a Story', she wrote:

> With a colossal humility then, but with a colossal self-confidence all the same ... Nobody who did not know beforehand what the Comedy was all about would guess from its opening the audacity of its scope and aim. Mr C.S. Lewis has well pointed out the reason for the 'ritual and incantatory' style of the Virgilian and Miltonic epic: 'the invocation, the formal opening, the grand manner', are all there 'to give us the sensation that some great thing is now to begin'.

The problem is that these grandiose features of the narrative voice are not anywhere near as fluent and accessible as the latest Agatha Christie whodunit.

My argument is that the entire project was intellectual from the start. The *canti* of the great poem need voluminous notes and explanations. What is avoided is how Dante's poem and its stories could keep a modern reader without the benefit of an Oxford education, turning the pages. There are a number of ways to see and understand this last magnificent project from DLS's pen. First, as Barbara Reynolds stresses, there was the joy, the 'gaudium', involved. Reynolds writes that the reader needs to perceive the nature of her friend Charles Williams's concept of 'The Affirmative Way' in order to see what the deep understanding of Dante gave '[t]o someone of her temperament, with such earthy zest for life, the Affirmative Way as mapped by Charles Williams was a liberating sanction. Enjoyment, *gaudium*, elation of the soul, was a virtue she did not find difficult to practise.'

As with all aesthetic and critical positions, there is another spin on the Dante enterprise, of course. Translating the *Commedia* was complete in itself, and was, as the cliché goes, 'art for art's sake'. My own experience as a writer qualifies me to comment on this. The embarkation for a journey into the *terra incognita* of a work of art is at the same time a thrill and a sense of possible despair. Over the optimism and feeling of motivation there is the shadow of failure, and what this does is intensify the determination to master a form or a structure. In a shapeless novel, that structure may be simply a series of stages of development; in a long poem in *terza rima* it is a directed ending with a defined task. All this for myself relates to a valid theory of how most writers develop from stage one to a sophisticated stage of ability. Greg Light, of the University of London, engaged in some research on the growth in creative writing expertise, and spoke on this at a conference in 1999 at Sheffield Hallam University. His findings led him to posit these stages of development: releasing – documenting – narrating (limited critiquing.). The last stage, a sophisticated level, relates to advanced creative practices. Summary concludes, in short, that when we begin writing our material is largely autobiographical, and then we gradually move through stages towards the sophistication of critiquing, which includes editing. The final re-reading of the script of a novel, for instance, will entail the application of all the acquired knowledge and skills. Most important, with DLS's writing and translating of Dante, is the notion of readership. At the early stage, we mostly do not think of an imagined reader.

Today, a writer producing a book proposal will most often be asked by a publisher or agent to describe the readership they have in mind for their projected work. This is a difficult task, and involves guesswork. However, in the writing done at the *early* stage of development, the thought of a reader the *reception* of the writing, will not be a factor in the creative activity. In my own writing life, looking back, I can see that my first twenty years were spent writing poetry and short stories without ever thinking of a possible or probable reader.

If this is applied to DLS, the response to her Dante project is obvious: she had 'burnt out' in writing the crime fiction for so long. In 1949 she wrote to Henry Wade:

> As for writing detective stories there are a thousand and one reasons why I can feel no desire for it ... the chief reason is ... that I have become so sickened by importunity ... that the thought of being pushed and hallooed into the old routine fills me with distaste.

Now, with the thought of the new challenge, she was done with 'readership' and writing to a defined audience. It was all about the 'work', and its demands and pleasures. The 'critiquing' stage has the kinds of aesthetic delights we associate with discovering something charmingly new and fresh. There had always been the poet in her, and this figure was the kind of poet who would have thrived in the Tudor court or in the Oxford of Thomas Gray.

We could add to this the argument of DLS the European. Her taste and sensibility partly lay with the kinds of literature she had found in the lays and *laisses*; deep in the Old French poetry of love and chivalry, and also in classical myth. Even her childhood love of adventure and romance had a Francophile flavour to it, with Dumas and Orczy. It went deeper than that, however; the entire linguistic traditions of medieval sensibility appealed, and now here was a great storyteller who had not encroached on her life and literary taste during her busy professional life.

No account of the Dante enterprise can be complete without some account of Williams's thesis in his book *The Figure of Beatrice*. The appeal this made to DLS was on several levels. Williams posited a *via negativa* and its opposite, the *via positiva*. The latter he defines as 'The Affirmative Way' and this relates to a concept of beauty that soon relates and applies to Dante's creation of Beatrice, the young women whom he sees and who becomes an ideal with multiple elements for him and his beliefs about the divinely created world. For Williams, this concept of beauty appears to apply to our access to life's most appealing and staggering exhibitions of purity and idealisation within what is thought of as beautiful. Williams wrote that 'The vision of the perfection arises independently of the imperfection; it shines through her body whatever she makes of her body.' He wishes to bring traditions of aesthetics which embrace both the common usage of the word 'romantic' and the 'Romanticism' as historians and scholars see it in the expressions of the Romantic Movement of the period c.1780–1830.

Williams wrote about the germ of this Romantic feeling: '"We cannot," wrote Dante in the third tractate of the *Convivio*, "look fixedly upon her aspect because the soul is so intoxicated by it that after gazing at it once goes astray in all its operations."' This all settles neatly into the proliferation of epiphanic visions and revelations at the heart of Romantic poetry, and in common life, and the stereotypes of romantic love, it is equally about radical change, about a transmutation from earth-bound experience to visions of some higher plane of perception and all this is something entirely outside the world of drugs or alcohol. The cliché about Dante which has been promoted in popular culture, is of his first sight of young Beatrice. One of the most entrenched images is in Henry Holiday's painting 'Dante and Beatrice'. This shows Dante standing on a bridge over the Arno, looking at Beatrice, who walks with two other young women; she seems to be trying to look at him, from behind her escort. More accurate appears to be the record that Dante's father took him to the home of the Portinari family and there he met Beatrice. She was to marry a banker, Simone de Bardi, in 1287, and Dante was to write his great poem sequence, *La Vita Nuova*, later, some time around 1293.

The images in popular culture play up the idea of 'courtly love', the secret nurturing of affection and service for a beloved lady. Charles

Williams also foregrounded the more religious and philosophical line of thought, that there is ideal and perfect beauty, but that beauty reaches into thinking such as the idea that the substance of God himself is conveyed in the perceived beauty. For DLS, Williams's thinking that essentially, romantic love is a method of seeing and absorbing grace. What was aligning in DLS's mind between c.1940 and her work on Dante was a confirmation of her growing belief that all her previous writing and talking about work, morality and the creativity reflected in the Trinity was indeed converging, and in Dante she saw a master at work: he, in creating a universe embracing hell, purgatory and paradise within a poetic vision was providing something she had always wanted to believe, something she had told in a simple way to an audience at a talk in Hull, 'To go from earth to faery is like passing from this time to eternity; it is not a journey into space, but a change of mental outlook.'

In spite of the reservations above concerning the motives behind this very demanding poetic project, one has to stress the results of DLS's efforts when it comes to the very highest levels of description and impassioned visions. This is evident in the portrayal of Beatrice, and much later in *Paradiso*, in Canto XIV we have this:

> But Beatrice appeared all smiles, and glowing
> with beauty such that I must leave it there
> with things outgone by memory in its going.

Then what follows is one of many instances of what DLS clearly saw as scraps of experience in a vision of what could be The Affirmative Way:

> With my whole heart, and in the tongue which all
> men share, I made burnt-offering to the Lord,
> such as to this new grace was suitable...

Of other successes in writing and theology which were fired by Williams and his ideas, perhaps C.S. Lewis's book, *Surprised by Joy* (1955) in which one of Lewis's persistent concerns is the nature of what he sees as 'joy', as applied to an elusive element in the experience of material reality is applied to something within the feeling that needs a German word to define it: the word *Séhnsucht*. This is related to 'an inconsolable longing' akin to the more familiar Welsh word *hiraeth*. The source of the book's title is the Wordsworth poem, *Surprised by Joy*, which is about the loss of a loved one. Wordsworth has the line 'Love, faithful love, recalled thee to my mind.'

If one lifts these feelings related to Lewis's 'Joy', the result is the kind of recurrent experience running through the *Commedia*. DLS obviously saw one of her key beliefs in the triune nature of God-spirit-mankind. That is, for Wordsworth, Lewis and Dante, one thing that makes common ground for them is the revelatory 'opening up' of these feelings of joy, as elements of Godhead become transmuted into the other areas of the creative Trinity.

One feels sure, from various biographical sources, that DLS had the happy experience of a number of aesthetic satisfactions and rewards coming her way as the translation advanced. She had, one feels certain, existed in a number of 'worlds' and although on the surface they might seem as different as earth from sky, there was common ground: this was in the fulfilment of having accepted and followed innate urges to create. Surely that word rippled through all her being, her thinking and feeling, as she moved from challenge to challenge. Her worlds had appeals to her talents as well as to her need for intellectual reassurance that the scholar in her was as capable as ever.

In the end, when all possible assessments might have been expressed, here was a writer who was always, after her own fashion, the 'scholar-poet' who could have found her true spiritual home at the end of any one of several roads. Yet she chose them all, and it was not through greed: it was through sheer, determined powers of creativity.

These were always there, and never let her down. The 'worlds' were packed with friends and encouragement, and in writing her biography, one feels that she was most warmly and rightly defined and celebrated as that young women in the Mutual Admiration Society who made others feel the joy in creativity and in storytelling that she knew had the potential to enrich life, in any context and in any condition. Reading her letters, one senses that whenever she said no to an invitation to contribute, it was always with an explanation that she perhaps never told herself with sufficient force.

On 17 December 1957, Dorothy Leigh Sayers, after spending some hours with friends and shopping, came home to Witham. Later, her body was found at the bottom of the stairs; she had been going to feed her cats. My personal reaction to that exit from the world is that first, it happened in the process of caring as well as from a desired routine, and second, that the deeply seated poet in her wrote some lines back in 1943 which say so much. They come from *War Cat*:

See now, I rub myself against your legs
To express my devotion,
Which is not altered by any unkindness...

Chapter 9

Reputation and Influence

At every word, a reputation dies.
                            - The Rape of the Lock, Alexander Pope

There is no doubt that the life of DLS has been thoroughly recounted, but where does she stand in regard to how her name and status fit into cultural reference? As she is now partly seen as a figure of high establishment in the Golden Age of crime fiction, her name is fixed in the firmament, in that ethereal location where 'classics' abide. One hint of this came in a news feature in *The Sunday Times* in 2023 concerning women's clubs. The University Women's Club, according to David Brown, has been seen as a 'sanctuary of civility'. He adds that 'Past members included Dorothy L. Sayers and Emily Davison', but now, the members want 'equal privileges' to those of men.

These privileges appear to be acts which include longer drinking hours and 'laddish' behaviour. David Brown stresses that 'A neighbour who has lived in the area for fifty years fears life will be "unbearable" if the club is allowed to host hen nights and wedding parties.'

DLS loved a 'gaudy', but would she have welcomed the raucous celebrations which are a mark of modern recreation? Her name, it seems, still links firmly to scholarship, conservative and cultural values dictating moral behaviour.

In academic and scholarly terms, assessments have been varied. One of the most mainstream judgements has come from critic Cora Kaplan, in her essay, 'Queens of Crime: The Golden Age of Crime

Fiction'. Kaplan summarises very usefully and succinctly the threads of thought and reference running through so much of the fiction. She writes, with reference to both Christie's Miss Marple and DLS's Harriet Vane in *Strong Poison*: 'they both debate the effects of the loosening of sexual conventions and the negative consequence of "free love" in the post-war period'. Also, Kaplan describes a more general effect of the changing detection story under the guidance of the 'Queens of crime' as explained by DLS herself in an essay: 'The lack of affect, morality and realist characterisation in the purely cerebral detective stories of her competitors was, she thought, itself a troubling sign of the social and ethical crisis of the times.' Added to this is the comment on readership of the 'Queens': 'books were not being read in "back kitchens" but in Downing Street and in Bloomsbury studios, in bishops' palaces and in the libraries of eminent scientists.'

Readership will, one might argue, be an increasingly negative factor; the course of crime fiction since the last reprint of the Wimsey novels has moved into a dizzying number of sub-genres, influenced in part by the increased interest readers appear to have for extreme violence, international themes, fast-paced thrillers, and variations on the serial killer category. The true crime and documentary interest has expanded also, along with the acceleration of popularity in crime podcasts.

Alternatively, and more optimistic for fans of DLS, the nature and scope of the 'cosy crime' novels has increased, and various levels of crime fiction dealing with the social contrasts and oppositions (which is strong in the Wimsey books) appear to have succeeded and grown recently.

What does her name suggest to modern readers and crime aficionados? One way to find some answers is to ask members of the Dorothy L. Sayers Society, and in an informal approach, I did exactly that. There was nothing statistical about my question; I simply wanted to know about impact and influence, whether they were readers or writers themselves. I also asked other readers and students, particularly those who had studied the oeuvre in literature courses. Some people offered quite a lot of biographical context to the discovery of the Sayers reading pleasures; others simply pinpointed a moment of strong impression.

Jasmine Simeone, Secretary and Bulletin Editor to the Dorothy L. Sayers Society, recalls hearing *The Man Born to be King* on the radio, and later the radio series of the Wimsey novels, with Ian Carmichael and then Edward Petherbridge. Jasmine's involvement in the Sayers experience has been far more than merely as a reader of the novels:

> Sayers has made me do several things: I read Golden Age detective fiction whenever I can, and more modern detective story writers as well to a much greater extent than ever before. I learnt bell-ringing, though for various reasons I no longer practise the art. I came to the conclusion my local church was not fulfilling my needs so I became a Roman Catholic as a result of reading Sayers' religious writings. I sang in a recorded performance of the incidental music to The Just Vengeance. I have travelled with the Society to France, to visit L'École Des Roches, to Germany for a conference in Freiburg im Breisgau, and another near Bonn ... I have learnt things about medicine, the law, murder, life in the 1920s and 1930s, and advertising between the wars, which I would not otherwise have even thought of.

DLS always said that if a writer concentrates on the facts and details regarding material in a novel that supports the pretence of reality, then the reader's involvement will remain steady and firm. I recall a talk once, given by thriller writer Angus Ross, in which he said that, at a talk he was giving, someone pointed out a mistake about a motor car in one of his novels; such a small thing could eat away at credibility.

Other respondents selected specific books that had an effect and changed attitudes. Gary Dobbs pinpointed *The Nine Tailors* in this respect – and says he was 'hooked' from that. He adds, 'The books have that cosy quality, but they are so well realised and there is a lot of humour in the interaction between Wimsey and Bunter, and rather than a master/servant relationship there is a solid friendship between the pair.' Gary adds a really important critical point: 'when Wimsey meets Vane his character grows on the page in a way that say Sherlock Holmes never did. Basically, Holmes is the same character in his first story as his last.'

Claiborne Ray expresses a 'total immersion' influence, saying that DLS 'permanently influenced my education, my dreams, my very way of thinking', but adds a negative: 'her intimidating example was part of the reason I never felt worthy of pursuing real scholarship or trying to write a novel'. Some of the intimidation as is often noted – relates to the learning carried in the fiction. Claiborne adds, 'I realised I needed more education to understand the allusions and the historical context.' But there is an entirely different literary force at work for Claiborne when it comes to her reading of *Busman's Honeymoon*, which 'opened my eyes to adult love and set an impossible standard for relationships. The idea of a marriage of equals helped make me an early second-wave feminist and a very poor prospect for matrimony.'

The religious writings certainly had an impact. Claiborne writes that they gave 'an intellectual context for my own Episcopalian faith'. The translations and radio plays also made an impression. For me, Christopher Isherwood was a similar influence, and like Claiborne, I just failed to contact him while he was here on earth. She writes, 'I sat down to write her a fan letter when I was still at high school. When I went to the library to find out where to send it, I learned that she had died a couple of years before...'

John W. Kennedy relates another influence of life-changing effect. He writes that reading *Gaudy Night* was the factor in change: 'over

the next couple of years I went through nearly the entire Sayers canon
… *The Mind of the Maker* also transformed much of my thinking.'

Responses, revisions and assessments tend to take a scholarly
stance; we are all so nervous about the kinds of extreme judgements
we make about art when pronouncements are rashly made. Opinions
of particular writers change in an individual at different points in their
lives. Then time elapses and a writer of any notable stature becomes
adopted and positioned as someone who fits into a compartment where
he or she may be studied (not necessarily read as every writer hopes to
be read). The name Sayers appears to have settled in a place that makes
her a 'modern classic' and that may often mean someone whose works
are not read but respected; the kind of name that would soon find its
way onto a university literature syllabus. After that, terrible phrases
may be used, such as 'of its time', or 'difficult to read now'. The latter
words are sadly applied in DLS's case. In conversation or in gibing
opinions on favourite reading, someone is likely to say that so much
needs to be explained, or that one needs to have Google to hand, or a
massive literary reference tome.

However, a true reader committed to having to work at a novel
will understand the point about 'particularity' that DLS makes in her
essay on Dante called 'And Telling a Story':

> Two kinds of excitement are blended together to make an
> excitement less heady than the excitement of either poetry or
> story-telling by itself … what the trick of particularity adds to
> the poetry is, I think, best described as a vivid conviction of
> fact – the sort of conviction that used to lead people to address
> letters to 'Sherlock Holmes Esq. 221, Baker Street.'

In fact, DLS's own Peter Wimsey illustrates this. During the war,
Wimsey made some appearances in newspaper pieces. He was destined
to be one of the handful of fictional creations who many imagined

walking around Britain, being his cheery and very dependable self. The particularity notion rests on the basic storytelling ploy of adding detail that appears to support the viability of the pretence. As an actor creates small movements and grimaces to build on a pretend personality, so a writer uses a narrative tone to steadily accrue the particular in the mortar of the bricks from which the structure of the story is made.

My own view is that DLS had two outstanding abilities as a writer: one was to master anything related to the structure of a linguistic artefact, whether that pertains to a stanza in Dante or to a complex plot such as the twists and turns in *Unnatural Death*. The twists and turns relate to a convincingly viable network of legal accoutrements in the novel, from authentic-seeming lawyers to references spinning out from legislation.

However we assess her work, what will remain is her consummate bundle of narrative skills and the inter-relationship of a scholarly attitude and a novelist's eye for making sure the story itself is open to be easily and compellingly shared with the reader. Her status may well become primarily that of a 'set book' writer, and a writer whose work is 'canonical' in the milieu of the schoolroom and the literary curriculum, but one feels that there will always be those readers who see and understand a special relationship with DLS the writer. I think that Barbara Reynolds, when she used the phrase 'life and soul' with regard to her biography of DLS did so with the rich double entendre of (a) the writer with a spiritual dimension, and (b) the woman who was the 'life and soul' of the party. She loved to laugh and she patently revelled in the humour running through the Wimsey novels. Particularly when she employs the metafiction of pretending that Peter refers to crime novels and amateur sleuths. That is an invitation to smile with the weird irony of it; then there is the amusement we feel when a 'type' is let loose into a wonderful monologue that both entertains and satirises.

The reputation, one feels, is secure; as to the readership, that is (as always in literature) a topic on which, as the cliché has it, the jury is out.

Chapter 10

A Summing Up

See how love and murder will out.

– William Congreve

Why should we read DLS now? Some of my own answers to the question are glib and obvious: to enjoy her achievements as an original crime writer; to go far beyond crime in our engagement with the literary themes and debates in modern writing; also to reflect, with her stimulation, on social and ideological topics which are now increasingly universal. Coming down to more earthy and plain replies, we might point to the phenomenal rise of what is called 'cosy crime', and what that says about society now.

With varying levels of unreality the crime genres thriving now show us the nature of the complexity of characters coping with the tough confrontation with modernity. After all, what is a fictional detective? How does Wimsey fit any definition? It is impossible to read a Sayers crime novel and not reflect on the prismatic views she gives us from which we respond to the shock of transgression. DLS purposely breaks the fictional spell of the 'pretence reality' of a novel in order to invite her readers to share in the strange link between the suspension of disbelief and the uneasy shadow of natural, irrational life. For each of us, life itself is a suspension of disbelief; religious belief, arguably irrational, as faith is per se, sustained by that suspension. The will to share a story goes hand in hand with the desire for rationality to impose meaning and purpose on the chaotic flow of sensual impression we have to label 'reality'.

It comes as no surprise to note that it was in the interwar years of the twentieth century that surrealism arrived, and it came along with challenges to the fabrication of such notions as 'the realist novel'. When Modernism came onto the scene, readers were open to read experimental narrative which purported to shine a light on the inner self, the unconscious and the 'real' nature of people beneath the social veneer. Interest in surrealism was growing, together with any other kind of innovative thinking and messing with the accepted representations of social reality. At one end of the spectrum, where youth was in a creative mood, there were the wild parties, as DLS describes in *Murder Must Advertise*; maybe George Melly's memoir explains a common attitude:

> 'Change life' the Surrealists had ordained. 'Tell your children your dreams!' From the few texts I'd read; from the reproductions of Ernst, Dali and Magritte I'd studied; I had derived amazing certainty that the marvellous was all about us, and if only we could escape from that mental labyrinth built in the name of morality, religion, patriotism and the family, we could all become poets; move through a reality where dreams and reality were indistinguishable.

Subcultures, deviants and the ordinary folk in rebellious mood, taking a chance, jumping off the treadmill of work and the harsh facts of existence make the meat and drink of the crime writer. The large-scale unrest on the world stage has its echoes in the cosy crime world of the vicarage and village green. What DLS did, with her Detection Club peers, was have her readers plunge into the fun, in spite of the chaos around them. Wimsey, her ace creation, is never fiddling while Rome burns; he is that charming paradox, the stealthy radical in the eye of an ideological storm.

There is no doubt that we still read DLS for an understanding of the women caught up in the results of the legislation regarding their lives and occupations in 1918–19. She projected much of her own inner strife and her ongoing oppositional writing regarding her own first-hand experience of trying to survive her London life. In those crucial few years of 1920–23, her sheer tough application to writing, and the opening with Gollancz, provides a paradigm for so many of her peers, and her own savvy approach to the fiction market stands together with similar success by Agatha Christie, Storm Jameson, Ethel Mannin and many more.

Some of these women writers didn't make the same rapid forward strides in the profession. This has been shown in a series produced by the British Library in their women writers series, which has the aim of showing 'a collection of novels by female authors who enjoyed broad, popular appeal in their day'. As writer Lucy Scholes points out, some were really destined to remain obscure, but some, such as Ursula Bloom, who was astoundingly productive, had some of DLS's qualities but never struck gold, as it were, in terms of extreme popularity: 'Mary Essex, for example is just one of the many pseudonyms used by the novelist Ursula Bloom who, in the course of her long life (1892–1984) was truly prolific, publishing over 500 novels and biographies, as well as short stories, newspaper columns and radio plays.'

The issues around the discussions of the New Woman, and the impact of the 1919 Sex Disqualification (Removal) Act, explain much of the changes taking place in society that led to such career openings as DLS needed, although only as stop-gaps. Her professional life was always going to be the singular and single-minded one of the woman novelist. Of course, the 1919 Act led also to the award of her Oxford degree, but if we take a broader view, as writer Jane Robinson did in her book *Ladies Can't Climb Ladders*, then the results of that legislation were not all pleasantly successful. In a review-essay on the book, writer Arianne Chernock points out an important aspect of all this: 'But the jauntiness of Robinson's prose belies the balanced nature of her analysis. Her women are no one-note crusaders. Instead, they are human: passionate about their professional paths but also prone to error, jealousy, revision and self-recrimination.' The lonely path of the successful writer made DLS an exception, but she saw these negative aspects in other professions.

More importantly, it has to be stressed that DLS saw and understood another notable aspect of the 1919 impact, as Chernock explains:

> the structural and psychological impediments to female advancement were so deeply entrenched that many men and women alike continued to play by the old rules. Long after 1919, women seeking employment were far more likely to become secretaries, nurses, teachers or hairdressers than architects, engineers or lawyers. And they usually terminated their employment if they married and had children.

There is also no doubt that, as has also been said of Colin Dexter's Morse novels, in the relevant Wimsey books there is a strong sense that the profound importance of Oxford for DLS is an element that seeps into so much of the writer's nature. In her experience at Somerville, she was fortunate to have Dame Emily Penrose as Principal and Mildred Pope as her tutor. In *Testament of Youth*, Vera Brittain writes of Penrose, 'whose austere personality and dominant mind were probably, through their grim concentration of purpose, more responsible than anything else for the fact that Oxford took advantage of post-war legislation to give degrees to women while Cambridge refused them'.

There have been disappointments in this question of reputation and popularity too. In 2022 Penguin Books issued their relaunch of their 'greenback' crime list; thirty titles were published, with more planned, but as I write this in early 2024, not only is it disappointing to report that DLS is not a name in that first list. Worse than that, as critic Muireann Maguire reported in a long review-essay, the new 'crime and espionage' imprint has very little female presence, and Maguire also argues that women are denigrated in the texts also. She wrote: 'Yet unlike Martin Edwards, whose long-running series of British Library Crime Classics prioritises the reprinting of forgotten female authors, Winder's selection policy leaves many stars of the Penguin back-list out in the cold and out of print.' She adds, 'To exclude female authors, to marginalise their contribution and to foreground fiction that essentialises and denigrates women is not acceptable.'

In many ways, the name Dorothy L. Sayers will define for fiction readers a startling instance of a writer of genius: her skills went far beyond mere whodunit precision and cerebral planning. Her novels have other dimensions that adhere to humanitarian values, Englishness, and the necessity for networks of moral values in a community. Yet above and beyond these assertions, there is the convincing reminder every reader surely feels, that here is a writer who has been inside stories as a scholar and outside stories as a spellbound listener. This is combined with a sure sense of how people from imagination are put on the page with the magic that stems from a steady ability with the craft involved.

Sometimes, comparisons are not odious. Sometimes they enlighten us on literary matters, and one feels that placing DLS in certain critical lines of thought tend to show up strengths as well as influences. The work of Raymond Chandler, one might argue, enlightens her achievement, in the context of the time. After all, both began to find success in writing at around the same time, and in terms of very different markets.

We should also take a wider view of her achievement, in the context of how and why the 'Golden Age' women writers expressed their themes with such enterprise and adventure in the context of an attitude to crime writing that was derived from Conan Doyle. The key word here is 'ratiocination.' DLS, in her editing and collecting of the stories for her Gollancz anthologies, saw the appeal of approaches which were markedly different from the male-centred fiction of the successors to Holmes. The ratiocination was working the seam of cerebral problem solving, which was most appropriate in the age of invention in Conan Doyle's time.

The notion of a *mystery* for the story of detection before the Wimsey novels was not far removed from the enterprise of an Edison. It was based on the idea that if the investigator acquired the relevant parts, he could assemble a product he could call a 'solution.' The neat package supplied in the denouement of the narrative and in the wrapping-up of the puzzle did not necessarily include something with the emotional depth we find in more recent crime fiction. In other words, there was a secondary place for the fundamental basis of a novel of relationships: a story about what people want and about what they fear.

Much may be made of Raymond Chandler's thoughts on crime writing in this respect. A comparison of Chandler and Sayers is a profitable critical road to take. Like DLS, Chandler had a classical education in his years at Dulwich College, and again like her, he saw the potential for serious, socially engaged fiction in the crime genre. But where they parted company was in the need Chandler saw for the detective to be embedded in the stuff of life, the world of the workers and of those outside the Bright Young People of the Jazz Age.

Also, like DLS, Chandler when young had written poetry, much of it published in the high culture Edwardian magazines, before he left England to serve in a Canadian regiment in the Great War. DLS was unfairly criticised in his statements about detective fiction, as he did not understand Wimsey's very complex and shifting attitudes to the class structure around him. Chandler assumed that Wimsey was a 'toff' and was a limited concept with too much of the stereotype in him. But Chandler was hunting for the right idiom to apply in stories set in Los Angeles, and within the *Black Mask* magazine approaches, which were purposely cynical, hard and disturbing.

Chandler explained his problems with the purely cerebral material and themes in the work of many of the post-Holmes writers of detection stories. Frank MacShane, in his biography of Chandler, quotes the kernel of Chandler's thinking on the matter, using Chandler's own words:

> To get the complication you fake the clues, the timing, the play of coincidence, assume certainties where only 50 per cent chances exist, at most. To get the surprise murderer you fake character, which hits me hardest of all, because I have a sense of character. If people want to play this game, it's all right by me. But for Christ's sake let's not talk about honest mysteries. They don't exist.

Here, he misses the point of many instances of the genre as it emerged in the 1920s. The difference between the lead sleuths of Chandler and DLS is easily seen in the accounts of the two, Wimsey and Marlowe. MacShane said of Marlowe: '...through his voice was what Chandler called the "controlled half-poetical emotion" that is at the heart of the work. In contrast, the same words could be applied to Wimsey's regular and sometimes extended poeticisms, but the difference is that for DLS the projection of Wimsey's words into wider society and into philosophical thinking generates much more than one insular world of a sensitive soul who has come through the hell of war. His layers of selfhood are much more interesting than that one perspective.

Like Chandler, DLS wrote short fiction for a number of popular magazines before her success with Wimsey, and the fact that when she saw where her real talent and success lay, there was a way to make her own version of realism. On the surface, Chandler and DLS could not seem further apart in their aesthetics, but the common ground is in the thick texture of Wimsey and Harriet's emotional (as well as in intellectual) powers.

Here we have an explanation of why so many women writers flourished in what we think of as the 'Golden Age' of crime fiction: it all rests on the after-effects of the 1919 Act, discussed earlier, in which the professions were opened up to women, and degrees could be awarded to them. This is profoundly related to the specific dilemmas in the life of DLS. Put rather brutally, it concerns the axis between women as the child-bearer or individual. This is the concept of the 'good wife' – the women meshed in the notion expressed in the German *Biedermeier* era of the mid nineteen century, which was all about comfortable domesticity and the woman as the heart of the home – and the free spirit.

The new freedom given to women after the Great War was of course not an instantaneous event. It was the beginning of a slow process of change, but it did reveal to novelists the possibilities of exploring these issues with creativity and deep interest. DLS, along with others such as Ngaio Marsh, Margery Allingham and Agatha Christie, saw the rich field of women and their fears and needs as a vital ingredient for a new kind of fiction. This was one in which the daily lives of women could be contrasted with the lives they aspired to. Alongside Harriet in *Gaudy Night* is the skivvy, the pot-washer and room-sweeper. Yet there are no true polarities because there is a deeper, shared range of feelings which have been eclipsed from fiction and art before, or sometimes subtly disguised, or eve explained through symbols, images and hidden themes.

There was a challenge to the male ratiocination then. The years after the Great War and the Edwardian male culture of cosy writing around successful literary careers generated an opposite, and this was the women who came from the shadows, with affairs of the heart to place alongside the cerebral dimensions of the post-Holmesians. This is a simplification, but it does pinpoint one of the principle virtues of DLS as a writer of detective fiction: the depth of her characters which lie hard against the stereotypes that many readers would have known and expected in their reading.

Creating a fictional world and community entails making a basis of convincing reality, but this may be superficial, often, as every writer knows, displaying the results of years or months of filling notebooks with character profiles. The result may only be a one-dimensional character, but there may be enough in the dialogue to sustain the 'willing suspension of disbelief' that stories demand. DLS was searching for the right vehicle for her art when she embarked on her first stories, and she became acutely aware of the need to collect a full range of techniques to back up the surface bubble of with and poetic tone given to Wimsey. She found the perfect formula for giving the reader the 'ratiocination' they expected, deepened by the demands made in the enjoyment of her novels by Wimsey's elusive and distracting intellect.

DLS loved nothing more than a fictional venture into a world of cerebral activity, with far more than a murder to solve at the heart; she had the brainwork in *The Documents in the Case* in abundance. But in the end we have to define her creation of Wimsey in comparison with Philip Marlowe as a mind at work on an expanding landscape (Wimsey) with one dealing with one body rotten with disease and corruption.

The brainwork also extended to something in the Wimsey profile and character depth: espionage. This was a playful activity of course, as has been pointed out by Joseph Hone in his account of T.J. Wise, the literary charlatan, *The Book Forger*. The link between some real espionage workers and Dorothy at the Gerrard Street Detection Club. Working with one of these, Graham Pollard, DLS concocted a 'fake' publication as a Christmas joke. Joseph Hone explains: 'When Sayers got round to sending a copy to Pollard, she inscribed the title page with a personal note from the fictitious 'author.' Pollard received the booklet with thanks, though his mischievous response speaks volumes about his desire to be thought of as a rival to Lord Peter...'

The fun with Pollard and the fake volume makes it clear that the people around her in the Detection Club, spending time in the office and sitting-room, just a short walk away from where she could talk to a real-life spy, leading a double life, did far more than sit in a corner and read in between talking about their latest publications. In fact, Joseph Hone pushes this link between Pollard and DLS a little further, noting the double life of the spy in contrast to the double life of DLS, who was a woman with hidden motherhood beneath the surface of the literary public figure.

The episode with Pollard shows exactly what the pleasures of collaboration were for DLS, as discussed in my account of the work on *The Documents in the Case*. But of course, writing and developing the core of a factional idea into a full novel is quite a different matter from being playful with something close to a practical joke with a friend. In the end, the various adventures in her actual life experience run alongside DLS' fiction very easily and naturally. One feels that her novels, although they might have been extremely difficult to construct, were still not without the pleasures we find in games and crosswords. Yet her achievements in fiction were well beyond a one-track series of small mysteries en route to a revelation and resolution of an intellectual puzzle.

A Glossary of Poetic Terms

Note: This is simply a minimum list of terms, all directly relating to DLS's poetry. Some of these are explained by DLS herself in the editions of her translations. For more detail, the reader is referred to either J.A. Cuddon, *A Dictionary of Literary Terms* (Penguin, see bibliography) or, for a shorter version, John Lennard, *The Poetry Handbook* (Oxford, 1995). I am offering simplifications here, but I feel that, in reading my chapter on the poetry, some readers may need a quick reference to terms.

Assonance
The repetition of vowel sounds that have a similar sound, as in a common half-rhyme, such as pairings of *home / harm; stone / stain; pain / pale*.

Caesura
A significant or important pause or break usually in mid-line such as: 'The thoughts that hurt him, they were there.' (A.E. Housman)

End-Stopped Line
A line in verse with punctuation at the end of the line, as in: 'He had wanted that, but never said so.' (S. Wade)

Enjambment
The use of a line that runs on to the following line, rather than being end-stopped, as in: 'He was never meant to be
in there in nothing but a box'. (S. Wade)

Laisse/Lay

In the above text, as explained, DLS uses for *laisse* a definition described by Eustache Deschamps, but a general definition relates it to the lai or lay: a poem to be sung or spoken, and often in octosyllables.

Metre

A term used to describe the patterns of line-length and stressed syllables in formal verse.

Metrical Feet

This refers to the patterns of stress on syllables, and feet can have two or three syllables in all the commonest forms. Two syllable feet: dominant are iambic: – / (stress on the second syllable) and trochaic: / – (stress on the first syllable). Three syllable feet: anapaestic: – – / (stress on last syllable) and dactylic: / – – (stress on the first syllable). The latter comes from the Greek word for finger, and the syllables reflect the three bones.

Octosyllabic Verse

This is essentially a tetrameter: a line with eight syllables. In formal poetry, these are usually iambic or trochaic feet; e.g. in Andrew Marvell: 'Had I but world enough and time.'

Rhyme

The use of words which have a matching sound when spoken, either at the end of a line or medially (in the middle of a line).

Terza rima

A poem or stanza with a rhyming pattern of: ABA-BCB-CDC-DED-EE.

Acknowledgments

There are many people and organisations to thank here. Dorothy L. Sayers had such a wide range of friends and social contexts that hunting down elements of her life has meant asking for assistance. Notably, I owe immense thanks to Debbie Rudwick and Andrew Edney at Bluntisham; Angela Barden at the Harvard Library, and Gwen Jones at the Bournemouth Little Theatre, who supplied not only the picture of Dorothy Rowe but also the centenary booklet of the Club.

I have to acknowledge contributions in discussion from novelist Kate Walker, who read far more popular fiction than I when she was a student and still does.

Special thanks are due to Seona Ford, Chair of the Dorothy L. Sayers Society, and to Jasmine Simeone, Secretary and Bulletin Editor of the Dorothy L. Sayers Society.

Illustration Credits

The cover image of Dorothy L. Sayers: thanks go to the Dorothy L. Sayers Society for the reproduction of the image in this book.

Thanks to Gwen Jones, Treasurer of the Bournemouth Little Theatre Club for permission to use images from their centenary booklet.

Thanks also to Stephanie Siddons Deighton, Chair of the Salisbury Civic Society for permission to use the Blue Plaque regarding Dorothy's time at the Godolphin School.

At the Marion E. Wade Center, Laura Stanifer was very helpful regarding possible illustrations, and the eventual use of two pictures.

For permission to use the images of St Mary's Church, Bluntisham, thanks go to Debbie Rudwick and Andrew Edney, whose help was invaluable.

Further thanks are due to members of the Dorothy L. Sayers Society, in particular Gary Dobbs, John W. Kennedy, Claiborne Ray, Jasmine Simeone and Laura Simmons for their contributions to my penultimate chapter.

For the use of the two photos of Dorothy and friends, acknowledgement of the courtesy of the Marion E. Wade Center is confirmed.

The reproduction of the image of Dorothy from the Cournos material is by courtesy of the Houghton Library: reference MS Eng 1074 Volume 1 Houghton Library, Harvard University. I must express my thanks to Jennifer Leahy for help with acquiring the photo of the young Dorothy.

Thanks to Ian Osterloh of the Canterbury Historical and Archaeological Society for permission to use the photograph of the Chapter House of the Cathedral. Ian Osterloh is the photographer.

Bibliography and Sources

Note: The first date, in brackets after the title, is the date of first publication.

Overview

There tends to be a great deal of information on Dorothy L. Sayers and her circle of friends and peers. A search soon reveals blogs, academic articles, cross-references to spin-off topics etc. There is even a fascinating thesis on DLS and her use of quotation, and some unexpected studies emanating from Christian apologetics.

Sayers Main Reference

The starting point for any new research or information-seeking has to be the Dorothy L. Sayers Society. To follow this, I would recommend a comb through the journals on JSTOR. For this, see the British Library material on the ITHAKA facility: http://www.bl.uk/

Gilbert, Colleen B., *A Bibliography of the Works of Dorothy L. Sayers* (Macmillan, 1979)

The Dorothy L. Sayers Society: https://www.sayers.org.uk

Online Summaries

https://detective-fiction.com

Justus.anglican.org/resources/bio/19.html

Works by Dorothy L. Sayers

Books: Editions Cited

Crime Fiction

Whose Body? (1923) (New English Library, 2003)
Clouds of Witness (1927) (Hodder, 2003)
Unnatural Death (1927) (New English Library, 2003)
The Unpleasantness at the Bellona Club (1928) (New English Library, 2003)
The Documents in the Case (1930) (Hodder & Stoughton, 2016)
Five Red Herrings (1931) (New English Library, 2016)
Have His Carcase (1932) (New English Library, 1975)
Murder Must Advertise (1933) (New English Library, 2003)
Hangman's Holiday (1933) (New English Library, 2003)
The Nine Tailors (1934) (New English Library, 2013)
Busman's Honeymoon (1937) (New English Library, 2016)

Drama

The Man Born to be King (Victor Gollancz, 1947)
The Zeal of Thy House (A play for Canterbury Cathedral) (Gollancz and Harcourt Brace, 1937)

Editorial Publications

Great Short Stories of Detection, Mystery and Horror: Part Six (Gollancz, 1934)

Prose Works

Further Papers on Dante (1957) (Greenwood Press, 1979)
The Letters of Dorothy L. Sayers (Edited by Barbara Reynolds) (Sceptre, 1995)

Poetry

Hone, Ralph E., (Editor) *Poetry of Dorothy L. Sayers* (The Dorothy
  L. Sayers Society, 1996)

Stories in Anthologies

Over the full period of DLS's career as a writer, the income from
publication in short story anthologies and from magazines was always
welcome, and as always tends to happen when a fiction writer meets with
success, the opportunities for print increase. Hence, her short fiction
appeared regularly in such popular magazine collections as *Argosy*,
which always had a mix of prominent authors alongside lesser known
ones. The issue for January 1952, for instance, has her story 'The Man
Who Knew How' in company with work by Martha Gellhorn, Truman
Capote and Ray Bradbury. The most recent collection is *Dorothy L.
Sayers: The Complete Stories* (Harper Collins, 2002).
Hangman's Holiday (1933) includes stories with Montague Egg, wine
  salesman and detective.
For a summary account of the short stories and DLS's highly regarded
essay on crime fiction, see David Stuart Davies, *Shadows of Sherlock
Holmes* (Wordsworth Classics, 1987) pp.viii-xv.

Translations

The Song of Roland (1957) (Penguin, 1967)
NB: A useful summary piece on various issues relating to the
translation of Dante is by Peter Hainsworth 'Coming to our senses in
a corpse-hued wood.'

Reference Works

Brewer, Ebenezer Cobham, *Dictionary of Phrase and Fable* (1895)
  (Wordsworth Reference, 2002)

Bronowski, J., *The Ascent of Man* (Book Club Associates, 1977)

Buck, Claire, (Ed.) *The Bloomsbury Guide to Women's Literature* (Bloomsbury, 1992)

Cuddon, J.A., *A Dictionary of Literary Terms* (Penguin Reference, 1991)

Lewis, H.D., *Philosophy of Religion* (English Universities Press, 1961)

Rossetti, Maria Francesca, *A Shadow of Dante* (Longmans Green, 1896)

Works Cited

Books

Agate, James, *Ego 7* (George Harrap, 1945)

Anon., *The Empire by Express* (Collins School Series, 1935)

Anon., *English Short Stories of Today* (OUP, 1939)

Anon., *Report of the Departmental Committee on Detective Work and Procedure* (The Home Office/HMSO, 1938)

Barbellion, W.N.P., *The Journal of a Disappointed Man* (1919) (Penguin, 1948)

Bentley, Phyllis, *O Dreams, O Destinations* (Gollancz, 1962)

Bishop of Truro, *The Gospel for Tomorrow* (Penguin, 1941)

Bramah, Ernest, *Kai Lung's Golden Hours* (1922) (Penguin, 1938)

Brittain, Vera, *Testament of Friendship* (1940) (Virago Press, 1989)

Brown, Janice, *The Lion in the Waste Land: Fearsome Redemption in the Work of C.S. Lewis, Dorothy L. Sayers and T.S. Eliot* (Kent State University Press, 2018)

Carey, John, *The Intellectuals and the Masses* (Faber, 1992)

Chesterton, G.K., *Essays and Poems* (Penguin, 1958)

Chesterton, G.K., *Generally Speaking* (Tauchnitz, 1929)

Christie, Agatha, *An Autobiography* (Harper Collins, 1993)

Connon, Bryan, *Beverley Nichols, A Life* (Timber Press, 2000)

Coomes, David, *Dorothy L. Sayers: A Careless Rage for Life* (Lion, 1992)

Cournos, John, *The Devil is an English Gentleman* (1932) (Farrar & Rinehart, 2009)

Cuthbertson, Guy, *Wilfred Owen* (Yale University Press, 2014)

Cyriax, Oliver, *The Penguin Encyclopaedia of Crime* (Penguin, 1993)

Dabby, Benjamin, *Women as Public Moralists in Britain* (Boydell & Brewer, 2017)

Davenport-Hines, Richard, *Auden* (Heinemann, 1995)

Davies, David Stuart, (Ed.) *Shadows of Sherlock Holmes* (Wordsworth Editions, 1998)

De Quincey, Thomas, *On Murder* (1827) (Oxford University Press, 2009)

Doblin, Alfred, *Berlin Alexanderplatz* (1929) (Penguin Classics, 2018)

Fowler, Christopher, *The Book of Forgotten Authors* (Riverrun, 2017)

France, Marie de, *The Lais of Marie de France* (Penguin Classics, 1986)

Gissing, George, *The Private Papers of Henry Ryecroft* (1903) (Harvester, 1982)

Gregory, Alyse, *The Day is Gone* (E.P. Dutton, 1948)

Grosse, Alfred C., *The Master Book of Detection and Disguise* (Quaker Oats Ltd, 1936)

Haining, Peter, *The Golden Age of Crime Fiction* (Prion, 2002)

Hanley, James, *Grey Children* (1937) (Methuen, 1937)

Harries, Richard, *C.S. Lewis: The Man and his God* (Fount Paperbacks, 1987)

Hitchman, Janet, *Such a Strange Lady* (New English Library, 1975)

Hobhouse, Christopher, *Oxford As it was And as it is to-day* (Batsford, 1939)

Hone, Joseph, *The Book Forger* (Chatto & Windus, 2024)

Jacobson, Howard, *Mother's Boy: A Writer's Beginnings* (Jonathan Cape, 2022)

Jameson, Storm, *Journey from the North* (Collins & Harvill, 1969)

Joannu, Maroula, (Ed.) *The History of British Women's Writing 1920–1945* Vol.8 (Palgrave Macmillan, 2013)

Jones, Terry, *Chaucer's Knight: The Portrait of a Medieval Mercenary* (Weidenfeld & Nicholson, 1982)

McDonald, Jess, *No Comment* (Raven Books, 2023)

MacShane, Frank, *The Life of Raymond Chandler* (Jonathan Cape, 1976)

Mannin, Ethel, *Confessions and Impressions* (Penguin, 1936)

Marnham, Patrick, *The Man Who Wasn't Maigret: A Portrait of Georges Simenon* (Bloomsbury, 1992)

Maugham, W. Somerset, *A Writer's Notebook* (1949) (Heinemann, 1952)

Mehew, Ernest, (Ed.) *Selected Letters of Robert Louis Stevenson* (Yale Nota Bene, 2001)

Melly, George, *Owning Up: The Trilogy* (Penguin, 1984)

Morgan, Iwan, (Ed.) *The College by the Sea* (The Cambrian News, 1928)

Morgan, Janet, *Agatha Christie: A Biography* (Harper Collins, 2017)

Moulton, Mo, *Mutual Admiration Society* (Corsair, 2019)

Nichols, Beverley, *Twenty-Five* (Penguin, 1926)

Olivier, Edith, *Without Knowing Mr Walkley* (Faber & Faber, 1938)

Orczy, Baroness, *The Scarlet Pimpernel* (1913) (Hodder, 2005)

Orwell, George, *Decline of the English Murder and Other Essays* (1965) (Penguin, 1975)

Owen, Wilfred, *Collected Poems* (Chatto & Windus, 1977)

Parker, Peter, *Housman Country* (Abacus, 2016)

Poe, Edgar Allan, 'The Man of the Crowd' in Kennedy, J. Gerald (Ed.) *The Portable Edgar Allan Poe* (Penguin, 2006)

Powys, Llewelyn, *Rats in the Sacristy* (Watts & Co, 1937)

Priestley, J.B., *English Journey* (Heinemann, 1934) (Mandarin, 1994)

Rawnsley, W.F., *Highways and Byways in Lincolnshire* (Macmillan, 1926)

Sartre, Jean-Paul, *Les Mots* (1964) Translated as *Words* (Penguin, 1969)

Smith, Stevie, *The Collected Poems of Stevie Smith* (1975) (Penguin, 1985)

Stallworthy, Jon, *Wilfred Owen* (Oxford University Press, 1974)

Sterne, Laurence, *The Life and Opinions of Tristram Shandy* (1759) (OUP, 1992)

Stevenson, John, *British Society 1914-45* (Penguin, 1984)

Sutton, Maureen, *We Didn't Know Aught* (Paul Watkins, 1992)

Williams, Charles, *The Figure of Beatrice: A Study in Dante* (1944) (Reading Essentials, 2019)

Wordsworth, William, and Coleridge, Samuel Taylor, *Preface to the Lyrical Ballads* (1799/1800) (Routledge, 1971)

Journals: Essays and Features

Anon., 'Fall of the German Government' *The Times* 24 November 2023 p.16

Anon., 'Lively Marriage Bill Debate' *Nottingham Evening Post* 16 April 1937 p.11

Anon., 'Living by the Pen' *Cheltenham Chronicle* 2 May 1936 p.8

Anon., 'Miss D.L. Sayers on Religious Plays' *Gloucestershire Echo* 22 July 1938 British Library Newspapers

Anon., 'Murder by Six Experts' *Gloucester Citizen* 16 April 1936 p.6

Anon., 'Paris Day by Day' *The Daily Telegraph* 25 November 1923 reprinted in *The Daily Telegraph* 25 November 2023 p.32

Anon., *The Book of Manchester and Salford* (George Falkner & Sons, 1929)

Anon., 'The Drama of Dogma' *Aberdeen Journal*, 6 June 1938 p.6 British Library Newspapers

Anon., *The Great War: The Murder Triumph of the Zeppelins* (Amalgamated Press, 1919)

Anon., 'Wireless Music from across the Atlantic' *The Daily Telegraph* December 1923 reprinted in *The Daily Telegraph* 30 December 2023 p.26

Anon., 'Zeppelin Activities: The Murder Raiders and the Aerial Handicap of Our Fleet'

'Book Exhibition in London' *Aberdeen Journal* 28 October 1936 p.2

Bostridge, Mark, 'Hectic Hysteria' *Times Literary Supplement* 4 May 2018 p.29

British Library Newspapers link.gale.com/apps/doc/JA32383566465/BNCN? U=lancs& sid=bookmark-BNCN&xid

Brome, Vincent, *J.B. Priestley* (Hamish Hamilton, 1988)

Brown, David, 'Women-Only Club demands drinking party with men' *The Sunday Times* Web Edition Articles 29 September 2023 p.1

Burgess, Glyn S., and Busby, Keith, (Ed.) *Introduction to The Lais of Marie de France* (Penguin, 1986)

Child, Harold, Review of Joseph Conrad's *Some Reminiscences* 25 January 1912 reprinted in *Times Literary Supplement* 19 January 2018 p.34 as 'The Undimmed Eye'

Cochrane, Harry, 'After Dante' *Times Literary Supplement* 31 July 2020 p.29

Downing, Crystal, 'Dorothy L. Sayers and Russian Orthodoxy' *Inklings Forever: Published Colloquium Proceedings 1997-2016*: Vol.4, Article 25 (see https://pillars.taylor.edu/inklings_forever/vol4/iss1/25

Hainsworth, Peter, 'Coming to our senses in a corpse-hued wood' *Times Literary Supplement* 11 May 2018 p.9

Hall, Lesley A., 'Contraception – Birth Control through the Ages in Principle and Practice' in Losovsky, Monty, (Ed.) *Getting Better: Stories from the History of Medicine* (Medical Museum Publishing, 2007) pp.88-108

Hampson, John, 'Movements in the Underground I', Lehmann, John, *The Penguin New Writing 27*, 1946 pp.133-151

Henderson, Sir Vivian and Burt, Dr Cyril, 'Causes of Crime' *The Listener* Vol.XI Bo.277 2 May 1934 pp.748–750

Hughes, John B., 'Voice of Christ on BBC' *Aberdeen Journal* 11 December 1941 p.2 British Library Newspapers

Jaffer, Nabeelah, 'Sleuths' *Times Literary Supplement* 24 May 2019 pp.38–39

Jameson, Storm (Ed.) *Fact* July 1937 (FACT 15 July 1937) p.6

Jensen, Hal, 'Sin is a Slithering Thing' *Times Literary Supplement* 22 December 2023 p.18

Kaplan, Cora, '"Queens of Crime" The "Golden Age" of Crime Fiction' in Joannu, Maroula, (Ed.) *The History of British Women's Writing 1920-1945* (Palgrave Macmillan, 2013) pp.44–160

King, Francis and Steele, Bruce, Notes to *Chaucer, The Prologue and Three Tales* (Longman,1983) pp.173–174

Light, Greg, 'Conceiving Creative Writing in Education' Papers from the Creative Writing Conference 1999 at Sheffield Hallam University Edited by John Turner et alia, School of Cultural Studies, Sheffield Hallam, 1999

Lohr, Marie, and Cheyney, Peter, 'A Debate on Marriage – is it Worthwhile Now?' *Evening Telegraph*, 12 November 1931 p.2 British Library Newspapers, link.gale.com/apps/doc/JE3237430447/BNCN? U+ lancs &sid=bookmark

Maguire, Muireann, 'Cherchez la femme' *Times Literary Supplement* (5 January 2023 pp.8–9)

Maitzen, Rohan, 'Agatha Christie and Shrewd Miss Marple' *Times Literary Supplement* 15 June 2018 p.38

Maitzen, Rohan, 'Straying onto the Grass' *Times Literary Supplement* 15 December 2017 p.25

Meade, L.T. and Eustace, Robert, 'The Story of the Man with the False Nose' *The Harmsworth Magazine* Vol.4 (Harmsworth, 1899) pp.559–567

News Chronicle Jubilee Parade 23 April 1935 (The Daily News Ltd, 1935)

Pring, Charles H., 'Women Medical Students' *The Last Cuckoo* (Unwin Paperbacks, 1927) p.51

Purvis, Libby, 'Introduction to *The Documents in the Case*' (Hodder & Stoughton, 2016)

Sieburth, Richard, 'Verse in their Sleep' *Times Literary Supplement* 29 June 2018 p.13

Shipley, Michael, *The Little Theatre Guild: A Brief History of 70 Years 1946 to 2016* see https://littletheatreguild.org>welcome.guild-history

Scholes, Lucy, 'Tales of Hopeless Husbands' *Times Literary Supplement* 8 January 2021 p.19

Shortt, Rupert, 'A slave in your place' *Times Literary Supplement* 30 March 2018 p.42

Stewart, Victoria, 'Constructing the Crime Canon: Dorothy L. Sayers as an Anthologist' *Literature and History* Vol. 30(2) pp.105-120, 2021

Stourton, Edward, *Auntie's War: The BBC During the Second World War* (Doubleday, 2017) *The Tatler* 3 June 1951 p.329

Werime, Marcia Satterthwaite, *Letter to The New York Times*, November 1993 section 7 p.75 (The full text available at https://nytimes.com/1993/11/14books/l-family-matters-559893.html)

Wilson, H.W., (Ed.) *The Great War* Vol.6 (Amalgamated Press, no date) *Argosy*, (January 1952)

Secondary Reading

Books

Barbera, Jack, and McBrien, William, *Stevie: A Biography of Stevie Smith* (Macmillan, 1986)

Brabazon, James, *Dorothy L. Sayers: A Biography* (Encore Editions, 1981)

Brilli, Elisa, and Milani, Giuliano, *Dante's New Lives* (Reaktion, 2024)

Bunting, Madeleine, *The Plot: A Biography of My Father's English Acre* (Granta, 2009)

Burns, Rob, (Ed.) *German Cultural Studies* (Oxford University Press, 1995)

Cana, Frank, *The Great War in Europe* (Virtue & Company, 1920)

Chesterton, G.K., *Essays and Poems* (Penguin, 1958)

Collins, Wilkie, *The Moonstone* (1868) (Penguin, 1997)

Dooley, Maura, (Ed.) *How Novelists Work* (Seren, 2000)

Freud, Sigmund, *Civilization and Its Discontents* (1930) (Penguin Classics, 2014)

Hall, Radclyffe, *The Well of Loneliness* (1928) (Wordsworth Editions, 2014)

Hardyment, Christine, *Slice of Life* (BBC/Penguin, 1995)

Holtby, Winifred, *South Riding* (1936) (Virago, 1988)

Priestley, J.B., *English Journey* (1934) (Mandarin, 1995)

Simenon, Georges, *Maigret* (1934) (Penguin, 2015)

Thompson, Laura, *Rex v. Edith Thompson* (Head of Zeus, 2018)

Journals / Newspapers (Historical)

Harmsworth Magazine (Harmsworth, 1900)

The Strand Magazine (George Newnes, July–December 1891)

The Idler Vol.3 July 1898 (Chatto & Windus, 1893)

Articles and Essays

Anon., 'Dorothy L. Sayers, Writer and Theologian: Biographical sketches of memorable Christians of the past' see Jusrus.anglican.org/resources/bio/19.html

Anon., 'Motoring Offences' *The Times* 8 May 1937 p.8 issue 47679 Col.

Anon., 'Murder by Six Experts' *Gloucester Citizen* 16 April 1936 p.6

Chernock, Arianne, 'The Wars Women Wage' *Times Literary Supplement* 5 June 2020 p.24

Davies, Dr Ross, Review of *Auntie's War* (see above) on *Reviews in History* website: https://www.review.history.ac.uk

Kennedy Smith, Ann, 'Fishy Thinking' *Times Literary Supplement* 30 March 2018 p.53

Lamb, Stephen, and Phelan, Anthony, 'Weimar Germany's Modernist Political Project; Theory and Practice' (see Rob Burns above) pp.56–62

Oliver, Sophie, 'Tragic Accomplice' *Times Literary Supplement* 29 June 2018 p.28

Rebstock, Sonja Irene Grieder, *Quotes as Clues: Intertextuality in Dorothy L. Sayers's Detective Novels* (Wissenschaft Verlag Trier) Studien zur anglistischen Literatur und Sprachenwissenschaft, 2013

Roberts, Michael, 'Editorial Notes' *The London Mercury* Vol. XXXIII April 1936 No.189 pp.573–577

Schaffner, Anna Katharina, 'Science to Justice' *Times Literary Supplement* 16 March 2018 p.13

Scholes, Lucy, 'Tales of Hopeless Husbands' *Times Literary Supplement* 8 January 2021 p.19

Websites/Podcasts

Sites

Greydogtales.com/blog/master-madame –detectives –l-t-meade

https://cburrell.wordpress.com/2023/03/20/williams-the-figure-of-beatrice/

https://www.cslewis.com/the-lion-in-the-wasteland/

https://hollisarchives.lib.harvard.edu/repositories/24/resources/2376

https://martinedwardsbooks.com (There is information here on the past and present Detection Club (founded in 1930))

https://sonetka.livejournal.com/169770.html
https://www.thegospelcoalition.org (Contains a chronology of
    broadcasts on BBC by C.S. Lewis)
https://ww1hull.com/air-raids-on-hull1/
https://thrillingdetective.com/2020/01/sexton-blake/

Unpublished Research

Noonan, Catriona, The Production of Religious Broadcasting: The
    Case of the BBC
University of Glasgow, Ph.D. thesis, 2008 see https://core.ac.uk

Podcasts/Blogs

Shedunitshow https://shedunnitshow.com Caroline Crampton
    The references in the text are to these podcasts: 'Miss Marple,
    Spinster Sleuth' and 'The Advertising Adventures of Dorothy L.
    Sayers'
Ridpath, Barbara, 'How the Malvern Conference of 1941 Set the
    Scene for Malvern 2017' see: https://williamtemplefoundation.
    org.uk/how-the-malvern-conference-of-1941-set-the-scene-for-
    malvern-2017/

Small Press/Ephemera

Clarke, Charles J., *Christian Courtship* (The Epworth Press, 1947)
Gray, Dr A. Herbert, *Are Sex Relations Without Marriage Wrong?*
    (Alliance of Honour, 1949)
Phillips, J.B., *The Way to Love* (United Society for Christian Literature
    no date, c. 1950)
Sierz, Aleks, 'Radical Agatha Christie' *Times Literary Supplement*
    2 October 2023 p.8

Lord Peter Wimsey: Chronology

The Wimsey fiction, though continued along with Jill Paton Walsh, and also in numerous stories for magazines, has this fundamental listing.

Whose Body?	1923
Clouds of Witness	1926
Unnatural Death	1927
Lord Peter Views the Body	1928
The Unpleasantness at the Bellona Club	1928
Strong Poison	1930
Five Red Herrings	1931
Have His Carcase	1932
Hangman's Holiday	1933
Murder Must Advertise	1933
The Nine Tailors	1934
Gaudy Night	1935
Busman's Honeymoon	1937
In the Teeth of the Evidence	1939
Striding Folly	1973

Index